The Pleasure Zone

The Pleasure Zone

Why We Resist
Good Feelings
& How to Let Go
and Be Happy

Stella Resnick, Ph.D.

CONARI PRESS
Berkeley, CA

Conari Press books are distributed by Publishers Group West

Art Direction: Ame Beanland
Cover Design: Nita Ybarra
Author Photo: Mitchell Rose
Interior Design: Jennifer Brontsema

ISBN: 1-57324-071-0

Library of Congress Cataloging-in-Publication Data
Resnick, Stella, 1939–
      The pleasure zone : why we resist good feelings & how to let go
and be happy / Stella Resnick.
            p.   cm.
      Includes bibliographical references.
      ISBN 1-57324-071-0 (hardcover)
      1. Pleasure.   I. Title.
      BF515.R47   1997
      152.4'2—dc21   97-15651

Printed in the United States of America on recycled paper.

10 9 8 7 6 5 4 3 2 1

For Alan,
the great love of my life
For Dad,
a constant caring presence

In Memory of
Holly Harp
Janet Lederman

Foreword

· ·

The Pleasure Zone is a remarkable book, a wise and practical book written by a wise and practical woman. It takes us to where we all live—our bodies—and offers simple, sensible tools to help us move toward what we all want: healthy and fulfilling lives.

For me, *The Pleasure Zone* is a particularly exciting book. I have spent the last two decades probing this question of pleasure. Why, when our most basic human yearning is for pleasure, has pleasure been vilified, forbidden, and often distorted into "pleasure" at the expense of others? Why do we carry so much negative luggage about pleasure? What can we do to accelerate what in my book *Sacred Pleasure* I call the pain to pleasure shift?

My own research has focused on the larger cultural and historical picture—on how we need to shift to a society that supports and rewards partnership rather than domination if we are to reclaim our birthright to pleasure. The more our society supports and rewards caring in all spheres of life, the more pleasure can be a part of our day to day lives. But personal and social change go hand in hand. The more pleasurably embodied we become, the more our day to day relationships become loving and the more sexually, spiritually, and socially healed our society becomes. *The Pleasure Zone* focuses on this personal healing—and it does this beautifully.

Unlike so many so-called self-help books, *The Pleasure Zone* is *really* helpful. It is grounded in sound research. It distinguishes between real pleasure and the escapism that, under the guise of "fun," leaves us feeling empty, disconnected, and in danger of becoming hooked on harmful, and in the long run painful, addictions.

The Pleasure Zone is also real in another way. Throughout, Stella Resnick speaks to us out of her own personal and professional experiences—and she does this with honesty, caring, and charm.

But that is not all.

The Pleasure Zone does not ignore the spiritual dimension of feeling good—what I have called sacred pleasure. On the contrary, there is a spiritual dimension throughout the book. But it is not the old disembodied spirituality that denigrates our bodies and the rest of nature. Rather, it is a full-bodied partnership spirituality that celebrates the wonder, and miracle, of our great capacity for love and creativity, for feeling good and helping others to do the same.

I consider *The Pleasure Zone* an important contribution to the reclamation of true pleasure. And I found it a pleasure to read!

—Riane Eisler

Contents

· ·

Part One: A New Understanding Of Pleasure, 1

Part Two: The Fundamentals of Pleasure, 75

Part Three: The Psychological Pleasures, 139

Acknowledgments

· ·

This book has been a long time in the making. I wrote my first article on "pleasure deprivation" for *New Age* magazine in 1978. Two years later, I followed it up with another on the connection between conscious breathing and the ability to enjoy both lasting love and fulfilling sex. From that time on, pleasure has been my life's work—and, contrary to what might be expected from such a seemingly benign issue, it hasn't been easy. Nor has it been without controversy. I'm indebted to all the people who have supported me over the years in a variety of ways, both personal and professional. I particularly thank Peggy Taylor, then editor of *New Age*, for mid-wifing that very first artcle through me.

I'm especially grateful to the people who have worked with me in private therapy, groups, and workshops, and to those who have learned to use a pleasure-positive perspective to transform their lives. Witnessing their success has been tremendously gratifying to me. I owe a special thank you to all those who have been disguised in this book and whose anonymous stories have been used to provide insight into the dynamics of pleasure-resistance and how to overcome it.

I have also continued to develop my ideas and methods in professional seminars and conferences. Particularly in the early years, my warmest receptions on the topic of pleasure were always among sexologists, sex educators, and sex therapists. I specifically want to thank the Society for the Scientific Study of Sexuality, a stimulating group of thinkers and researchers which, for over fifteen years, has been an endless source of valuable professional development and collegial support. I am also grateful to the Association for Humanistic Psychology and the Somatics Community of the Association for Humanistic Psychology for many years of support and exchange of ideas.

Since I have been researching the topic of pleasure over a long period of years, I fear that I may fail to acknowledge all those whose work has influenced mine. Though it's not possible for me to list them all, still I want to extend my appreciation to any I have failed to specifically mention, who nonetheless have contributed greatly toward clarifying my ideas on the importance of pleasure in everyday life.

Committing my ideas to the page has not been an easy task for me. I'm grateful to Nancy Bacal, my friend and teacher, and all the women of the now defunct Wednesday group, who for six years cheered me on as a writer.

In the many years it has taken me to research and put together a coherent manuscript, there are two people whose specific help has been invaluable. I owe a special debt of gratitude to Diane Rapaport, author and cherished friend, who helped me separate wheat from chaff in early versions of this book. I am also indebted to Dr. Carol Cassell, another cherished friend and a colleague, for her continual encouragement, no-holds-barred feedback, and other useful input in both early and final drafts.

I thank my agent, Elizabeth Kaplan, who instantly recognized the value of a book investigating pleasure and who worked hard to find the right publisher.

I owe a special thank you to my publisher and editor, Mary Jane Ryan, for her help in cutting and shaping the vast amount of material I considered essential to this volume—and for convincing me that I would find a home in future projects for my treasured gems which had to be cut from this book.

I extend my appreciation to my friend and colleague, Dr. Marjorie L. Rand for her useful comments in reading the final manuscript and to Steve Andreas, Linda Marks, and Andrea Cagan who have read all or portions of the final manuscript and whose comments have been highly valued.

Some people deserve my gratitude because they have made an impact on more extensive areas of my life. I thank my father, Nat Resnick, who has always been there for me. I thank my mentor, Fritz Perls, for teaching me phenomenological existentialism as both a therapy and a lifestyle. I thank my brother, Lou Siegel, for his friendship. I thank my nephew, Isaac, and my niece, Emma, for all I'm learning from them about the purest love of all—the unconditional love of a growing child.

Lastly, and most importantly, I thank my husband, Alan Kishbaugh, for his sweet love and for being, all these many years, my greatest champion, my guinea pig, my most literary editor, and, at the core of it all, my deepest sense of home.

Opening to Pleasure

Our collective philosophy about pleasure and pain is as fundamental to how we lead our lives as are our notions of good and evil. Contrary to popular thought, pleasure is not only about fun and games, or relishing sensual and sexual delights--it's that and a whole lot more. How we enjoy ourselves affects our health. How well we can enjoy intimacy determines the depth and quality of our connection with others. How much pleasure we allow ourselves daily determines how fulfilled we are throughout our lifetime.

Think of the pleasure zone not as a place but a process. It's an active way of focusing your attention that centers you in the present moment, releases enormous stores of vitality and optimism, and makes whatever you're doing considerably more enjoyable.

For thousands of years, in cultures all over the world, pleasure has been disdained and demonized. It's time to reclaim our birthright. It's time to proclaim the true wisdom of a life informed by pleasure.

PART ONE

A
New
Understanding
of Pleasure

Chapter 1

The New Pleasure Principle

*Discovering the connection
between happiness and pleasure*

. . . .

We cannot say what joy is.
We must go the further step and
discover its true nature for ourselves.

—*Robert A. Johnson*

We're not as happy as we might be—not in our everyday lives, not in our love lives. And it's not because our lives or our loves are so lacking. Rather, it's because most of us have lost the ability to fully take pleasure in what we have.

Happiness involves skills for everyday living that few people consistently practice. Instead of taking pride in our accomplishments, we tend to be self-critical. Instead of holding positive visions of the future, we run worst case scenarios, thinking that's the way to be prepared for emergencies. Rather than regularly expressing appreciation to those we love, we find fault with them, hoping to make them "better." Genuine pride in a job well done, maintaining hope even during hard times, spontaneously expressing gratitude to someone—these are some of the simple pleasures that can enrich and vitalize our everyday lives, which we just don't enjoy often enough.

As a psychotherapist, I'm often aware of the opportunities for inner pleasure my clients routinely deny themselves. One man in his early forties would see me weekly and in each session I'd suggest he take a few breaths and check in with himself, and each time he would tell me his body was tense—his shoulders were tight, his neck and back hurt, and his chest was heavy. It always felt good to him to breathe and relax during a session; he would think more creatively and have some good insights. Yet, when I suggested that he stop periodically during the day to stretch and relax for a few minutes, he would shrug and say that he kept forgetting. One day he admitted that he was afraid that if he let himself relax, he wouldn't work at all.

I've heard this attitude expressed in so many different ways by so many different people—that if they're not all wound up, they feel like they're not working hard enough. Somehow, they think they'll get more out of themselves if they grit their teeth and stay in pain. Finding energy and purpose through relishing the pleasurable possibilities of the situation sounds hopelessly naive to them as a way of getting anything accomplished.

The same is often true in intimate relationships. We seem to hold a curious philosophy that what brings people closer is talking about how they displease one another. I've seen couples who could easily itemize what was lacking for them in the relationship—carefully spelling out their resentments, disappointments, and sexual complaints—who would resist saying how much they appreciated one another. Eventually they would acknowledge that while they do have a lot of love and high regard for one another, they felt that expressing tenderness would hinder, not help, them in getting what they want from one another.

The fact is that our whole society diminishes the value of pleasure. We think of pleasure as fun and games, an escape from reality—rarely as a worthwhile end in itself. Amazingly, we don't make the connection between vitality—the energy that comes from feeling good—and the willingness to take pleasure in moment-by-moment experience. As a result, we fail to appreciate the truly significant role pleasurable experience plays in leading a meaningful and fulfilling life and, more specifically, in maintaining deeply satisfying relationships.

A Personal Odyssey

That was certainly my story. After years of graduate study and training, I became a successful therapist with a thriving practice in San Francisco. I bought a home, made many friends, and traveled widely giving talks and seminars. The only problem was that I wasn't happy.

By the time I was thirty-two, I had had two brief marriages and had embarked on a stormy three year relationship that was full of anger, with lots of fighting and hurtful tears. After that breakup, I kept myself constantly on the go. Every night I scheduled work, business meetings, or dinner with friends. I told myself I was leading an exciting life. In truth, I was lonelier than I had ever been and was doing everything I could to keep from being home alone.

Yet here I was—a therapist. I clearly had something worthwhile to offer others; my practice was full. Why wasn't it working for me? I had been in the best therapy for years, with the leaders in my field. I had my insights, my dramatic breakthroughs when I would erupt into tears and rage over the pain of my childhood—my parents' divorce when I was five, the years living with a neglecting mother and a physically abusive stepfather. I did yoga. I meditated. I exercised. I became a vegetarian. Why did I still suffer? Why wasn't I happy?

When I turned thirty-four, I learned that my mother was dying of cancer. I decided to take a leave from my practice and go back to New York to see if I could make friends with her before her death. That August I rented an apartment in Manhattan and began taking the subway to Brooklyn twice a week to sit with her at her hospital bed. Unfortunately, even as she lay dying, my stepfather continued to poison our relationship by saying things that made her mistrustful and guarded around me. When she died in July of the following year, I felt profoundly sad, not so much because I had lost my mother but because I never had one.

At that point, I felt I couldn't just go back to my hectic life in San Francisco. It was time to confront my pain and loneliness and discover what was keeping me so unhappy. A month after my mother's death, I moved to Mount Tremper, New York, a town in the Catskill Mountains near Woodstock. The few people I knew there had summer homes, and in winter they came up for only an occasional weekend. I found a small house surrounded by woods, without a TV, and signed a lease for a year.

I spent that year in the country more alone than ever before—but this time it was a chosen solitude. For guidance, I read Henry David Thoreau's *Walden*, the famous nineteenth-century account of a similar retreat in Massachusetts. Like Thoreau, I had a pond full of croaking frogs in the summer, which froze over in winter. Like Thoreau, I had a visitor now and then and made regular forays into town for supplies. And like Thoreau, days and days would go by when I neither saw nor spoke to another living being.

At first, my days were terribly lonely. I cried a lot and felt sorry for myself. I read, wrote in my journal, and took long walks in the woods. Sometimes I would find myself staring at a wall, not knowing how long I had been sitting there or what I had been so lost in thought over. On better days, I could spend hours looking out the window, fascinated by how the birds fought over birdseed at the feeder in the tree. In winter, I chopped kindling to feed the fires in the two potbellied stoves and fireplace that kept me from freezing. I cooked plenty of soups and stews. Some nights when the cold winter wind blew especially hard, I would stay awake stuffing newspapers between the planks of the uninsulated walls of this summer house, grumbling to myself and wondering how this was ever going to make me a cheerier person.

What I began to discover during those endless days was how little I knew about how to be happy on a daily basis. I knew how to drive myself to succeed. I knew how to criticize myself for how I wasn't good enough. But I didn't know how to take on a day and enjoy it.

I nagged myself constantly. I played old movies in my head of past events I regretted and of the people in my life who had done me wrong. I resented my father for leaving me when I was five with my badgering mother in Bensonhurst, a working-class section of Brooklyn, even though I had begged him to take me with him. I resented my stepfather for ten years of beatings, when he would throw me against walls and hit me on the face and head. I resented my mother for not standing up for me, and instead provoking him further into trembling, uncontrollable rages with her incessant complaining about me.

I hated them both for what I had to do, when I was eighteen, to make it stop. Coldly, I told my stepfather that if he ever laid a hand on me again, one night while he slept, I would drive the big kitchen knife through his ugly heart. He must have believed it because that ended his violence toward me.

I felt disgust when I remembered the rage I let out in fights with other sullen girls like me who hung out on rival street corners. I could still call up the heartache I felt at the odd mix of kindness and cruelty from my first boyfriend, the leader of my neighborhood gang. I never felt lovable enough for the men in my life. I resented men for denying me the male closeness I craved—but I also felt guilty. Obviously I wasn't good enough to be loved.

I thought I had dealt with this in therapy. Yet despite all my cathartic tears and rages and all my insights into how my past contaminated my present, I still didn't know how to do things differently. I knew all about what didn't work. But I didn't know what did work, and in the absence of any real skill at having an enjoyable inner life, I fell back on old patterns of negative thinking and painful feelings.

Finally, just as I was getting settled into the quiet of my country retreat, I had the flash of insight that would turn everything around. I suddenly realized: It isn't enough to know what you are doing wrong, you have to know how to do it right. You have to learn how to enjoy this life—this brief blip in eternity that is yours.

Carpé diem, dammit! I railed at myself. Lighten up! Learn how to enjoy your life—moment by moment and day by precious day.

Like so many people, I wasn't happy because I didn't know how to be happy. I had no role models of happiness in childhood. I knew how to have a good time and to distract myself from my frustrations and disappointments with external pleasures. I could be amused and entertained; I could enjoy parties, fancy restaurants, and the theater; I could relish being admired by others and indulge myself in a material success that was beyond anything this poor little girl from Brooklyn ever dared dream. But I didn't know how to get off my own case and relax, to enjoy the inner pleasures of a quiet mind and ease within my body. I didn't know how to invest myself in activity out of enthusiasm for the task, rather than to prove that I could do it better than anyone else.

So that became my grand revelation, what I had intuitively placed myself in exile to learn. I had not come to figure out what was wrong with me. I was already an expert on that. I had come to experiment with how to do things differently. More than that, I had come to discover what was truly right with me.

One of the first actions I took was to turn all the clocks toward the wall and to tape over the clock on the stove. Even though I was completely alone, I still found myself fixated on time—what time to wake up, when to eat a meal, how much time was left in the day, and how late I was staying up. I realized I was uncomfortable with open-ended time. I remembered the terror I would sometimes feel, back in San Francisco, when I had nothing scheduled on a Sunday and no one to be with until Monday when I could gratefully get back to the office.

It was hard at first, but I came to appreciate the freedom in the open space. Since there was nothing to do and nowhere to go, I started to give myself permission to enjoy whatever there was to enjoy.

When I released myself from the tyranny of time, I became more attuned to my own natural rhythms—what felt good to do now, when my interest ebbed, what I felt stimulated to do next. I also became more aware of how my incessant inner voice of self criticism was even worse than my mother's nagging. If there was a choice at any moment either to give myself a hard time or to treat myself kindly, I saw how easy it was for me to be hard on myself. More and more I began to choose kindness.

Much to my surprise, instead of dreading each day, I began to awaken each morning with a new spirit of adventure. How would this day unfold? What would I experiment with? What insights would I have? How could I enjoy my own company? I began to notice that when I read, I was less impatient and more invested in what I was reading. Sometimes I listened to music with my legs draped over the arm of the couch. Sometimes I danced to the Temptations, other times to Bach and Vivaldi. Chores like cooking and cleaning became opportunities to be creative, and I stretched and did leg raises as I waited for pots to boil. I found myself energized rather than exhausted by chopping wood and felt a distinct sense of pride that this city girl could build a fire and keep it going all day. I felt more lighthearted and actually began to like myself better. I finally comprehended what Thoreau had meant when he wrote, "I love to be alone. I never found the companion so companionable as solitude."

Toward the end of my stay in the mountains, I met a man who was briefly to become my lover, and my friend for life. Our relationship was immediately different from any other I had known before. I didn't try to impress or control him because I didn't need him. I liked him; he liked me. No preconceptions. We were free to be ourselves.

And if we had a fight about something, we got over it. It didn't mean anything. It certainly didn't mean I could never be happy with any man, as I had been prone to think after disagreements with past lovers.

Pain Is Not the Route to Happiness

When I returned to California that next summer and resumed my practice, I soon recognized in my clients the same incapacity to enjoy their everyday lives that had blighted my own. Like me, many of them had spent years in therapy digging into the unresolved issues of their early childhoods and had come to terms with them. Yet, while most felt that therapy had been helpful, still they couldn't really say they had been able to translate their insights into actually doing things differently. Many felt that the same issues kept cropping up time and again and that some of their greatest hopes and desires still seemed elusive.

I began to see that while understanding and releasing pain is certainly crucial for lasting results in psychotherapy, it's not enough. Getting good at struggling with problems just makes you more skillful at struggling with problems. To enjoy your life more, and especially to have more love, it's better to become skillful at what inspires your enthusiasm and generates vitality and good feelings.

Because having an intimate connection was so important to me, I began to focus on working with people, individually and in couples, on their dissatisfaction with their intimate relationships and their sex lives. Deep down inside, I suppose I felt that if I became an expert on loving relationships, maybe someday I, too, would have one. Happily, my hunch paid off. Though we've done our share of struggling, I've now enjoyed more than seventeen years with the only man I've been able to both love and live with.

I certainly have learned a lot over the years, watching people at the office grapple with their need for love and their sexual longings, and then watching my husband and myself grapple with these same issues at home. A major factor that goes unaddressed in most relationships because it is so completely taken for granted is the common tendency to make matters worse by inflicting pain on ourselves and the people we care about—all in the name of trying to make things better. We punish ourselves; we punish each other. We withdraw and act cold, whine and sling guilt, attack each other verbally, or withhold affection and sexual contact. Apparently, few of us have had good role models for how to deal effectively with emotional and sexual differences in a relationship, while maintaining a loving and supportive manner.

It's clear to me now that you can't get positive ends by using negative means. The way to resolve differences in a relationship so that everybody's happy is not to strongarm each other into submission, but to draw upon one another's love, empathy, trust, affection, and emotional excitement—all pleasures of the heart.

I have also come to see how important a good sex life is to feeling fulfilled in a relationship. Oddly, withholding sex often seems to be the preferred way to have power over your partner, but doesn't it make more sense to expect people who give each other loving physical pleasure to be more emotionally available and in tune with one another?

It's actually contrary to how we're been trained, but the route to happiness is not through pain and sacrifice. If there is a path to the highest levels of well-being, it is lined with what nourishes us the most and brings us joy.

The Connection Between Happiness and Pleasure

Until very recently, psychologists rarely studied happiness; unhappiness seemed a lot more fascinating. But times have changed. Suddenly there's a burgeoning scientific interest in finding out what makes people happy. Social scientists run surveys and ask people to rate their level of "subjective well-being" and to say what makes them happy; physiologists and medical researchers study our genes and brain chemistry to seek the same answers.

Happiness, we're discovering, doesn't depend on income level—except for people who are very poor, the richest people are no more or less happy than people of moderate means. Nor does happiness depend on social status—whether you're blue-collar or white-collar—or on your level of education. Happiness doesn't depend on how young or old you are, whether you are male or female, or remarkably, even whether you've won the lottery or had a life-altering accident. In fact, within six months or so of either a big success or a major setback, most people usually return to how they were feeling right before the significant event.

What does make a difference, however, relates much more to a person's level of enthusiasm, energy, and their willingness to derive pleasure from ordinary life. In a variety of different polls, people who say they're happy tend to feel good about themselves, are optimistic, feel in control, enjoy other people, have learned to relax and quiet their minds, can manage their negative thoughts and feelings, and, rather than focus on what's lacking in their life, they tend to take pleasure in what they have. In terms of having achieved some of their goals, the happiest people are those who say they have fulfilling work and satisfying relationships.

The bad news, however, is that most people's baseline level of happiness doesn't change much over their lifetime. Some psychologists suggest that happiness may be largely a matter of heredity. They submit that we have a set-point for happiness, a concept similar to a set-point for weight, which contends that some people will still be overweight no matter how much they diet. In the same way, set-point proponents say that certain people will be happy or not no matter what happens in their lives. To support their theory, they point to studies showing that identical twins, siblings who have exactly the same genes, are alike in their level of happiness 44 percent of the time, while fraternal twins who are genetically no more alike than other siblings, are alike in happiness only 8 percent of the time.

But there is no real proof that people tend to maintain the same level of subjective well-being over a lifetime because they were born that way. Most researchers agree that even if there is a gene for happiness, it wouldn't be a completely determining factor. A biological propensity for happiness might account for only a small portion of your mood, but the predominant influence would still be related to how you learn to interpret your life circumstances and to enjoy what you do have.

Rather than a happiness gene, what's much more likely is that people's happiness level stays the same over a lifetime because most people take for granted the narrow range of pleasures they tend to rely on to bring fulfillment. Not many of us have ever considered the notion that we could raise our sense of well-being directly by learning to expand on, and intensify, our basic ability to enjoy everyday pleasures.

The Connection Between Pleasure and Health

This burst of interest in happiness has actually been spurred by a host of other scientific findings, which have demonstrated that there is a strong correlation between a wide variety of pleasures and good health. In the relatively new field of psychoneuroimmunology (PNI), biologists, psychologists, and sociologists are accumulating impressive evidence to show that pleasurable experiences and positive states of mind can actually enhance the immune system.

We've known for a long time that worry, self-sacrifice, and a lack of loving physical and emotional contact can be hazardous to our health. Hostility and stress are highly correlated with a tendency to develop illnesses such as high blood pressure and heart disease. Chronic depression has also long been recognized as a factor that may impede recovery from physical ailments.

Physiological studies show why that happens. In one experiment when subjects were made to feel helpless, their negative feelings actually slowed down the motion of disease-fighting white cells in their bloodstream, making those cells sluggish and less efficient. In other studies, people who were pessimistic, depressed, under stress, or in mourning over the loss of a loved one were found to have a deficit of active natural killer cells. Adrenaline and other stress hormones also seem to cause us some of our greatest health problems, particularly related to the heart and circulation. Triggered by anxiety, anger, or stress, adrenaline constricts the blood vessels all over the body and particularly in the heart, raising blood pressure, potentially causing damage to the heart muscle and arteries, and increasing the risk of stroke.

But even more profoundly, today's scientists are finding that positive feelings like confidence and peace of mind are associated with good health. In other words, pleasure can actually prolong your life. The PNI research shows that positive emotions strengthen and enhance the immune system. Having faith or courage, as opposed to despair or panic, can help us to resist disease and to recover more quickly from an illness. For example, women who have undergone mastectomies and have faith in their chances and a fighting spirit possess a far better rate of survival than women who feel hopeless.

Even pleasant experiences can help. Psychologist Robert Ornstein and physician David Sobel have collected concrete evidence to show that simple pleasures not only enhance mood but have a profound effect on our healing powers and overall health. Patients who listened to music before and during surgery had a lower level of stress hormones in their blood than those who didn't; patients recovering from surgery with a view of a park from their hospital bed, on average, left the hospital one to two days earlier than patients recovering from similar surgery with a bedroom view of a brick wall. It also turns out that feeling hopeful or confident, having sensuous experiences like being hugged, getting massaged, or making love, or even just daydreaming about doing so are all associated with signs of enhanced immunity. From an increased count of disease fighting white blood cells, to a slower heart rate and the release of hormones into the bloodstream that can regulate and balance practically every system of the body, research shows that feeling good is good for us.

The chemical messengers of all these good feelings, the neurotransmitters that course through our bloodstream and relax and open us up on all levels, are endorphins. Endorphins are the body's own natural painkillers, responsible for "runner's high," the feeling of euphoria that comes over you after you have been in vigorous motion for some time. Endorphins stimulate dilation of the blood vessels and a relaxed and open heart, and they have been linked to a stronger immune system, faster recovery from illness or surgery, and a healthier old age. When you're feeling great, you can be sure your endorphins are flowing.

Any activity that stimulates the flow of endorphins is usually good for us, and one such activity is sex play. Not only does substantial evidence exist showing that enjoying the pleasures of sex can have a very positive effect on relationships, but we now know that good sex can also enhance physical fitness. Sexual activity can boost the immune system, strengthen the heart, and counter stress. On an emotional level, people with fulfilling sex lives tend to be less anxious, less depressed, and have greater self-esteem than people who say their sex lives are lacking.

The Positive Effects of Pleasure on Aging

In the face of all this evidence, it makes sense to expect that people who know how to relish their lives will reach their mature years, on average, healthier than older people who have suffered through their lives. Today, we have vital people older than ninety who are running marathons, teaching ballet classes, publishing bestsellers, and doing comedy routines for young audiences in Las Vegas. We have an active jazz sax player Benny Carter, who recently turned ninety, and ceramist Beatrice Wood, who's more than a hundred years old, and both are still going strong. No doubt their ability to take pleasure in their art contributes greatly to the enormous store of vitality they continue to enjoy.

One inspiring example of a courageous love for life was Mr. S. L. Potter from Alpine, California. Mr. Potter celebrated his hundredth birthday by doing a bungee jump from a 210 foot tower. When his physician of many years advised him against it, he simply got a new doctor. According to his seventy-year-old son, since the bungee-jumping tower had opened three months earlier, his father had dreamed of nothing else.

We used to believe that sex was not one of the pleasures available to older people. We thought men reached their sexual prime at age eighteen, that women did so at thirty-five, and that older people's sexual appetites and ability to function seriously deteriorates with age. Research now shows that this is simply not true. Healthy older people can have highly fulfilling sex lives well into their eighties and nineties, and in the health-conscious generations to come, very likely even beyond. According to a survey conducted by sociologist Reverend Andrew Greeley in 1992, 37 percent of married couples older than sixty make love at least once a week, and these couples were the most likely of all to report that they were leading happy, exciting lives. In fact, rather than assume that old people lose interest in sex, a more accurate way of looking at it may be that people who don't lose interest in sex don't get old.

Peak Experience: A Reference Point for Great Times

Lately, most of our interest in "peaks" has been on the peak performance visualizations and affirmations that Olympic athletes use to break world records or that motivationally oriented business people use to bolster their financial success. Yet, in the late 1950s, when psychologist Abraham Maslow developed the notion of peak human potentials, it wasn't with performance but rather with peak experience that he was most intrigued. Maslow was one of the first psychologists to say that, in the exclusive study of distressed and unhappy people, researchers were missing a valuable source of information about human psychology—individuals who were happy and enjoyed their lives.

Peak experiences are intensely pleasurable times that can last for just a minute or for several weeks or more. They're periods of complete happiness and fulfillment—and while they're not common events, they're not necessarily rare, either. Whenever they occur, they're perceived as great moments, as very fine times in a person's life. Maslow found that certain individuals—people he called "self-actualized"—enjoyed a much higher frequency of peak experiences than did individuals in the general population.

The self-actualized people Maslow studied came from all walks of life—they were working people, artists, homemakers, and famous people, as well as people known and loved only in their own circles. What determined their inclusion among the self-actualized was their high degree of personal satisfaction. They felt fulfilled in their lives, motivated not by need, but by the desire to grow. And while they continued to want to develop their capacities and talents, they were also people who knew themselves and accepted their own intrinsic nature.

Maslow asserted that in his own studies he was able to find self-actualization only among older people. He theorized that this might be the case because it is usually in maturity that individuals can move beyond the struggle with such youthful issues as insecurity, identity, or social acceptance. He found that these older people often felt at the peak of their powers, and indeed were, because they were no longer wasting effort fighting themselves.

The fact that our society today is more interested in peak performance than peak experience says something very significant about our popular values and why it can be hard for people to hold on to their happiness. Whether we're Olympic athletes or not, most of us can get very focused on performing—what we're supposed to do and how we're supposed to do it. We think doing things right will earn us a particular outcome—everything from approval to love to making more money to having better sex. But by being so focused on performance and achieving goals, we can lose touch with our experience— how what we're doing is making us feel. Consequently, we can fail to be guided by what feels right for us and what doesn't.

When the focus is on performance, engaging in an activity primarily for anticipated rewards, we don't always reap the prize we think our sacrifice has earned, and that can lead to bitterness and frustration. But when the focus is on experience, every moment counts. The quality of life we gain by opting for good experiences is its own reward. Besides which, when we're guided by our good feelings, things usually turn out well.

Personal Milestones

Though we may not yet have reached our peak in life, we've all had peak experiences that can alert us to how good things can be. No doubt you can look back at your own past experiences and identify several key moments that were wonderful for you. For however long they lasted, you perceived the world and yourself in a unique way. It may have been a time when you felt enormous love for someone or were profoundly moved by a momentous event. It may have been something you accomplished or completed after many years in preparation. It may have been as simple as a time when you were overwhelmed aesthetically by a painting or a symphony. Or it may have been as complex as a religious or mystical experience where you actually comprehended the continuity of all things, and were given a sense of the eternal.

What's so important about peak experiences is that they provide a kind of reference point for how good you can feel in your body, and what you can accomplish while feeling good. Your best times tell you what is working in your life. For the moment, you feel no self doubt; you have no self imposed limitations. You feel inspired, courageous. You have a greater than usual sense of appreciation for yourself and a grander feeling of love and empathy for others. And even though the episode itself may be short-lived, the positive after effects of the experience tend to be very lasting. Life returns to normal, yet you continue to bask in a kind of psychic afterglow that makes you feel more generally hopeful about things, more confident, more connected to the world at large. Your peak experiences alert you to your vast potential for pleasure in all aspects of your life.

Pleasure-Resistance: The Hidden Saboteur of Happiness

While we now have a substantial body of evidence showing that feeling good is good for us, the grand irony is that most people, to varying degrees, hold themselves back from feeling as good as they can. We deny ourselves in many different ways.

For example, few people allow themselves a broad range of pleasures. One woman I know gets most of her pleasure in life from going to the theater and all of the activities around seeing the latest shows and planning theater parties. She laments, however, that there is little intimacy in her life, and she feels like her days and nights are filled with dozens of acquaintances and not one true friend. A man who works long hours at the office gets most of his enjoyment from sex, and if he doesn't get to have sex every night with his wife, he feels sorry for himself. His wife is ready to leave him, complaining that she feels used, coerced into having sex every night whether she wants to or not, and says she is not interested in his working out his tensions on her.

Some people know only to go to movies to get away; others bury themselves in a book, take drugs, or run off to go shopping. Not surprisingly, many of the addictive behaviors people find themselves trapped in are the only pleasures they know how to enjoy.

Unfortunately, most of us have had a lot more practice at being negative than at being positive. If we're not careful, we can find ourselves spending a good deal of the day complaining, regretting, worrying, denying, arguing, and saying no (if only to ourselves) than appreciating, relishing, relaxing, accepting, and saying yes. The old saw that if it feels too good it's probably illegal, immoral, or fattening is no joke. Deep down inside, many of us believe it.

In fact, our entire culture, with its roots in Puritanism, has a distinct antipleasure bias. Since early childhood, it's been drummed into us that life is full of sacrifices and that the pursuit of happiness, though a guaranteed freedom in the American constitution, is nevertheless a selfish and petty enterprise. We learn that it's morally superior to deny yourself and to suffer. We learn to perform rather than experience. We learn that pleasure is not a birthright; it's a reward for hard work—a time-limited vacation from "real life."

Our pleasure-negative society, in both subtle and not-so-subtle ways, encourages us to seek pleasure outside of ourselves—through consumerism, material gain, social validation, or passive diversions—rather than through more intrinsic pleasures. As children, there are many ways our enthusiasm is dampened. We learn to restrain our natural need for physical affection, to be fearful of our sexuality, to withhold our exuberance, and to abandon our interests in favor of more practical endeavors. We learn to invalidate our own personal experience and do as we're told. As adults, we learn to live with less than what we truly yearn for, and then to make up for the deficit by buying more gadgets and toys, bigger cars and houses, better seats at concerts, and fancier clothes to hang in our closets.

The cultural emphasis on the negative is particularly obvious in how we think about intimacy. When two people first get together, what draws them to one another is how much they enjoy each other's company. Yet as soon as that relationship starts to get serious, not uncommonly the pleasure aspect of the relationship is relegated to the superficial realm, and what passes for depth in their connection is more related to the working out of problems.

When I listen to my clients talk about their relationships, I become keenly aware of how many of our concepts about relationship are dominated by society's antipleasure philosophy. Over and over I hear that love is about sacrifice, intimacy is about revealing weakness, and closeness is about sharing pain. Again, the emphasis is on performance, not experience, on *proving* love, rather than on *feeling* love. No wonder we have such a hard time making relationships work!

Body Psychotherapy and Somatic Psychology: The Body-Mind Approach

Psychotherapists have traditionally focused on mental and emotional pain, practicing with their clients what Freud called the "talking cure." The theory is that if we can simply articulate our distress, in full emotional honesty, the pain will go away. Gone would be the tension, the anxiety, the depression, the food binges, the dependence on alcohol and drugs, the unfulfilling relationships, the bad sex, and the settling for less. Unfortunately, while talking about hurt and resentment is often essential for letting go of pain, usually it's not enough.

In fact, too much valuable time and effort can be devoted to talking about dissatisfaction rather than developing genuine skills at making things better. These are actually two distinct approaches to mental health which can yield very different results.

Traditional therapy, focuses almost exclusively on how we think and, in many ways, is steeped in our culture's pleasure-negative philosophy. Most traditional therapists know a lot more about anxiety, fear, anger, anguish, resentment, guilt, shame, grief, child abuse, narcissistic injury, and traumas than they do about gratitude, love, laughter, faith, trust, sensuality, desire, passion, orgasm, and inner peace.

However, a new approach to psychology is steadily gaining ground that includes an awareness of the body and is more focused on learning positive skills for living an emotionally healthy and fulfilling life. It's grounded in the "wellness" model that has become popular in the area of physical health as a direct outgrowth of the PNI research. This mind-body approach says that since physical health, and mental and emotional well-being are clearly interrelated, when people are physically ill, their mind, body, and spirit have to be included in the healing process.

We know this philosophy works. People recovering from life-threatening illness or surgery have dramatically improved their chance of survival by developing all sorts of positive skills for good living. However, until recently, most of the emphasis on the mind-body connection has been on how the mind affects the body. It's been a notion of health that primarily has encouraged people to think more positively and to use meditation, visualization, and talking to develop a more positive mental attitude.

But it's also true that the body affects the mind. Since the mind and body are inseparable, we can also contribute to a positive state of mind by being more attuned to our bodies. We can foster good thoughts, positive visions, and the kind of sharing that brings people closer by focusing directly on what's happening in our bodies. We can become more attentive to the quality of our bodily experience instead of continually trying to mentally assess how well we may be performing. We can learn to be more guided by authentic feelings—unmistakable sensations in the body—that can motivate us in positive directions.

This body-mind approach to emotional well-being—also known as "somatic psychology"—is like the mind-body approach only the emphasis is on how states of the body affect the mind. Practiced by therapists who incorporate an awareness of the breath, body sensations, and physical energy, these body psychotherapists are usually grounded in a wellness perspective, shifting from the damage-control of traditional psychotherapy to a greater interest in skills-development and personal mastery. The body-mind approach teaches that an open, pleasured body can stimulate an expansive mind and spirit.

One psychologist who has spelled out the major factors involved in a psychological approach to wellness is Dr. Emory Cowen, the director of the University of Rochester Center for Community Study. Dr. Cowen suggests that any mental wellness program needs to specifically train people in four major areas: developing greater competence in sharpening practical skills for solving problems, building resilience and an ability to thrive and emerge stronger from difficulties, changing troublesome social situations into positive environments that can enhance health, and helping people gain a greater sense of empowerment and control over their lives.

Pleasure is the visceral, body-felt experience of well-being—it's the embodiment of happiness. With pleasure as our guide, our actions can be informed by what feels right deep down inside—especially in our heart and in that mid-section we call the gut. These areas are our body-based, positively-no-denying-it truth detectors. When we feel something here, no matter that our heads are telling us something different, we know our body holds the truth. The body never lies.

This book is about how living a life informed by pleasure can gain us genuine body-mind wellness through a greater sense of competence, helping us to become more resilient during stressful times, and strengthening our capacity to make good things happen. It's about developing the skills for becoming more optimistic, enhancing our capacity to give and accept love, maximizing the enjoyment and fulfillment of sex, and honing the ability to enjoy solitude and spiritual peace. It's about the fact that—for mental and emotional well-being, physical health and immunity, and maximum satisfaction in our intimate relationships—we actually need to relish life's joys.

With less energy going into explaining anxiety, we can invest more into building courage. With less obsessing on managing depression, we can focus more on what inspires excitement and enthusiasm. And if we can get off the tedious fixation of controlling our bad habits, we can concentrate more on widening the range of natural pleasures that are ours to fully enjoy.

Pleasure-Enhancement: The Eight Core Pleasures

The common thread linking optimism, feeling good about ourselves, experiencing emotional fulfillment in love and intimacy, enjoying deeply gratifying sex, good physical health, and positive aging, rests in the ability to fully enjoy eight core pleasures: the primal pleasure of timelessness, pain relief, play and humor, as well as mental, emotional, sensual, sexual, and spiritual pleasure.

These eight pleasures are fundamental sources of gratification that have been diminished and discouraged in many of us and have left us stunted in our ability to fulfill ourselves naturally. This book shows the critical value of each pleasure and offers a comprehensive experiential program for cultivating that pleasure so that, no matter how happy you may be now, you can be even happier.

For most of us, having and maintaining a genuinely fulfilling intimate relationship is critical to our happiness. We can all benefit from looking at how to accentuate the pleasures of a love relationship and how to develop the capacity to enjoy, rather than work hard at, emotional, sensual, and sexual intimacy. This book offers positive new tools for resolving difficulties in a relationship, reducing power plays and vindictiveness, and building on what's good about a relationship rather than incessantly trying to fix what's wrong.

We'll also see how strong moral values and a concern for the welfare of others are in complete harmony with a deep respect for the value of pleasure in everyday life. The individual pursuit of pleasure is neither selfish nor a danger to society. Rather, a person who feels good is likely to have greater goodwill and generosity of spirit than one who feels deprived.

A pleasure-motivated person moves toward what inspires interest, enthusiasm, and excitement rather than simply avoiding pain. Pleasure-motivated people are less likely to be controlling, autocratic, jealous, demanding, angry, intimidating, greedy, vindictive, or violent toward others. People whose basic needs are met, who feel secure in their ability to love and be loved, are those most likely to be kind, flexible, and democratic. Such a person gives more to others because, being fulfilled, he or she simply has more to give.

There is an enormous untapped potential for pleasure in every one of us that has yet to be fully explored. We can reconnect with our most authentic joys, and the more we do, the more deeply and unequivocally we can contact our truest self and the truest selves of the people we love.

Chapter 2

Why We Say No to Pleasure

*How we have been trained
to resist pleasure*

. . . .

Pleasure-anxiety is the foundation of the fear
of a free, independent way of living.

—*Wilhelm Reich*

If you're like most of us, you were indoctrinated with anti-pleasure messages very early on. They may have been subtle, but they permeated every area of your young life.

You may have watched your parents struggle with their lives or with each other, and now you can't shake the feeling that life is hard and relationships are always problematic. Maybe you learned from religious training to deprive yourself as a way of improving your character, yet now, no matter how much you sacrifice, you still feel like you're not good enough. Maybe you were shamed after being caught touching yourself sexually, and now you're in conflict over what turns you on. Or maybe like me, you acquired your negative bent as an abused child, feeling more and more humiliated and worthless with every verbal barb or physical blow, and now you're always on your own case, giving yourself a hard time.

So here you are, twenty, thirty, fifty years later, and very likely, in more ways than you know, you continue to do exactly what you were programmed to do—limit your full enjoyment of life. You may complain about the way things are, but now it's likely to be you and you alone who is keeping you from all the joy, excitement, enthusiasm, good feelings, and exuberance that life can afford.

Programmed for Unhappiness

The eminent psychologist Erich Fromm was one of the first to acknowledge that happiness (or unhappiness) is learned. Fromm saw happiness training as the mother's realm, though no doubt he was reflecting the cultural bias of his time that took for granted absentee fathering. In any event, he said that a mother's love is like the promised land flowing with "milk and honey." Milk is the aspect of love that is care and sustenance; honey has to do with appreciating the sweetness of life. Fromm felt that most mothers are capable of giving milk but not honey. To give honey a mother must not only be a "good mother" but a happy person, and few people, said Fromm, have achieved this aim.

From my observations, you can fail to learn to appreciate the sweetness of life from either parent. If you're a man whose father typically came home drained and emotionally unavailable, you might have learned that that's the way a man is supposed to be. Whether you unconsciously see it as your right, your curse, or your revenge on your childhood, now that you have the power, you are very likely to repeat your family pattern. As a result, you may miss out on the sweetness of a happy home life and loving children just as your dad missed out on you.

Women often learn to deny themselves in the same ways their mother denied themselves. Leah, a young attorney, told bitingly funny stories about the lengths her mother would go to keep herself unfulfilled. Though she had a master's degree, her mother never worked outside the home and never had any hobbies either. Her career, she said, was keeping her husband and two daughters fed and functioning, and this she did well. But Leah remembers her mother as forever talking wistfully about what might have been, and she was openly frustrated about all the things she would have loved to do if she only had more time. Yet, now that her girls were grown, she still didn't seem to be able to do some of the things she had said for years that she wanted to do—like taking a pottery class. One day Leah urged her to take the class, but again her mother said she had no time—only now it was because her retired husband had no interest in pottery, and she would feel guilty getting involved in something that "shuts him out."

"Do you believe it?" Leah said incredulously. Yet, in her next breath she told me she strongly regretted that she wasn't going to accept a highly desirable position she had been offered by a prestigious law firm because it might require somewhat longer hours than she had previously worked. Though she has no children and nothing to prevent her at this stage of her life from going for it, she demurred. "My husband would get really upset, and I'd just rather not hassle with him over it." But she never even brought it up with him.

For both Leah and her mother, the man was her excuse for holding back and the woman had neither the right to have what most excites her, nor skills for sitting down with him and talking it over. She didn't even want to see if the man was in fact threatened by her moving more in the direction of her own interests. He might actually be delighted to have more time by himself—or was that something each woman secretly feared? What Leah discovered as she investigated her deeper motives in my office was that she was afraid to venture out and challenge herself, so she blamed her reluctance on wanting to please her man—just as her mother did.

The Culture of Self-Denial

Despite the often heavy hand of early conditioning, our ingrained negativity is not born solely of our personal histories. Throughout the history of Western culture, society at large has encouraged a pain-based rather than a pleasure-based worldview. The implication is that the finest people are those who renounce their own pleasures, sacrificing themselves for the good of others. On the other hand, making choices and taking action based on what feels best—as opposed to what is right—is essentially seen as small minded and corrupt.

It appears that a fundamental mistrust of pleasure is deeply embedded in Western culture. The great twentieth-century French philosopher, Michel Foucault, traced the association of the virtuous hero with self-restraint over bodily cravings all the way back to the pagans. It wasn't until the Greeks, however, that this way of thinking blossomed into a model for proving one's moral superiority. For the Greeks, renouncing sexual pleasure, in particular, was considered a mark of extreme virtue. Abstaining from sex was linked directly to greater access to wisdom, truth, and spirituality and, in the communal life of the Greek thinkers, was seen as a sign of self-mastery that resulted in greater status and power over others in the intellectual community.

Religious training that teaches children to deny and suppress their natural sexual urges can turn pleasurable feelings in the body into painful feelings of guilt and shame. Not only does this doctrine often make people confused about their feelings, but it can also do harm by making essentially good people think ill of themselves. One male client of mine who was raised in a sex-negative religious home was a truly kind and compassionate human being. Yet he thought of himself as defective because his strong sexual needs led him to fantasize about sex and to masturbate. He despaired of his "character flaws" and harbored a low opinion of himself, despite the fact that he was unusually conscientious as a caseworker in a low-income health clinic, going out of his way to personally help his patients and their families cope with the effects their illnesses.

The denial of pleasure, particularly sexual pleasure, is typically seen as a basic requirement of civilized living. Sigmund Freud, the originator of psychotherapy, argued in *Civilization and Its Discontents* that human suffering was the unavoidable price we paid for the benefits of society. To live together, human beings had to repress their most basic instincts, those of sex and aggression. In addition, we had to postpone the gratification of even our most fundamental needs, such as expressing genuine feelings or seeking pain relief. Freud was the one who coined the term "the Pleasure Principle" to describe the guiding force we're born with to seek gratification. But to him, pleasure was nothing more than the absence of pain, a temporary filling of a need, not something distinct and complex in its own right.

Scholar and mythologist Riane Eisler, however, in an extraordinary study of how pleasure came to be suppressed in Western culture, has shown that human suffering is not an inevitable byproduct of society. Rather, Eisler offers compelling evidence to show that pain has been institutionalized in our society—through our myths, laws, belief systems, in how we're taught to feel about our bodies, and especially in male-female relationships—because we have evolved a way of relating to each other that is based more on a dominator rather than on a partnership model. In a partnership way of relating, social as well as intimate relationships are based on cooperation, emphasizing the links rather than the differences between people, and as a result, interactions can be bonding and nourishing. A social system of this sort—and apparently there have been a few in our historical roots—tends to value our human capacity for pleasure. On the other hand, a dominator way of interacting tends to place greater value on pain, and those who are socially sanctioned as stronger often prevail by inducing pain or fear in those who are weaker. Relationships of all kinds—especially those between parents and children and between women and men—tend to encourage punitive means of control, emphasizing obedience and a renunciation of personal gratification. Unfortunately our society shows strong signs of operating along a dominator morality and nowhere is this more obvious than in how children are often raised.

The Punishment Ethos

One of the most damaging aspects of our culture's war with pleasure is the belief that the way to control undesirable behavior is to make people suffer when they do wrong. Whether or not this belief system has any merit when it comes to controlling deviant behavior in society is subject to debate. But there can be no doubt that when it comes to raising children, or having a loving intimate relationship with another adult, or feeling good about yourself, this way of thinking and acting can be a real disaster.

Love and approval are nutrients that, for everyone, are as basic as food. Infants come into this world craving physical contact; they want to be held close to the heart, smiled at, and talked to. Young children want nothing more than to please and be enjoyed by their parents; they want to play with them, and they love it when they can make the grown-ups laugh.

As a child, your parents didn't have to wallop you physically to punish you. They may have been physically undemonstrative without intending to be punitive; they may have denied you loving touch and spontaneous hugs and kisses simply because they were denied to them, and they didn't know how else to be. Even so, if that was your childhood experience, you would most likely have interpreted your parent's lack of affection as a sign that you were being punished for not being worthy of his or her love.

On the other hand, your parents may have been purposely cold and unloving to hurt you for not meeting their expectations. They may have criticized you subtly, condemned you outright, or been verbally abusive. In any case, if your parents punished you to get you to shape up, very likely you now punish yourself in very similar ways when you're not satisfied with the way things are.

The punishment ethos instills in us a tendency to make ourselves feel guilty or ashamed. We tell ourselves we're not good enough and then we try to beat ourselves into being more disciplined. We punish ourselves with self-recriminations when we're not satisfied with our own performance—as though recounting our inadequacies will give us the energy to do better. However, feeling bad only makes us want to run away and hide from whomever is doing the punishing, even if it's from ourselves.

Enthusiasm for the task is the best way to generate the positive energy to get things done. Interest, curiosity, and excitement animate us to take action. Our bodies feel alive and move us forward. Yet it's remarkable how unaccustomed some people are to being motivated by what naturally attracts them.

A normally spry and energetic woman in her seventies one day was telling me that an attack of bronchitis had kept her homebound for almost a month. I told her I thought it would be good for her to get out in the warm spring sunshine and to take a little walk around the block to get her lungs working a bit. She agreed that it sounded good to walk by the well-tended little gardens that dotted her neighborhood. Yet she responded with a sigh and said she really ought to "force" herself to do it.

Why should a person have to be coercive with herself to do something that sounded good? I told her all she needed to do was to close her eyes and imagine how good it feels to walk, basking in the sun's warmth and seeing the signs of spring in the greenery and flowers blooming everywhere. I suggested that if she inspired herself with positive images, she wouldn't have to play this game with of push-and-resist herself.

If you punish yourself, it's very likely that you also punish those who are nearest and dearest to you when they fail to fulfill your needs and expectations. That's because the punishment ethos teaches us to withhold love, to be hurtful and vengeful toward the people we love as a way of trying to get them to do what we want. It's the dominator approach to love. Power comes from being capable of causing pain and then, when we get our wishes met, of undoing the painful conditions and providing relief.

It's amazing how much we are governed by this unconscious attitude. One young woman in therapy talked about keeping her boyfriend jealous and insecure as a way of getting him to be more thoughtful about her feelings—as though being motivated by his fears of losing her was as beneficial to their bond as being motivated by his ability to empathize with her and by his desire to give her pleasure.

This is only one of many subtle and not so subtle manipulations I see among couples. It's as though there is an unquestioned assumption that if you want something you're not getting from the other person, your best chance for getting it is to be critical, cold, distant, aggressive, or physically unavailable. Such a notion comes directly out of the punishment training we had as kids that made us think that punishing someone will get us what we want. One man bangs cupboards and doors when he's in the mood for sex and his wife isn't. Does he think petulant behavior is the way to turn her on? A woman sits in the car staring out the window as her boyfriend drives, clearly annoyed with him but not saying what his offense is. Her only hint to him is that his not knowing what's wrong is a big part of the problem. In both cases, the punishing mates may get their partners to be more responsive to their needs, but in a resentful, back-against-the-wall way that takes its toll on the relationship.

The Broad Reach of Pleasure-Resistance and Pleasure-Anxiety

Using punishment and manipulation as ways of motivating ourselves and others, rather than reward and encouragement, is a telltale sign of pleasure-resistance, a concept originally developed by Austrian psychiatrist Wilhelm Reich. A contemporary of Freud, Reich was the first to call attention to the fact that people actually learn to resist pleasure and that the resistance shows up in chronic tension in different parts of the body.

Reich wrote that as we struggle in childhood to avoid punishment by controlling our natural urges and needs we develop a kind of "armoring in the body." It's as if the muscular tightness created by holding ourselves back emotionally or sexually hardens and rigidifies our bodies in characteristic ways, such as in how we stand and move. This body armor not only numbs us and makes us less aware of our persisting pain, but it also renders us less comfortable with, and less capable of, enjoying pleasure.

But it goes deeper than that. Reich observed that it is possible to actually come to fear pleasure. Anything intensely pleasurable can be threatening because we're afraid that if we lose our restraint we'll be completely out of control. As a result, we learn to clamp down on the expansive feelings of energy streaming through our body, which are natural indicators of pleasure. Instead, low-grade pain becomes a more constant companion.

Even when we do allow ourselves pleasure, we may resist feeling quite as good as we otherwise might because the increased feelings of expansiveness oddly bring up a sense of dread. For example, the extra flow of energy throughout the body during times of sexual excitation or even times of emotional closeness with a lover, can feel overwhelming. So we pull away or do something foolish, without realizing that it's our pleasure-anxiety that's causing us to sabotage a perfectly wonderful situation.

Low Pleasure-Tolerance

When I first arrived in Woodstock, it was August and the upstate New York summer was lush and hot. The air was moist and thick with the bouquet of plant life. Flowers were in bloom everywhere. Vines of purple or white morning glories rolled along fences and crept up the trunks of trees. Willows hung over ponds. Maples and sycamores were heavy with mature leaves.

Driving along the little country roads, I would look out onto rolling fields where cows grazed. I would pass horses standing in corrals near charming, well cared for little cottages. Just behind my house, I would walk through the forest to a beautiful meadow and sit and read under a tree. I would ride my bike to hidden ponds and creeks. Off in the distance, the low, rounded Catskill Mountains provided a backdrop to it all, intense furry green ridges against vivid blue skies, where wisps of white clouds occasionally floated by.

It was glorious, and when I first arrived I had the distinct thought that it was impossible to be unhappy surrounded by such awesome natural beauty. How wrong I was. The irony was not entirely lost on me, however, that while I was telling myself that my life was horrible, I felt secure enough to take a year off from work to live in a lovely little cottage in an idyllic setting. How bad could my life be—really?

As I discovered for myself, every day in countless ways, consciously and unconsciously, most of us persist in denying ourselves our full measure of pleasure. We may push ourselves, worry, neglect our emotional needs, work mostly to please others, and be stingy with ourselves when it comes to granting time-out for play. We may even make ourselves uneasy when too many good things happen, expecting that, any minute, it's all going to come crashing down. The cumulative effect of these bad habits results in what I think of as "low pleasure-tolerance."

It may be odd to think of pleasure as something to tolerate, as though pleasure is something to put up with. But because of our inherent suspiciousness of pleasure, good feelings are not so easy to sustain.

For example, imagine that two men are offered promotions to a job that not only brings a substantial increase in income but also additional responsibilities. At first, both are thrilled and excited about their new positions. But while Joe maintains his enthusiasm for the challenge, Jack starts to generate self-doubt and anxiety.

Jack worries that his job will be too demanding and that he doesn't really have the background for some of the new tasks he'll be taking on. He pushes himself to work much longer hours and feels the need to go over his work several times to make sure he's done it right. Joe, on the other hand, feels a sense of pride that his boss has confidence in him, and while he knows he has a lot to learn in his new position, he's determined to do well. He does some research into his new assignment, finds an area that particularly interests him, and plans a creative project on that topic. While Jack is having a hard time sustaining his excitement at his good fortune, Joe is having a good time, which is generating energy for inventiveness. Who do you suppose will have the stamina and vision to move ahead? Even if both continue to do well, who do you think will have more fun? What about yourself—are you more like worried Jack or happy Joe?

Low pleasure-tolerance involves many self-limiting habits that hold us back on every level—mental, emotional, physical, and spiritual. Usually, we resist joy across the board, although we may resist a little more in some ways, a little less in others.

Mentally, we hold back from feeling as good as we can by thinking pessimistic thoughts and, in our mind's eye, picturing worst case scenarios and threatening images of the future. We make ourselves tense by running self-critical inner dialogues that trigger anxiety, guilt, shame, or resentment.

Emotionally, low pleasure-tolerance shows up as a tendency to withhold love from oneself as well as from others. We're perfectionistic, and our first reaction to a person or a situation is more likely to be fault-finding, rather than seeing the good in it.

Physically, low pleasure-tolerance shows up in chronic tension in the body, particularly in those places where we are most resistant and most undernourished. A low tolerance for pleasure may make it hard for us to get out of our heads and to savor our senses. It may render us incapable of wholeheartedly giving ourselves over to love, to become fully aroused sexually, or to enjoy intense orgasms.

Spiritually, low pleasure-tolerance can keep us from enjoying moments of quiet reflection, from counting our blessings, or from feeling a sense of reverence and awe.

How about you? How long can you sustain your good feelings before you're finding fault with the situation, the other people involved, or with yourself?

Here's a questionnaire that will enable you to determine your own pleasure-resistance. Take a few minutes now to see to what degree you may be automatically and unwittingly preventing yourself from feeling as good as you can.

The Pleasure-Resistance Profile

. . . .

1. Do you typically deny yourself what you most enjoy — foods you prefer but have convinced yourself are bad for you, work breaks to relax and replenish your energy, little treats and presents?

   Sometimes, usually

2. Do you usually feel guilty that you're not doing enough for someone or accomplishing enough?

   yes

3. Do you rehearse in your mind worst case scenarios, figuring that unless you anticipate disaster you won't be fully prepared for it when and if something bad happens?

   yes, yes, yes

4. Are you a naysayer, more likely to say no to an invitation or a new idea than yes? *NO*

5. Do you get superstitious when good things happen, knocking on wood while you wait for the other shoe to drop? *No, sometimes*

6. Do you have a hard time acknowledging your success, feeling like an impostor at times or denigrating your accomplishments?

   yes

7. Do you live your life as a melodrama, playing tragedy-king or queen, making scenes in public and dramas with intimates that involve strong displays of negative emotion? *Sometimes*

8. Do you secretly or openly think of yourself as a victim, powerless to do anything about a bad situation? *No, sometimes*

9. Are you abusive toward people who love you or who treat you well? *No*

10. Do you believe that love requires sacrifice and that the only way anyone will love you is if you forfeit your own needs and desires to theirs? *No*

11. Do you abuse food, alcohol or drugs, and do you feel you can't have a good time without your favorite substance? *No*

12. Is sex less than wonderful, marred by guilt or shame, limited in passion, and resulting in mediocre orgasms, if any? *No*

13. Do you have to be in control of a situation, getting competitive

with companions who make alternate suggestions and finding it difficult to kick back and relax? *yes*

14. Do you feel uncomfortable with solitude, making busywork for yourself to keep yourself occupied when you're alone?

yes

If you have answered yes to any or all of these questions and are ready to broaden your ability to enjoy your life, you've come to the right place. The rest of this book is about how to do just that.

Chapter 3

Keys to Reaching Your Pleasure-Potential

What pleasure actually is and how to be positively motivated

· · · · · · · · · · · · · · · ·

Without the feeling of pleasure,
happiness is only an illusion.

—*Alexander Lowen*

Alec was an attractive, soft-spoken, shy young man in his early thirties who was feeling uninspired by his life. A civil engineer, he was completely detached from his job, though he took some modicum of pride in a few of the city projects to which he had contributed. He would have preferred being a musician, and since he made good money at work, he indulged himself in a keyboard and some fine quality musical equipment to dabble in at night and on weekends.

But he considered his music making a way of wasting time and judged himself harshly for not having had the confidence to devote himself to music while he was still young enough to be taken seriously. So he didn't enjoy his work, and he didn't enjoy the love of his life—music.

"What do you enjoy?" I asked him the first time I saw him. He shrugged sadly, "Nothing much." His shoulders stooped forward, and he stared at the carpet with a blank unfocused look. "Maybe if I had a good relationship with a woman I would enjoy my life more," he mumbled with little conviction. "The trouble is that I keep picking the wrong woman. Then, when I realize it, I'm afraid to hurt her feelings, so I stick around resenting her and feeling controlled. Eventually we break up, and it's always a bad scene."

Alec had a hard time finding an example of anything he enjoyed past or present without immediately finding fault with it or with himself for liking it. He enjoyed playing soccer in high school, but he wasn't good at it. He was fascinated by archeology as a college student but abandoned the major when he decided he didn't want a career that, "to do right," required traveling. He liked riding his bicycle on the bike path near the beach, but he resented all the strollers and roller skaters who also used it.

Finally, he managed to recount the story of the first time he laid eyes on the woman he was currently seeing, at a friend's Christmas party. He didn't even know what it was about Karen that captivated him. "Whatever it was," he recalled with a laugh, "I was so drawn to her that I was in her face the next second—and I have no idea how I got through that crowd so fast. When I reached her she gave me a big smile, and I could tell she was interested."

In that brief moment, I saw Alec sparkle with energy. But the light in his eyes quickly dimmed as he started to talk about how, after he and Karen started to see each other, she turned out to be a disappointment. She was too temperamental, and she hadn't lost the few pounds she'd gained over the holidays. Still, there was that moment of genuine enthusiasm, and it was that glimmer of light that was the baseline on which we could build.

Pleasure Is Positive Motivation

Alec's story highlights some of the leading indicators of what makes for a pleasurable experience. The first is that it energizes you—it excites you, fires up your enthusiasm, and makes you feel alive and tingling. Secondly, a pleasurable experience is always expansive—it propels you out, broadens your horizons, expands your perspectives, and stimulates openness and discovery. For these reasons, pleasurable excitement is always positively motivating—it urges you to move forward; you are drawn toward what attracts you.

Pleasure is life-affirming. In fact, the roots of the word *dead* are the prefix *de-* meaning "without" and the suffix *-ad* meaning "outward movement." To be dead is to be without energy to move out. To be dead is not to expand.

While pleasure gives us positively motivated energy, pain generates negatively motivated energy. Painful feelings automatically trigger movement away from the source of pain, but unlike pleasure, they don't give a clue as to where to move toward. They simply propel us away. Panic, for example, is pure random movement—it could send a person running directly into the path of a moving car or drive a stampeding herd to its death over a cliff. Pleasure, on the other hand, always gives a clear direction. Alec was energized just looking at Karen at the party and felt like he was being drawn by a powerful magnet directly toward her.

While pleasure is expansive, pain makes us contract. We hold our breath, tense up, and want to run and hide. When we can't escape— backs against the wall and tightly wound up—we lash out in anger. Painful feelings grip us; pleasure relaxes the hold. Pleasure lets us breathe and let go.

Unfortunately, many of us have learned to be negatively, rather than positively, motivated. We've learned to make choices based on avoiding criticism and worst case scenarios rather than on what inspires enthusiasm and our greatest hopes and aspirations.

Vitality: The Embodiment of Positive Motivation

Vitality is a zest for life. It's the mental and physical vigor that we usually associate with good health and optimal enjoyment of life. Vitality completely depends on being able to be both energized and relaxed at the same time.

Think about what it's like for you to experience a moment or situation as pleasurable. Maybe you get totally absorbed in a project or listening to a favorite piece of music. You could be playing with a pet or getting a great shoulder rub, or dancing, or kissing someone and getting turned on. In each case, even though you feel energized by the activity, your body stays open and relaxed.

Internally, we actually do expand in pleasure and contract in pain. A system of nerves—known as the autonomic nervous system—runs between the head and all the organs and glands of the body and has two subdivisions that act antagonistically. One side, the sympathetic system, responds to possible danger by shooting adrenaline and other stress hormones into the bloodstream and triggering the emergency or fight or flight reaction. Then, when the danger is past, the parasympathetic side of the system takes over, releasing calming biochemicals such as endorphins, that induce relaxation and the restoration or rejuvenation reaction.

When we're in a state of fear or anger and the sympathetic nervous system is predominant, our insides contract. Our arteries, veins, and capillaries get narrow and all the muscles in the body shrink, including the heart and the viscera—our internal organs. The heart gets smaller and tighter yet it has to beat harder to pump the blood into the more constricted vessels. Blood pressure builds with emotional pressure. The chest feels tight or in pain. Breathing comes quicker and is more shallow; the pupils constrict. Energy moves out of the brain, heart, stomach, and gut, down into the legs and up into the shoulders and arms. You may not be able to think or feel clearly, but your legs will have the strength to run away, your arms to fight, and your hands to curl into fists and become weapons.

When the danger is past and we feel safe and in a state of positive emotion—whether relieved, thankful, loving, celebratory, or all of these—the parasympathetic system becomes more active. At this point, our insides expand. Our arteries, veins, and capillaries relax and widen, and blood pressure lowers. All the muscles and organs in the body begin to let go. The heart relaxes into a slow and steady beat. Blood flows back into the center of the body—back to the brain, the heart, and the gut. Breathing slows and becomes more rhythmic; the eyes become moist and sparkling. Once again we can think rationally, feel more expansive emotions, and operate on a more integrated level.

However it's not like one side of the autonomic system is bad while the other is good. For example, both systems come into play during sex; the sympathetic raises the excitement level and the parasympathetic stimulates the male genitals to erection and the female to lubrication. The sympathetic system also fires during other times of pleasurable excitement like hearing a favorite song, riding a roller coaster, or watching a thrilling sporting event.

It's when the two sides operate in sync—in a state of autonomic balance, when we don't contract with the extra excitement but stay open—that we can most feel the pleasure of energy. Energy streams through our body, and we allow it to do so by expanding with it. On an everyday basis, when we are in a state of relaxed excitement, we feel at the top of our form. We're alert, energetic, motivated, and at the same time, feel open, expansive, and calm. We're positively motivated, drawn to what we're doing, not negatively motivated and driven by fear or anger.

One thing is for sure; we don't feel so great when only one side of the nervous system predominates. If we keep ourselves in a state of emergency a good deal of the day, staying tense and hyper-alert for any sign of danger, we feel anxious, under pressure, and often hostile. An overactive sympathetic response creates wear and tear on the body—the worst consequence of this state of stress—and makes us more susceptible to breaking down. But an overactive parasympathetic reaction is not good either and can go hand in hand with depression and lethargy. Balance is best.

Four Cornerstones for Reaching Your Pleasure-Potential

Even when it comes to achieving something as obviously positive as taking greater pleasure in your life, growth is never without some challenge. To enjoy more pleasurable excitement than you may be used to, you have to welcome it, and you also need to be able to relax into, rather than contract against, the burst of extra energy. This is not always easy to do.

Throughout the book, we'll be exploring ways to become more open to some of life's greatest delights. At the end of each chapter, you'll have an opportunity to personally experiment with some of the ideas presented. When you experiment, be prepared to meet your pleasure-resistance head on. You may find times when you experience a particular pleasure—or even just consider doing so—that a negative inner voice kicks in with fear messages or self-recriminations. Keep in mind that any time you devalue yourself or your good feelings, or get scared of being too open and relaxed, that's where the most growth can occur. Of course, if you don't experiment at all with any of the exercises at the end of each chapter, however you may rationalize it, it may just be your low pleasure-tolerance keeping you from pushing your limits.

Often, life's most cherished pleasures occur in loving intimate relationships. If you are presently in an intimate relationship, you will have many opportunities during the course of this book to enhance the pleasure-potential of your relationship through what you and your partner can do for, and with, one another. Even so, a major portion of the exploration of your pleasure-potential entails stretching your own limits on pleasure and taking responsibility for your own capacity to be expansive.

If you want to be in a loving relationship and are not, it is especially valuable to develop your pleasure-potential on your own. The more pleasure you allow yourself, the more likely you are to attract a lover who is beyond suffering a relationship and is ready to love and share joy.

Stretching your pleasure-tolerance and increasing your capacity to enjoy good feelings rests on what I think of as the four cornerstones of pleasure: excitement, challenge, authenticity, and courage.

Excitement: Enjoying the Sensation of Energy

Excitement is energy and, like every other kind of energy—electricity, solar power, the water wheel—it generates movement. When you're excited, you can feel the life force pulsing through your body. You feel like moving and you have a keen sense of where you want to go. You're not tethered to the past or to the future. You're alive and well and living in the present.

Pleasurable excitement comes in different forms. You can be mentally stimulated, emotionally charged, physically aroused, or spiritually revitalized. You can enjoy your curiosity or be spurred on emotionally by feelings of warmth and affection. You can be energized sensually by appealing visions, sounds, or smells, and you can be sexually turned-on by all of the above.

There are also many different degrees or intensities of excitement. You can be energized in only one part of your body or buzzing everywhere all at once. You can feel a nice quiet hum of contentment or, like James Brown, you can be so outrageously exuberant it just "makes you wanna shout." Excitement is better medicine for depression, hopelessness, boredom, and loneliness than anything that comes in a powder or out of a bottle.

But there's a fine line between excitement and fear. Both are physical experiences where there is an activation of energy. In each case, the heart beats faster, the pulse is stronger, and more blood flows into our different muscles and organs. When a situation is interpreted positively, we'll make good mental pictures and tell ourselves good things about it. That way, the heart stays open and relaxed, the blood vessels dilate, and blood flows easily. The excitement feels warm, energizing, and expansive.

When our ability to enjoy pleasure in a particular area is limited, excitement can be interpreted negatively and bring up fearful thoughts and feelings. If so, we're more likely to conjure up negative mental pictures about doom and disaster that set off an emergency stress reaction. Now the rapidly beating heart contracts in fear, muscles tighten, vessels narrow, and blood pressure builds. Excitement turns into fear and feels terribly uncomfortable.

That's what happened to Alec, the young man we met at the beginning of the chapter. At first, he enjoyed being turned on by Karen, but time and again, especially when things were going well, he would start to feel trapped and to question whether Karen was the right woman for him. Then he would close himself off to her and start to feel anxious. A few times, after a particularly enjoyable night of lovemaking at Karen's apartment, Alec had to get up from bed and go home because he said he was feeling nervous and couldn't sleep.

Alec had a hard time staying relaxed when he felt excited and, as a result, couldn't just surrender to his good feelings and let himself be. One of the most critical skills he needed to develop was to let go and enjoy the sensation of energy streaming through his body, without having to clamp down on it with his sour thoughts.

Challenge: Staying Relaxed During Difficult Times

To stay stimulated, we need to continually challenge ourselves to negotiate new terrain. It's easy to get into a rut and to keep repeating what we know works. When we do, however, potential sources of pleasure in our lives get narrower and narrower.

This is true because our entire sensory system is built to respond primarily to change and to turn off when the stimulation is unvarying. We cease to hear the neighbor's lawnmower or the TV in the next room, for instance, unless it suddenly gets louder or softer. Whenever stimulation is constant we adapt to it, even in the case of low-grade pain, and we can become progressively less aware and less responsive to the world and the people around us.

If we settle in and opt for the familiar over the challenging, the whole body adapts, becoming less sensitive and sharp. In the sixties, Bob Dylan sang, "He who isn't busy being born is busy dying." There's a basic truth to those words. There's no such thing as maintaining and staying the same. If you're not getting better with time, you're getting worse.

As I see it, the key to success in all things—whether in business, at love, or on a spiritual quest—is to be able to stay open and relaxed during difficult times. If we can do that, we can stay expansive when we feel challenged or threatened, and instead of clamping down and doing something destructive, we can develop our competence to acting wisely. The biggest challenge of all is to look at a problem from the bright side—as an opportunity to move creatively through stuck areas and into potent and positive new directions.

Authenticity: In Touch with Your Inner Compass

To experience life's greatest pleasures you have to be true to yourself. Nobody knows better than you what feels good to you and what doesn't. Nobody has the right to tell you what should or shouldn't feel good to you. It either does or it doesn't. The only real truth is your subjective truth.

We are all born with an "inner compass"—a grounding in truth that is body-based—that often renders children more in touch with what's real than adults. If your feelings as a child were rarely validated, and you learned to question your heart and gut reactions, you can lose your inborn sense of knowing. As the French say, you can "lose north."

Without a strong inner compass, you can lose the sense of certainty about what feels expansive and right versus what's contractive and wrong. Most importantly, you can become completely dependent on other people to tell you what to do. But of course, what's good for them isn't necessarily what's good for you.

In order to cultivate your pleasures and follow *your* truth, you have to be able to know the truth. That means you need to be in touch with your authentic self—the true sensations of your body and your true likes and dislikes, not just what your head tells you you're supposed to like. The experiments at the end of each chapter will orient you to look for your authentic pleasures, to discover what naturally sparks your excitement, and to practice enhancing those experiences.

Courage: Facing Your Fears

Courage is the antidote for anxiety. Being able to tolerate high levels of pleasurable excitement without scaring yourself with anxious thoughts, approaching a painful situation as an opportunity to grow, and being true to yourself even when you meet with disapproval from people who are important to you—these situations require a boldness of spirit.

The word *courage* comes from the Latin word *cor,* meaning "heart or spirit." To have courage is to enter a potentially dangerous or painful situation, one that arouses your fear, and to face it instead of withdrawing or running from it. Standing up to something that doesn't really scare you can't rightfully be called courageous. But if your heart pounds and you can stay open instead of contracting, then you can have the energy to face any challenge and to deal with it resourcefully.

Some people have lots of courage when it comes to taking physical risks. They can dive hundreds of feet to the bottom of the sea with nothing but an aqua lung and a harpoon to keep them from becoming lunch for a shark. But when it comes to being completely honest, saying a clear no instead of a couched one, or revealing a personal need or a sexual desire to someone they love, these same intrepid adventurers may suddenly become cowards. For these people, emotional risks can be much more threatening than gambling life or limb.

Yet facing emotional hazards with alertness and dexterity can make you feel good about yourself in the same way that overcoming physical peril does. Some people may be able to temporarily increase their sense of self-worth by repeating affirmations to themselves or by fishing for compliments and validation from others. But nothing compares with the genuine pride that comes when, in the spirit of adventure, you bravely face a personal challenge and turn it into a pleasurable delight.

Enhancing your ability to accept and sustain pleasurable experiences relates to personal mastery. Mastery is the opposite of coping. When you're just coping, it implies that you're getting limited satisfaction and putting up with a bad situation. You may be doing the best you can, but "the best" is often based on repeating old ways of doing things. When you meet your life with an attitude that involves the four cornerstones of excitement, challenge, authenticity, and courage, however, you become less interested in what you can't do, or can't have, and you become absolutely fascinated by all that you can do and can have. Mastery depends on being positively motivated. When you're inspired by good feelings, there's no end to your energy.

The experiments that follow are for exploring your inner experience of pleasure—particularly by examining how pleasure vitalizes you and energizes your body.

Personal Experiments

. . . .

1. Make a list of five of the most memorable experiences of your life.
Describe one to someone this week and try to jog your memory to remember more
about it. See if you can conjure up a strong sense of what that experience actually felt
like in your body, then see which images can actually reawaken some of those same
sensations again.

2. Notice how it feels to describe a good experience to someone. Do you feel
uncomfortable talking about it, like you're bragging? Do you feel superstitious, as
though you could be tempting fate? Do you feel exhilarated recalling your good fortune
or adventure?

**3. Think of a time when you had the nerve to do something exciting that
also scared you.** How did you find the courage? Can you recapture the actual sensation of courage in your heart as you recall the experience? What specifically did you
gain by challenging yourself in that way?

**4. Think of a time when you were tempted to go along with what was
expected of you, and instead, you opted to be true to yourself—and it
turned out better than you could ever have imagined.** What danger did you
face at exposing your true feelings, and what persuaded you to act on your authentic
self? Are you still glad you did it?

**5. Periodically, remind yourself that the more you are true to what you feel
in your body, the healthier and happier you will be, and the greater your
vitality.** As the poet Theodore Roethke put it, "We think by feeling. What is there to
know? I hear my being dance from ear to ear." What makes your being dance from ear
to ear?

The Eight Core Pleasures: A Developmental History of Delight

....

Recognizing the full spectrum of pleasures

· · · · · · · · · · · · · · · · · ·

Once we fully recognize the consequences of
our treatment of babies, children, one another, and ourselves,
and learn to respect the real character of our species, we cannot
fail to discover a great deal more of our potential for joy.

—Jean Liedloff

My nephew Isaac was the first baby I had any extended contact with. I admit I didn't diaper and feed him that much, nor was I there when he fell and needed stitches, and I didn't sit with him nights when he was feverish with the flu like his mom and dad did. I was more what you might call the enchanted auntie. I spent most of my time with him in play, totally captivated by seeing him in apparent and spontaneous joy. Every good researcher needs a little firsthand knowledge of her subject, and Isaac was part of my fieldwork into the inborn human capacity for pleasure.

Studies in child development have traditionally provided detailed accounts of the kinds of developmental traumas during childhood that lead to adult disturbance. We have an extensive body of knowledge about all the things that can go wrong in one's earliest years that make for insecurity, low self-esteem, shame, suppressed hostility, anxiety, guilt, narcissism, resentment, and anything else that might trouble us.

To reconnect with all of life's possible pleasures, however, we need to re-acquaint ourselves with our earliest, purest, most natural capacity for pleasure. These are the basic building blocks of human pleasure—the childhood experiences that prepare us for the pleasures of a lifetime. In the chapters that follow, we'll explore each of these realms individually and practice ways to reclaim our birthright. To begin with, let's first identify these eight innate pleasures that define our human capacity for enjoyment.

Primal Pleasure

For almost a hundred years, psychologists have described birth trauma as the prototypical experience for all later pain and anxiety. The theory is that we start out in virtual paradise suspended in the amniotic sac, deriving all our nutrients for growth from our mother's body. Wanting for nothing and totally fulfilled, prior to birth, we are suddenly jolted from this state of perfection, thrust down a cramped tunnel into a world of searing air, harsh light, and thunderous noise many decibels above the comforting heartbeat, which was our familiar universe.

That all makes sense. But how come nobody ever asked, "If there is such a thing as Primal Pain, there must also be Primal Pleasure, and what can we learn from it about human development?

Primal Pleasure begins with floating, cradled in a sac of warm fluid, connected to a source of complete nurturance without any sense of separation or boundary. Whatever gets recorded as our earliest memories must have something to do with the sensation of floating weightless and timeless in suspended animation, gently rocked, nutrients flowing in and waste out, and in sync with surrounding organic rhythms. If birth is the primal pain, signaling separation, danger, and anxiety, then the experience of floating—of being buoyant—must be the primal pleasure, signaling connection, safety, and love.

Think about it. The physical experience of bliss is fundamentally an experience of buoyancy: You literally feel like you're soaring. That's probably why feeling good is so often described as "just going with the flow." Indeed, much of our language reflects the pleasure and joy we associate with being buoyant. When good things happen, we say we feel like we're "walking on air." A cheerful person, undaunted by hard times and optimistic, is described as having a "buoyant spirit." People who use drugs are looking to get "high." The word *elated* comes from a Latin root meaning "to be lifted up" and *exultation* literally means "to leap." Infants love to be buoyant. They are comforted most from their pain by being picked up and rocked, especially when the bleary-eyed mama or papa is pacing, affording the full antigravity experience. A few months later, a favorite activity, judging from babies' volumes of cooing and giggling, is being tossed into the air. I would gasp as I watched my brother toss Isaac high into the air and catch him. I always felt a little tense watching him in flight, his arms and legs outstretched like a skydiver, in gales of laughter. My brother, on the other hand, seemed more fascinated by Isaac's fearlessness. "Look at this," Lou would say to me, "complete trust."

The desire for weightlessness never goes away. Older children like to twirl until dizzy,. then flop giddily on the floor and watch the world spin. You may remember your own early pleasures with floating, perhaps in the playground, screaming "higher, higher" as you got pushed on a swing, wanting to feel more lift, more wind on your face, and more excitement beating in your heart.

There is a freedom of spirit in defying gravity. As we get older, we graduate from merry-go-rounds to Ferris wheels to roller coasters and, for the most adventurous, sky diving or leaping off bridges with bungee cords tied to the ankles. Going for a little less adrenaline, you might prefer to find your buoyancy jumping on a trampoline, or something even more mellow like floating in a pool. At its most intense, orgasm can feel like a total loss of boundaries as you merge with your partner, completely replicating the unbounded state of the original pleasure—the sense of timeless buoyancy. At the simplest and perhaps most profound level of primal pleasure is the pure joy of completely letting go of the need to do something and instead to "just be."

The Pleasure of Pain Relief

Since the birth process itself is painful, the first pleasure encountered in the new world is the relief of pain. After our personal expulsion from Eden, pleasure comes with being comforted and soothed, held close to our mother's familiar heartbeat, and being enveloped by the warmth, the softness, and the smell of her familiar flesh.

Affectionate human touch is the most naturally healing physical pleasure. A wailing, frightened infant finds comfort in human contact that can soothe an ache or spasm, relieve a need, and reassure fear. Babies crave holding and stroking and, without it, can die of a phenomenon known as "infant marasmus". They literally waste away and lose interest in living. But none of us ever outlives the need for warm, empathic touch. Grown-ups who don't get enough touching, it seems to me, can also suffer from "adult marasmus."

That's because nothing feels quite so good as another's caring hands gently holding and hugging you, or perhaps massaging you, smoothing the knots in your sore muscles and otherwise soothing your tensions. We all have a body hunger for physical connection and crave the warmth of empathic touch and the healing relaxation it brings.

This desire is so strong that humans have domesticated dogs and cats to be their "pets," literally creatures to touch affectionately. Indeed, studies have shown that people who live alone with a pet, recover from illness twice as quickly as patients with similar illnesses who live alone without a pet. People deprived of a daily embrace get depressed more often and feel pain more keenly—probable symptoms of marasmus.

The Elemental Pleasures: Laughter, Play, Movement, and Vocal Expression

Once the infant is sufficiently soothed and nurtured and starts to get comfortable with her new surroundings—with loving touch it could be very soon after birth—she begins to enjoy her budding existence. She smiles. What a marvelous survival mechanism Mother Nature builds into babies' complete dependence on adults: When they're treated well, they're so delightfully appreciative. Babies have warm, generous, adorable smiles for anyone who treats them lovingly. And when you play together, they can laugh like the funniest thing just happened.

For grown-ups as well as for babies, a good belly laugh is a decidedly physical pleasure. Your whole body shakes and vibrates, and your breathing rhythms are profoundly altered. Deep inhales occur reflexively, and exhales are vocalized, often loudly. We're all aware that a good laugh can induce a state of relaxation and well-being. Yet it has actually been demonstrated in the laboratory that mirthful laughter can decrease heart rate and substantially reduce muscle tension and blood pressure.

To play is to engage in an activity just for the fun of it, just for the sheer excitement or stimulation of it. You enjoy what you're doing, and the pleasure is like an energy factory—your battery is charged, and it keeps you going and going. When you play, you're fully absorbed in the here-and-now and anything you do in a playful spirit, even if it's work, puts you into that flow.

Play often has a distinctly energetic component to it. The most characteristic feature of children's play is their boundless energy—it seems they would always rather run than walk. Starting in the first few months of life, healthy babies are constantly moving. They shake their arms and kick their legs. They twist their bodies and reach for your nose or pull your hair. They pick things up, stick them in their mouths, then see how far they can fling them. First they scoot around; then they crawl. Soon they pull themselves up by the furniture and move about, exploring their environment on unsteady feet. No sooner do they learn to walk than they're running, skipping, jumping, and chasing the dog, the cat, and other kids. Until they drop from exhaustion, they're in perpetual motion.

Closely related to the joys of movement are the joys of making sound. Spending a few hours alone with Isaac when he was ten months old clued me into how much babies enjoy accompanying their movements with sounds. For two hours, he crawled on all fours, hauling himself up by chairs, door knobs, and open drawers. He climbed and dangled from every piece of furniture, pulled things off shelves, played with toys, tossed balls, and punctuated each of his accomplishments with shrieks of delight.

His cries were like hoots in celebration of the discoveries of the moment, and I could tell he was impressed with the sound of his own voice. He'd giggle and do it again, his eyes getting big with wonder. At one point, I mimicked his shriek and made a big hit with him. He had been sitting on the floor facing me, and he laughed so hard he fell over. When he got back up he shrieked again, this time stretching his neck, squinting his eyes, and really letting 'er rip. Again I parroted his sound and again he fell over in paroxysms of laughter. I felt enormously amusing. We kept it up, off and on for almost an hour. It was our first real conversation.

Making appreciative sounds is a way of being energetically

expressive. Thrill to a favorite musician in concert and you let out a whoop of appreciation as you applaud a great solo. Singing is a form of jubilant self-expression and is especially satisfying when you can really belt it out. Bite into a creamy delicious eclair dripping in chocolate or get rubbed on the shoulders in just the right spot and you let out a moan of rapture. Uninhibited people often find themselves incapable of making love without making sounds, typically crying out as they orgasm.

Mental Pleasures

An infant comes into the world predisposed with a curiosity to search out and get to know her environment. Research has shown that, from birth on, the human brain craves information. Newborns' brains are fed first by the mental nourishment that begins with a smiling, bobbing face and melodious voice no more than eight inches away. Very soon after, interest progresses outward, as the infant is eager to comprehend a universe of stimulation.

Learning is among life's earliest pleasures, and if we are allowed to follow our own interests, curiosity and wonder will propel us into exploring ever-new situations. When we're kids, we crave stimulation, and the worst thing in the world is to be bored. Understimulated children get cranky and restless. Parents know how uncomfortable it can be, for example, on a long car trip with two little kids in the backseat who have exhausted their supply of games and are whining and moaning about not being there yet.

Isaac now has a beautiful little sister named Emma, just two and a half years younger than he, and I am fascinated by how absorbed she can get in a task. At three years of age, I watched her repeatedly put together a three-dimensional puzzle, take it apart, and then put it together again, totally entranced. Even though she had a cold at the time and could breathe only through her mouth, she seemed oblivious to everything but finding the right piece of puzzle for the right space.

The great variety of mental pleasures all relate to how to enjoy the life of the mind: the intellect and imagination, as well as the internal dialogues we engage in with ourselves all day long. Especially critical is the habitual way we narrate the events of the day to ourselves. How do we interpret other people's actions? When our mind wanders, to where does it wander—a pleasant fantasy or an unlikely hazard? To the degree we allow ourselves the freedom to pursue our natural interests, we can continue to enjoy learning, the sudden insights that rearrange how we think about something, and even an occasional epiphany.

Emotional Pleasures

Early psychological research suggested that we are born with three primary emotions out of which all later emotions grow—love, fear, and anger. Each of these emotions represents a direction: Love moves us forward toward what promises nourishment; fear moves us away from danger, to hide or shrink from it; anger moves us against a threat of harm, and we want to destroy it. Fear and anger are usually thought of as negative emotions, but they can be positive in that they can be very informative. Genuine love is always a pleasure. When love brings pain it's not the love that hurts; it may be the disappointment of losing love or not getting what you want from the one you love. But the feeling of love is always expansive, always a strong energy moving you forward.

Love usually starts in a mother's arms. Mother carries life-sustaining fluid in plump silky sacs right up against her heart, with its recognizable pulse signaling safety and buoyancy. Mother looks into the eyes of the child in her arms and smiles and makes soft, melodious sounds of praise and appreciation. Baby's eyes lock onto mother and he smiles back. This is known as bonding—a wordless dialogue based on a combination of heartfelt warmth and playfulness.

Love is the prototype from which all purely positive emotions derive. You may like something or someone, feel thankful, hopeful, trusting, eager, enthusiastic, all the way through to exultation, jubilation, ecstasy, or bliss—they are all variations of love. Your heart feels warm and relaxed—and at the same time stimulated and open. These good feelings propel you forward. You feel trusting, attracted, drawn to what's in front of you.

As we get older, emotions become more complicated. Fear can be a pleasure—like at a horror movie. Though, that's because in two hours the lights are going to come back on and we can get up and go home. Anger can sometimes feel good—like when we let our frustrations out by yelling at someone. Though we usually have to deal with hurt when they then yell back or leave.

Revenge also holds a certain satisfaction. Sometimes it feels good to get back at someone who has hurt you, like when you were a kid and you clobbered the bully who took your toy. But revenge is never-ending negativity—it's has been around since before the Bible was written, and the same protagonists are still causing each other grief. As Gandhi said, "An eye for an eye makes the whole world blind." That kid you clobbered now owes you one—and you can be sure he'll get you back, and then some.

Love also gets more complicated, turning into disappointment when someone you care about lets you down; or into grief, when you lose a beloved friend. Then, emotional pleasure comes with the release of tears and with comforting words to soothe the sadness that has gripped the heart.

Ultimately, variations on love are the most consistent source of good feelings, with the fewest negative side-effects. Enthusiasm, gratitude, hope, faith, courage, pride, falling in love, infatuation, true love, devotion—these are some of the higher level positive emotions that are among life's most exquisite joys.

Sensual Pleasures

Babies emerge from the dark womb without much vision, but with a number of other senses already intact, and with some very distinct preferences. Just twelve hours old, a newborn who has not yet tasted mother's milk will respond with a gurgle of satisfaction to a drop of sugar water on its tongue and with a pained grimace to lemon juice.

Babies hear long before birth and, apparently, enjoy and can fall asleep most easily to the sound of the human heart or to familiar music played to them in utero.

From birth, we get information from our world through our five senses—sight, hearing, touch, taste, and smell—but to be sensual is to take delight in, and to linger over, the stimulation. Babies are very sensual—that's how they explore their world. They stick everything into their mouths, even dirt. They like to smear food and smell hair and watch mobiles of dolphins bobbing overhead. One toddler I know likes to carry a fleecy blanket and stick fuzzy balls pulled from it up into her nose. Another sucks his thumb and smells his fingers at the same time. Most children have very definite food preferences. My niece Emma, at two years of age, loved pickles and pitted olives but hated bananas.

All healthy children are sensuous. As we get older, however, sensual pleasure becomes associated with sex and, except for an aesthetic appreciation of the arts, we tend to downplay these natural sources of nourishment. To enhance our joys in life, sensual pleasures are critical components in the pleasure equation. We not only need to remember to smell the roses along the way, we also need to make room in our lives to admire their crimson petals, to listen to the rain, to really taste dinner, and to really touch a friend.

Sexual Pleasures

Boy babies have erections while they are still in their mother's wombs. After birth, they can have erections during breast feeding, when being diapered, bathed, or at other times of social interaction. We don't know yet if female fetuses have clitoral erection but girl babies are known to lubricate shortly after birth. This kind of research provides definitive proof that we are sexual from birth, fully capable of arousal from infancy on. Obviously, the capacity for sexual arousal is separate and distinct from the reproductive system, which doesn't begin to function until puberty.

Between six and eight months of age, boys will discover their penises; girls on average just a few months later will discover their vulvas. According to Dr. Thomas Mazur, the director of psychoendocrinology at the Children's Hospital of Buffalo, New York, by the beginning of their second year boys and girls both will become more focused on genital stimulation. They will use repetitive hand gestures and will rock and squeeze their thighs or straddle objects and toys and put pressure on that part of their bodies. Often, they will smile and coo and make affectionate gestures toward their mothers following this kind of self-stimulation. How the mother responds naturally becomes one of the earliest of the many factors that impacts the child's sexual development.

Sex play with other children has been observed in children as young as three. From age four on, children allowed to play freely will engage in what looks like pretend intercourse, changing sexual positions and roles, and enormously enjoying their activities. Most children, male and female, will stimulate themselves sexually and some develop real skill at masturbation.

We're no different from monkeys and other primates when it comes to sexual development. The young of both species engage in sexual rehearsal play, and as a result of this experience, grow up capable of having sex and reproducing. When monkeys grow up in isolation and are deprived of this kind of juvenile sex play, as adults they don't know how to have sex. With humans, it's a little more complicated. Though juvenile sex play is a natural developmental stage in a healthy adult sex life, the experience is complicated by a strong cultural taboo against childhood sexuality.

The persistent need in our culture to maintain the fiction of childhood sexual innocence probably does more to influence our eroticism and to determine what turns us on sexually than any other single cultural factor. The danger of being caught in sex play—the anxiety, embarrassment, shame, conflict, and self-recriminations—have the paradoxical effect of intensifying sexual arousal, not only in childhood but as adults as well. It's ironic that the social force meant to contain our sexual urges has the completely contrary effect of intensifying them. As a result, forbidden fruit often tastes the sweetest, and sex in marriage with a long-term partner, not uncommonly, becomes the most difficult sexual liaison to keep exciting.

Along with sexual arousal and eroticism, orgasm is another main sexual pleasure. The explosive burst that scientists have measured as two to five genital contractions each lasting eight-tenths of a second long is the generally agreed upon prize of genital play. Many adults remember their first orgasm in adolescence as a milestone of their sexual life, whether or not it was had by their own hand. While boys can have nocturnal emissions and some girls can be awakened by a spontaneous climax, most of the joys of orgasm are learned through practice, and masturbation is the easiest way to learn. The greater tendency for boys to masturbate during adolescence than girls may account for the greater ease with which males have orgasm over females. As adults, skill plays an important role in sexual pleasure, and by all accounts, when competence is combined with affection for one's partner, the result can be one of life's most intense pleasures.

Spiritual Pleasures

I heard a story several years ago that touched me deeply. After her baby brother was born, a three-year-old girl begged her parents to leave her alone with the baby. Fearing the child was jealous of the newcomer the parents refused, but the girl persisted. The parents were troubled about denying their daughter and, not knowing what to do, spoke with the family pediatrician on their next visit. The doctor suggested they honor the child's request and leave her alone with him in the baby's room with the intercom on so they could hear what was going on. If there were any suspicious sounds they could rush into the room and protect the newborn.

The little girl was delighted when she was told she could be alone with the baby. The parents ushered her into the room, closed the door, and rushed into their bedroom to listen. They heard the little girl approach the crib and, in an urgent whisper, say to the baby, "Quick, tell me about God. I'm starting to forget."

I don't know if the story is true or not; I like it for the reminder that children are close to the infinite and enjoy a spiritual awareness.

For me, a sense of the spiritual came when my mother told me at age four that babies grew in a mother's tummy and then were born from her body. It was at that point I knew that, if there was such a thing as birth, there was also death. It scared me. When Isaac asked his father what happens when we die, he was told that some people believe that your soul flies up to heaven and that the soul is the part of you that lives forever. Isaac pondered the answer for a few moments and seemed satisfied, but then had another question, "Will the sun hurt my eyes?" "No," his father confidently reassured him.

 I don't think a belief in God or the immortal soul are necessary aspects of spirituality. All that is required is to feel a part of something good that is larger than oneself. To be in touch with the spiritual is to identify yourself with the whole: with the family of man, woman, and child, and with all of life.

Spiritual pleasures can be sensed most particularly when the mind is quiet—no thoughts, no inner dialogues, no fantasies—just the silence of inner peace that allows us a direct experience of the infinite.

Empathy, morality, and altruism are other important spiritual pleasures. The enjoyment of empathy has to do with feeling so connected to another, or to many others, that their joy is your joy and their triumphs your triumphs. The most rudimentary forms of empathy show up almost from birth: babies act distressed when they hear other babies crying or when they feel their mothers tense.

A pleasure-based morality is not about doing only what feels good to you and everybody else be damned. Rather it's about having a keen sense of right and wrong—a clear moral compass—so that doing what feels right is immensely satisfying.

Altruism is about giving wholeheartedly to another and has been shown to have very positive effects on the immune system of the gift-giver. This is especially true when the giver can witness the receiver benefit from the gift.

These spiritual pleasures represent some of our highest human qualities in that they inspire good feelings and provide a loving safety net all around us. The capacity to be moved through spiritual pleasure can be witnessed in very young children, but it needs to be reinforced throughout childhood to be sustained. As adults, an enjoyment of spiritual pleasure is healing in many ways. A good deal of evidence now exists, for example, showing that both meditation and prayer are associated with a deep sense of inner peace and an enhanced ability to recover from serious illness.

These, then, are the eight core pleasures we will look to enhance. Each is critical to happiness because each supports a lifestyle based on a healthy balance of emotional, physical, and spiritual gratification. However, as children, we learn to favor some over others. We learn to put all our eggs into only a few baskets, because some pleasures seem unavailable or are outright forbidden. Yet when any one source of pleasure is overused it can become toxic. If we get most of our pleasure in life from eating, a sensual pleasure, we overeat; from sex, and we suffer a lot of morning-afters; from caretaking and overindulging in love, and our own lives will drift aimlessly by. As healthy individuals in a state of balance, we need to be able to partake of all of life's pleasures.

A Continuum of Pleasures

The ability to enjoy pleasure is cumulative. If we hold back in any one of these eight core pleasures, every other pleasure will be limited by that restraint. Our capacity to enjoy each of the developmentally earlier and more basic pleasures effects how well we'll be able to enjoy the developmentally later, more complex joys.

Primal pleasure sets the pace. The more we can let go to primal pleasure and surrender physical tension, the more we can surrender everywhere. It makes sense that the more we can surrender physically, the more we can let go of pain, and then, the more playful we can be. The more we can enjoy these most basic of pleasures, the better we'll be able to let go of limiting mental habits and cultivate a more positive outlook. The more we can enjoy our minds, the more positive our emotions will be. The better we can enjoy all these other pleasures, the more fully we can savor our senses. And as a result of letting go in our bodies, in our minds, and in our hearts, sexual arousal and release can become that much more intense. Finally, ability to enjoy the spirit deepens and brings greater meaning to all other pleasures. Each time you allow greater pleasure in any one realm, it informs every other pleasure and opens you up to greater pleasure everywhere.

With each of the eight core pleasures, there are also different intensities of energy and of enjoyment. There are nice times and there are wildly fabulous times. They're both good, both expansive. What's critical is your ability to stay open to the pleasure, to explore it, and to enjoy the experience.

In every pleasure, the first level of intensity is mostly about relaxing, letting go of negative feelings, becoming more in touch with what feels good, and more attuned to the present moment. The second level of intensity comes with not just being relaxed, but energized at the same time. Second level pleasures are about sustaining and intensifying positive excitement and becoming more animated by your good feelings. The third level is the most charged and intense, where words such as *thrilled, ecstatic,* or *jubilant* may apply.

In the mental realm, for example, first level pleasures may involve curiosity and gaining new knowledge; second level pleasures may entail insight and a deepened comprehension and awareness; third level pleasures may involve a profound revelation that changes the course of one's life. In sex, first level pleasures have to do with enjoying the early stages of sexual interest and desire; the second level has to do with feeling lust and passion; third level pleasures may involve experiencing explosive full-body orgasms.

Before we start our journey into pleasure, take some time to explore your own developmental history of delights.

Personal Experiments

· ·

You may choose to just think about the issues raised here and catch whatever spontaneous insights you may have that way. You may choose to have a conversation with an intimate friend who may also be interested in investigating his or her own pleasure history. Or you may write these questions into a journal, and then answer them for yourself.

If you choose to write, try a stream of consciousness kind of writing where you write from the heart, putting down the first thought that comes to you without censoring. Describe memories, and just tell the story rather than try to analyze it. You will learn more when you go back and read it than when you write it.

1. Recall some of your earliest memories of pleasures. What made you happy? What made you laugh? When did you feel most in the flow?

2. Which pleasures have you favored over the years? Trace some of your current favorites to their earliest beginnings.

3. Which pleasures have you lost over the years? How do you account for that? Which do you miss most?

4. How do you imagine your life would be different if you were fulfilled in all ways? Does that thought sound arrogant? Unrealistic? Shameful? Foolish? Inconceivable? Even if it does, imagine it anyway, just for the fun of it. What's the biggest change in your life you imagine total fulfillment would bring?

Now we are ready to explore each pleasure separately, starting with primal pleasure; I recommend that you explore each in the order it appears. It wouldn't make sense, for example, to skip everything else and head directly for sexual pleasure, because the heights of sexual excitement and release completely depend on developing skills in each of the other pleasures first.

The first three pleasures—primal, pain relief, and play—can be considered the basic building blocks of pleasure on which all others depend. These are the fundamental joys we need to reconnect with to shift from a pain-based to a pleasure-based awareness. If you have a clear appreciation for these basics, you can apply what you've learned to each of the other pleasures, so that you can better surrender, release hurt, and be playfully spontaneous everywhere else.

The next two pleasures—mental and emotional—can be thought of as the psychological pleasures. Becoming more skillful in each of these allows you to let go of limiting thoughts and feelings and opens up more expansive ways of using your mind and giving and receiving love.

The last three pleasures—sensual, sexual, and spiritual—can be thought of as the consummate realms for reaching your pleasure potential. Becoming more sensuously attuned to every one of your senses opens up the possibilities for enjoying the full spectrum of sexual delights from building maximum excitement to boosting the intensity of release. Ultimately, however, the most complete fulfillment depends upon coming to terms with the deeper issues of life and death and of clearly comprehending your place in the whole scheme of things, as a part of something good, something divine.

PART TWO

The
Fundamentals
of
Pleasure

Chapter 5

Primal Pleasure: Sweet Surrender

*The first step in intensifying pleasure
is learning to let go*

. . . .

Power returns to the person when rewards are
no longer relegated to outside forces . . . Instead of
forever straining for the tantalizing prize dangled
just out of reach, one begins to harvest
the genuine rewards of living.

—*Mihaly Csikszentmihalyi*

We all have a basic desire to return to the womb. But that doesn't have to be interpreted negatively, as though all we want to do is to crawl back in and hide in the dark. It's more about acknowledging a basic need for the most fundamental pleasure there is—the pleasure that preceded all others: timeless buoyancy, the ultimate expansiveness of being completely in the flow. Reconnecting with primal pleasure is about letting go and relaxing, getting out of your head, and releasing your bodily tensions. Essentially, it's about surrender.

This kind of surrender is not about a loss of power, as in surrendering in defeat. Nor is it about giving up, succumbing, and submitting to a superior force. Rather, it's an internal surrender—you give up the struggle within yourself, and you choose to let go. I think of it as sweet surrender because it feels so good just being.

As we shall see throughout, every pleasure, at every stage of intensity, involves yielding to primal pleasure. The sweet sensation of surrender is, at a very basic level, a physical experience, because the control that you're letting go of is in the grip of the muscles, felt as tightness and restraint in the body. On the mental level, when you surrender you ease up a bit on the dictatorship of the rational mind, and for the moment, you gladly give up trying to figure it all out. Surrendering emotionally is about releasing yourself from the clutch of fear and resentment and allowing positive feelings like love, courage, and forgiveness to come through. Sensually, you surrender by abandoning yourself to beautiful sights, appealing sounds, delightful fragrances, delicious food, sensitive touch, and an inspired imagination. Sexual surrender involves eroticizing each of these pleasures and giving in to the excitement—enjoying uninhibited arousal and unlimited orgasm. And finally, spiritual surrender has to do with trusting in a benevolent universe, believing in the essential goodness of humanity, and trusting and believing in your own essential goodness.

The Paradox of Control

Mihaly Csikszentmihalyi, a University of Chicago professor who has spent many years researching optimal experience, has observed a quality present in his subjects when they are happiest, that is very similar to what I call sweet surrender. He calls it "flow" and suggests that happiness depends on the capacity to enjoy yourself to the degree that you become completely engrossed in an activity so that nothing else seems to matter. The great paradox, he says, is that when people enjoy a flow experience they have the distinct impression that, while they feel like they've totally let go of control, at the same time they feel more in control than ever.

This is the great paradox of control—the more you let go, to the experience, the greater your sense of genuine power. Csikszentmihalyi found this to be the case even when, in the midst of a flow experience, a person loses any sense of self as being separate and distinct from his or her surroundings.

For most of us, however, it's not that easy to let go. As children, an important aspect of becoming socialized is learning to control ourselves. That's certainly a valuable quality to have. Over the years, however, we may have learned to be overcontrolled, continually trying to figure things out, unable to relax, and fearful of not being totally in charge. As a result, we may have learned to hold on too tightly and to keep ourselves in check at all costs.

Anyone who is overcontrolled and has trouble being in the flow, has trouble being relaxed and energized at the same time. The feeling is that if you're not in control, you're out of control, and that means you're either going to totally lose your head and do something foolish or hold yourself open for abuse. The truth is for most of us, letting go is not that simple.

Fear of Loss of Control

Though timeless buoyancy is the most fundamental element of pleasure, as adults, feeling free and without boundaries can be very anxiety-provoking. Some people have been so conditioned to keep a grip on themselves that if they do let go and feel a sensation of ebullience, their excitement may stimulate a fear of being overwhelmed. The perceptible sense of expansiveness can put them into a terror that if they don't really hold on, they're going to fall apart.

This is the very essence of low pleasure-tolerance and a clear sign of pleasure-anxiety. As a tense person becomes more stimulated, rather than relax and enjoy, his or her muscles may contract even more. As the pressure builds, inner voices of self-condemnation or unpleasant memories or images may be triggered in alarm to the siren song of temptation. Feelings of love may trigger fears of engulfment; intense sexual pleasure may trigger fears of loss of consciousness; success may trigger fears of emotional heights and a resulting incompetence in handling good fortune. Under these circumstances, low pleasure-tolerance, not uncommonly, results in an unconscious tendency to sabotage things when they're going particularly well.

Holding On

Harry wanted nothing more than to fall in love. He was a successful business man and enjoyed his work, but he was lonely and wanted to get married and maybe raise a family. He had had a long series of short relationships that typically ended in boredom or with lots of fighting and rancor. Then he would move on to yet another woman whom he would eventually also come to see as hopelessly flawed. By the time Harry reached me, he was despairing of ever finding the right woman. Harry's a good example of someone so tightly in control that he sabotaged his own happiness.

We looked at Harry's background. He grew up in Newark with a single mother who worked days, partied most nights, and neglected Harry and his younger brother. When she was around she found fault with him, especially with how he took care of things at home. Harry was not only resentful of his mother, but was disappointed in his dealings with most women. To Harry, women were demanding. He had stories about how he had been hurt by women who cheated on him, who demanded more than he could give, or who were angry with and resentful of him for no good reason.

Finally, after many months of looking into the psychological baggage he brought into his intimate encounters with women, Harry fell in love. He was ecstatic. He had found the perfect woman; Margot was beautiful, intelligent, accomplished, fun-loving ("she laughs at my jokes"), she amazingly also loved both opera and swap meets, and with her Harry said he had the best sex, what sounded like marathon sessions of sweat and passion.

The bubble lasted three weeks and burst loudly one evening when they had gone to a banquet for his company and Harry felt Margot had been too friendly with one of his associates. He lambasted her in the car on the way home for "playing him for a sucker." From that point, their relationship shifted into another gear. Harry grew suspicious of Margot and questioned her whereabouts when they weren't together. He ceased to find her as physically attractive and became too tired to have sex with her on many of the nights they spent together. When she said she missed their passion, he interpreted that to mean that she was going to start dating other men again and he became enraged that she was "so fickle." Whenever Margot tried to talk to him about any of it, he accused her of trying to control him.

Harry was having trouble letting go. It wasn't just that he was having trouble loving, he was also having trouble relaxing and maintaining his feelings of buoyancy. His work kept him tense and under pressure during the day, and it wasn't that easy for him to let go and surrender to his good feelings with Margot when he was away from the office. Invariably Margot would do something he was critical of, and he would feel resentful toward her and tell her what she should have done instead. Margot told him that while he accused her of being controlling, she felt like he was the one who was controlling, because no matter what she did, it was never right.

Most of us have come a long way since we were that infant

delighting in free fall. Like Harry, life has banged us up a bit too, and our usual response is to try to be in control by tensing up and keeping our feelings in. That's a realistic survival strategy for a child who can be punished for being too spontaneous. Unfortunately, if we hold on to that strategy as adults, we end up as control freaks—doing battle with ourselves, the people we love, and things the way they are. We drive ourselves to do things we don't—or won't allow ourselves to—enjoy. We find it hard to let go in our relationships and be accepting of others' idiosyncrasies. Or we don't let go sexually, finding it difficult to get out of our heads long enough to get totally turned on.

Whatever our degree of control, we can all benefit from learning to, periodically, kick back more and become more buoyant.

Getting High by Getting Down

Because primal pleasure is such a basic drive, risky though it might be, we all have our habitual ways of letting go. You may use alcohol or drugs to get yourself to surrender, with tranquilizers, a beer, a martini, or a joint helping you to relax and enjoy some "down time." You may be into electronic drugs. Television is the drug of choice for people who like to "veg" out in front of the tube and cable surf—or you may prefer to surf the Internet and drift in cyberspace. Maybe you eat too much, until you get numb and your belly distends, so that you couldn't move even if you wanted to. Maybe you're a shopper who relaxes best at the mall, ambling from store to store, trying on clothes and spending money.

None of these palliatives is necessarily harmful, as long as a person knows how to use, rather than abuse, their substance of choice. Moderate drinking has actually been shown to increase life span, and a number of people report that, for them, the disciplined use of marijuana can be very relaxing and without harmful effects. Spacing out for an hour or two for an evening of episodic television or chat rooms doesn't turn you into an electronic junkie. And you can stuff yourself as a weekend treat or enjoy window shopping without having to bring home a lot of things you don't need. However, the more limited the rest of your repertoire is for letting go, the more likely you will be to overuse your "fix" to the point of toxicity.

UCLA professor Ronald K. Siegel, who has researched drugs and drug use for almost thirty years, has suggested that we actually have a natural inborn drive that generates pleasure through intoxication. He finds that every culture in the world, along with many species of animals, enjoys the disoriented feelings and pleasant befuddlement associated with getting tipsy.

In fact, the research suggests that a big part of what people enjoy so much about "getting high" is the sweet surrender of the most primal of all pleasures—just floating in space. Dr. Siegel's studies show that, at least a part of what attracts drug users is what they describe as the pleasant sensations of floating outside their bodies—having a sense of detachment from their worries and tensions and a generalized feeling of well-being. Dr. Siegel may be on to something—we may indeed have an innate drive for intoxication, and it may very well be that the need to enjoy altered states of consciousness is universal and inescapable. If so, it particularly makes sense to cultivate the ability to get high in ways that are gratifying, but still safe and life-affirming. That's why it's so valuable to expand our repertoire for sweet surrenders on a daily basis.

Overcontrol/Out-of-Control Versus Moderation

In Ancient Greece, as the story goes, over the stone entrance to the Oracle of Delphi, the highly revered prophetess of Apollo, were carved the two key principles for leading a life of wisdom and mastery. One was "Know Thyself;" the other "Nothing Too Much." Psychotherapy, spiritual practice, self-help, and self-improvement disciplines of all sorts are based on the first principle. But the second principle hasn't made as much of an impact. We don't really know how to "do" moderation very well.

Most of us have been brought up believing that if you're not in control you're out of control. It's the kind of reasoning that operates for people who have trouble having only one or two drinks and thereafter saying "no thank you," or working an eight-hour day, and then going home to a relaxing evening and leaving work at the office. We mouth the words that it's best to be moderate in all things, but when it comes to certain compelling pleasures, we don't quite know how to do that. It's not that uncommon, for example, in whatever unique way each of us plays it out, to feel as though we can't give in to temptation at all because if we're going to eat a slice, we may as well eat the whole pie.

But you can't achieve moderation bouncing from one extreme to another and figure it all balances out in the end. Instead, we need to learn to relax and surrender, a little bit here and there, throughout our day.

The Discipline of Letting Go

It may sound odd, but the way to give up being overcontrolled is to become more disciplined about letting go. We ordinarily understand self-discipline as having to restrain our self-indulgent urges, denying ourselves things we shouldn't have. But any kind of power struggle, whether it's within yourself or between you and another person, can use up a lot of energy to go nowhere, just to keep yourself or someone else in check. Rather than repress our needs, we can learn to express them effectively and safely. Rather than holding on tightly so that the only time things change is when we're in a crisis, we can grow a little more every day. That way, with practice, growth and fulfillment become a natural part of everyday life.

Discipline is a concept we Americans usually have a hard time with. We tend to associate discipline with punishment and self-denial. When we were disciplined at school, we had to do extra assignments, or we might have had to sit in the principal's office. Discipline at home also usually meant being sent to our room or not being able to watch television for a week. We learned from these lessons that becoming a more disciplined person means depriving yourself, fighting your hedonistic urges, and doing what you're supposed to do, not what you feel like doing.

In this authoritarian form of self-discipline, the "good you" punishes the "bad you" to get you to be good or else—just like the authorities did in your childhood. You force yourself to do things you don't want to do, and you may be very good at this denying form of self-control, feeling chronically undernourished and sorry for yourself. Or you may feel like you've been deprived enough in life, and while you may torture yourself for being self-indulgent, the victim-child in you always seems to win. In which case you will act in self-destructive ways that are momentarily gratifying but often hurt you in the long run.

Becoming more disciplined about letting go, on the other hand, involves setting aside time to relax everyday. You can think of it as "conscious hedonism" and as a new model for fitness. That way you never get so wound up that, at the end of the day, you can't unwind or shift into something more mellow.

Just Being: Enjoying the Moment

At the simplest level, to surrender is to stop resisting. So first and foremost, the resistance you want to give up is the struggle with yourself. Physically that means releasing the isometric grip of tension in the muscles throughout your body. Mentally it means, just temporarily, giving up any inner voices of self-conflict, negative thoughts, regrets of the past, or worst case scenarios for the future.

Emotionally, again just for a while, you want to park your fears, resentments, combativeness, defensiveness, unfinished business, and bad mood and remind yourself what you have to feel grateful about. The whole idea is to get into the flow of the present moment, find your delight at being alive, and just be.

Think about the last time you let yourself surrender like that. Maybe you were getting a massage from someone who could not only read the knots in your neck and shoulders through his or her fingers but knew the absolutely right pressure to apply to release them. Maybe you were floating in a tub of hot water, the bathroom dark except for the glow of a single candle, and you had your favorite music playing softly in the background. Maybe you were lying on the couch after an early Sunday dinner hanging out with your family or alone doing yoga or making soft, tender love with your sweetheart. Maybe you were hiking a mountain trail, the smell of pine in every inhale, the song of birds and the whoosh of wind the only sounds piercing the silence. Whatever it was, you were enjoying the pleasures of just being—fully awake, calm yet energized, and very much in the moment.

The Key to Surrender: Deep Breathing

I'm about to give you the basic power tool for expanding your ability to experience primal pleasure, and each and every one of the other pleasures as well. You may be tempted to pooh-pooh it because it seems too simple. But withhold your judgments until you experiment for yourself. The simplest truths are often the most profound, and I can guarantee with absolute certainty that if you learn to use this tool, no matter how good your life is right now, it will become better. You will have a greater sense of personal mastery and enjoy yourself more over a wider range of areas. The method is this: To expand your potential for pleasure you need to master a certain kind of deep breathing. I'm convinced that the key to health, happiness, true love, and fulfilling sex lies very simply in how we inhale and exhale. It's like putting the paradox of control into action—thus, the more you let go, to relax and fully experience the moment, the greater your sense of genuine power. You can practice letting go as a discipline by developing a very powerful kind of control: breath control. Essentially, what you're doing is generating extra energy and then surrendering to it. It's sort of like taking a running leap and then letting go as you vault through space.

The Discipline of Breath Control

Everyday living is task-oriented, and for many of us that means restrained, focused movements and shallow breathing. The more stressed we are, the worse our mood, and the tighter we hold our-selves—in every muscle in the body but particularly in the jaw, chest, and diaphragm. We hold it all together by not exhaling much and tak-ing short quick inhales. This breathing style barely moves the stale air out of the lungs, so there's not much room in there to allow fresh air to come in.

Most of us are closet breathers; our exhales just seep out of us unconsciously. It's not even considered proper in polite company to breathe too fully. Try taking a few sighs in a social situation just to relax. The people you're with will probably ask you what's wrong.

Deep breathing is an important part of becoming more receptive to good feelings. This is especially true if you're dealing with physical or emotional pain, troubling thoughts, conflict with a loved one, or any other kind of difficulty. When we're having a hard day or a diffi-cult interaction, we usually hold our breath and tense our muscles as a way of resisting what's happening. Breathing into the pain or uncomfortable feelings, not only releases the spasm but feeds the brain and can actually make us think more clearly.

Think of it this way. When we encounter any kind of difficulty or stress and we get tense and hold everything in, the negative feeling is trapped in there and very likely to fuel our actions. In other words, if we get anxious or angry and hold our breath, we'll automatically think and act out of fear or anger. If we take a deep breath, and let go of the contraction, however, we can think and feel more freely, and then we have a choice in how we want to act.

That's why breathing awareness is such an important part of yoga, the martial arts, and many spiritual disciplines. One spiritual teacher, Yogi Ramacharaka, wrote that learning to do conscious breathing can not only cure disease in ourselves and others, and prac-tically do away with fear, worry, and anger, but it can also enable us to contact and develop our latent powers.

I have no doubt that there is a great deal of truth to this, and as we explore the rest of the core pleasures, you will see how there are times when learning how to use your breath in particular ways can enable you to change your mood, your thoughts, and your energy level, and it can empower you to make positive choices. Success in any area of life—whether we're talking about personal contentment, relationships, business, sexual satisfaction, or spiritual development—literally comes with learning to breathe into stressful feelings, rather than hold the breath and resist the feelings.

There are three basic breathing rhythms we'll be experimenting with as we move through the various realms of pleasure. Consciously breathing in these ways affects your energy and the intensity of your experience. You'll have an opportunity to practice these breaths in the Personal Experiments section of this chapter and the ones to follow.

The cleansing breath involves inhaling through the nose all the way up to the top of the breath and then blowing out through slightly puckered lips all the way down until you run out of air. This breath gets rid of surface tensions, and focuses your attention on the present moment and on what's going on in your body.

The sighing breath is a deep inhale and a soft exhale through the mouth. This breath releases deeper tensions and emotions and can be used to highlight and enhance pleasurable feelings.

The charging breath is a way of panting in and out through an open mouth. This breath builds excitement and ability to relax as pleasurable stimulation grows increasingly intense. We very naturally use these different breaths when we let go spontaneously. It can also be very helpful occasionally, to simply tune into your breath for a moment without changing it, just to check in with yourself.

Each of these three different breathing rhythms often automatically accompanies the three intensities of pleasure I spoke of in Chapter 4. First intensity pleasures have to do with relaxing, and when you've been tense and you start to let go, you may notice that you have a spontaneous tendency to blow the tension out in long exhales. You may also notice that when your breath naturally slows down, more of your torso begins to move as your muscles awaken. When you're more fully relaxed, alert, and energetic—as in second intensity pleasures—there's a tendency to breathe slow and deep, every so often taking some deep sighs. Then, if you start to get very enthusiastic or excited—as in third level pleasures—your breath will usually quicken. When you're really turned on, whether you're making love or walking in on a surprise birthday party being given for you, you will, very naturally, start to breathe heavily.

It makes sense then that you can make yourself more receptive to the pleasures of the moment by practicing breath control. The cleansing breath can facilitate first intensity pleasures by helping you, at least briefly, to let go of tension-producing mental habits and negative feelings and to focus in on good feelings. The deep sigh can help you to intensify your expansive feelings even more and to surrender to present experience. The charging breath can support third level pleasures and take you over the edge and into the realm of altered states.

Most importantly, consciously controlling your breath for a few minutes at a time can enable you to stay open and expansive to the pleasurable possibilities of the moment. When you can breathe into your feelings and be informed by them rather than tense them back and deny them, your ability to enjoy all sorts of new pleasures will be dramatically multiplied.

If you do no other personal experiments in this book, I urge you to at least explore the three breathing styles and see if you can develop some expertise in using them for a few seconds here and there throughout your day. You will be pleasantly surprised at what an enormous effect a little breath control can have on the quality of your daily life.

Getting High Naturally

When we're under stress, feeling anxious, or angry, the sympathetic nervous system fires a fight or flight reaction by shooting stress hormones into the bloodstream. We feel an adrenaline rush. The whole body gets speeded up, and we're off and running—terrified of missing a deadline or in a snit about something that didn't work out. But while we may feel energized, every part of the body is also contracting at the same time. Internal pressure builds and, if it becomes too much to handle, may burst out in self-destructive ways, in illness, or in rage.

Regrettably, many people depend on adrenaline to motivate them. Adrenaline junkies feel that if they're not driven to perform by their insecurities or fears of failure they would probably end up doing nothing and become lazy sloths. Adrenaline junkies can also become addicted to anger. I once knew a successful agent who had relied on his outrage to get things done. He decided to learn more positive ways to motivate himself only when, in his early forties, he started to feel painful spasms in his heart.

When the sense of danger has been real, and it passes, the parasympathetic system stimulates a replenishment response through the release of endorphins. The heart, gut, and skeletal muscles relax, and blood flows back toward the brain. This is an endorphin rush. We still feel a lot of energy, but it's an expansive rather than contracting kind of energy. On the other hand, when the sympathetic system is continually triggered, as in a habitual stress pattern, the person under stress eventually burns out and ends up in a state of utter fatigue.

Any scary activity that's fun usually stimulates a big adrenaline rush, which is followed by a big endorphin rush; in popular terms, we call that a thrill. Any kind of dangerous sport like race car driving or even just scuba diving is thrilling for the biochemical rush that makes us feel high. But we can also become addicted to endorphins—as in compulsive exercise; in fact, it's possible that it's the endorphin rush that makes people compulsive overeaters, shoppers, or gamblers.

The good news, however, is that you can trigger an endorphin rush, in a healthy way, through deep breathing. Just do a minute or two of the cleansing breath, and it will immediately calm and refocus you. If you're feeling anxious, breathing into your chest will stimulate your courage while breathing into your belly will relax you. If you're angry, taking a few long, slow, cleansing breaths can prevent impulsiveness, widen your perspective, and allow you to choose an effective action.

For our physical health, emotional well-being, and the health and happiness of all the people who have to come in contact with us, we are far better off driving up our energies through endorphin, rather than adrenaline, rushes. Adrenaline pumps us up with emergencies that aren't genuine emergencies, and it depletes our reserve tank. At the end of an adrenalized activity, we can feel more than spent—we can feel as though we've crashed—and it can take a while to recover.

Endorphins, on the other hand, fill us with energy, yet all the organs, tissues, and blood vessels in our body stay open. Good feelings flow; we feel like we're glowing. No wonder, during such times, people enjoy being around us.

Anything that gets you into the frame of body-mind that encourages relaxation—whether it's for sixty seconds, an hour, or a whole weekend—contributes to your letting go to every one of the core pleasures.

The Spa: Healing Waters

Some of the best ways to let yourself be involve getting into warm water. One method encouraging surrender in water involves the use of a floatation tank. Originally developed as a sensory deprivation experience by Dr. John Lilly, a floatation tank is a soundproof capsule about seven and one-half feet long with about ten inches of water that, with the door closed, is completely dark and loaded with so much Epsom salts that anyone can easily stay afloat.

Contrary to its original purpose, floating in a floatation tank is not experienced as sensory deprivation. In fact, what is so illuminating about lying buoyant in the complete darkness is the ebb and flow of all the different kinds of thoughts, memories, novel images, creative insights, even geometric patterns that spontaneously arise and fade from consciousness. For most floaters, an hour-long float in the darkness and temperature-controlled water of a floatation tank is a highly enjoyable experience that relieves muscle tension, decreases blood pressure, reduces anxiety and physical pain, and stimulates the flow of endorphins.

Another way to surrender in water is through water therapies that are intended to recreate the womb experience. One such therapy is known as Watsu. Another is called Waterbalancing. In both, the client and therapist together enter a pool of body temperature water, and while the client floats on her back, the therapist keeps her buoyant, either by cradling her under her shoulders and knees or by putting an inflated air pillow under her neck and what look like foam rolling pins under her knees. The therapist then gently moves the client through the water in slow, rhythmic, side-to-side sweeps, long fluid movements that stretch her spine, hips, and legs, and release tension throughout her body. The therapist can also massage her shoulders, hands, and feet. In Waterbalancing, toward the end of the session, the client is fitted with a nose clip and after each inhale is pushed underwater. The client exhales by blowing out in a slow stream of bubbles, while the therapist coordinates the client's exhales with dancelike underwater movements of sensitive shoves and tugs.

But you don't need a water massage to experience sweet surrender. Just get into a tub of comfortably hot water, light a candle, play some relaxing music, and let go.

Hanging Out in the Empty Spaces

Developing any level of mastery at letting go to pleasure depends completely on allowing yourself to enjoy timeless, buoyant moments, just being. Most of the time we have so much to do—people to give our attention to, appointments to keep, and obligations to fulfill. We get used to the speeded-up pace, and when we take time off, we usually do it in typical ways—going to a movie, to dinner, to a show, or on an afternoon outing. These are certainly good times.

But just being is somewhat different. It's not about where you go so much as it is about creating an empty space to relax in, giving yourself a moment of timelessness, where the only thing that matters is being at peace. It's the ultimate breathing room. Rather than distracting yourself, you're committed to just letting go; then, whatever is going on inside of you can drift to the surface of your mind, bob there for a few moments in your restful attention, then sink back below the surface. You haven't a care in the world, because temporarily you've chosen to blow those cares off your mind and out of your chest and gut.

When you keep emptying your mind of thoughts and freeing your body of the contractions of fear, you reach a place where nothing old is happening. For the moment, you've transcended your history,

Personal Experiments

. . . .

Remember, the key to surrender is in the breathing. We begin our experiments with the three basic breaths. When you practice breath control, keep in mind that you want to do conscious breathing for only a minute or two at a time. Breathing is an involuntary act, as it should be. These are simply ways of changing your energy for a few moments at a time.

Taking breathing space—whether you bracket off two minutes or two hours—is valuable healing time. It's like pushing the reset button and putting your inner counter back at zero-zero-zero. All the experiments that follow are opportunities to practice the primal pleasure of surrendering to the moment and just being.

1. The Cleansing Breath: Welcome to the Present

This breath brings you into the present moment and makes you more aware of what's happening inside your body. The object of this exercise is to slow the breath down by elongating each inhale and exhale. It's cleansing because it pushes carbon dioxide and other metabolic waste out of the lungs and makes room for more oxygen. An added dose of oxygen lightens you up on many levels, and exercising the respiratory muscles increases the elasticity of the lungs and relaxes and awakens the torso—massaging the muscles of the throat, shoulders, chest, back, ribcage, abdomen, pelvis, and all the internal organs.

Sit comfortably in a chair with both feet flat on the ground, your head straight and your chin parallel with the floor. Take a deep breath slowly, through the nose, all the way up to the top of the inhale; feel your chest lift as your lungs expand. When you can't fill up any more, pucker your lips softly and blow out in a steady stream of air all the way down to the bottom of your exhale. Suck your abdomen in slightly as you push out the last bit of old air remaining in your lungs. Keep exhaling until whatever little bit of air still left in your lungs is pushed out and the inhale happens spontaneously and naturally.

Feel the muscles of your torso moving like a bellows; become more attuned to the sensations of tension as some parts of your body try to move with the breath but remain tight. Imagine you can direct that tension out of your body with every exhale as though it were a smoggy brown haze you can blow out of your system like Jack Frost blowing a winter wind. With your cheeks puffed, blow out that stream of brown haze that darkens your insides.

If you find yourself lifting your shoulders to get a deeper inhale, try relaxing them instead on the next few breaths. If your throat gets tense, try taking a quick gulp of air through an open mouth when you reach your upper limit through your nose. Stop reading now and let yourself breathe like this for three or four consecutive breaths.

Now take a moment to notice how much more relaxed you are and more aware of your body. You can purposely trigger endorphins periodically throughout your day to counteract stress and to stimulate a brief parasympathetic response through deep breathing. Do a few cleansing breaths and consciously make your exhale twice as long as your inhale. Now how do you feel?

2. The Deep Sigh: Going Deeper

This breath will help you let go and get more in touch with your emotions, your senses, and your sexual excitement. It's a particularly good breath to practice consciously for a few moments during sex, to increase arousal and sexual surrender.

Take a deep sigh in and out through an open mouth and a relaxed throat. Feel your upper back widen, your "wings" stretching apart on the inhale, releasing on the exhale. Let the breath out in a deeply aspirated "hah" as though you were steaming up a pair of glasses you wanted to wipe clean.

Now take three deep breaths in a row. If you find yourself yawning a lot, let it happen. It's only your body's homeostatic mechanism operating to correct your oxygen/carbon dioxide balance. If you get lightheaded, close your mouth and breathe in and out slowly through your nose. See if you can enjoy the floating sensation for the few seconds it remains.

3. The Charging Breath: Building Excitement

The object of this breath is to build energy. It charges the system bioelectrically and intensifies feelings of vitality. At first, you may not feel completely comfortable with the sensation of floating or the experience of energy streaming through your body like electricity, but if you practice, you will find that this breath is like an instant pep pill. As with any energy boost, the effects of this way of breathing can be very powerful, and you want to be very disciplined in your use of it.

This breath is like panting very deeply. When you're ready, open your mouth wide, suck air all the way into your chest, and let it out all at once in a big "hah." Relax and notice how you feel. If you liked the way that felt, do it five more times in rapid succession.

Very likely the charging breath will soon make you feel lightheaded and even a little high. If so, begin breathing in and out through your nose and allow yourself to relax into the floating feeling—it's only the sensation of unbounded energy streaming through your body. While it's normal for the mouth and fingers to start to tingle and sometimes even to stiffen in reaction to the quick shift in the balance of oxygen and carbon dioxide, it's not productive to pursue these feelings. When you close your mouth and breathe normally, in and out through the nose, these sensations will subside. Notice if you feel a surge of energy and hyperalertness right after using this breath.

Don't abuse this breath. Even though it's only something as natural as air that you are playing with, you don't want to get to the point where you start to hyperventilate, and your body gets stiff. If you find yourself hyperventilating, you can breathe into a paper bag for a few minutes or even just into the neck of your shirt. That way, you get more carbon dioxide into your lungs and correct the deficit.

Here are some other ways that you can enjoy the primal pleasure of surrender at various times throughout your day.

1. Learn to take a few brief time-outs periodically throughout your day. You don't need more than thirty seconds at a time to do a few cleansing breaths and energize yourself with some endorphins.

2. When you're tense about something try "bracketing." Setting things aside briefly to deal with later is not necessarily the sign of a procrastinator. It can also be a valuable skill. If you're worried, or you have to make a difficult decision or tackle an unappealing task, you can choose to shelve it for a few minutes and let yourself relax. Do a few cleansing breaths. Picture yourself somewhere beautiful, surrounded by nature, on a lovely day. Lose yourself there for a few moments. When you come back, you'll find you can approach the issue with a renewed sense of vigor and a clearer course of action.

3. Take decompression time. Relax after a stressful day by taking some time alone. If you have a partner or a family that you want to spend quality time with at the end of a tense day, you'd be doing them a big favor if you first spent some time alone in decompression. A half hour alone can make you a friendlier, more available person. But just five or ten minutes at a time is also good and may be all you need to replenish your energy. Close your eyes, take some deep breaths, and let your mind drift. If your work day tends to be inactive, unwind by doing something active like taking a walk or doing some physical exercise.

4. Take a pleasure soak in a tub of hot water. Light a candle and turn off the electric lights. Close your eyes, take some cleansing breaths, and blow out the emotional nicks and bruises of the day and the rushed pace. Let your mind and tensions go. Let yourself float. Breathe high up into your chest, flutter your cramped fingers and toes, soften your eyes and cheeks, slacken your jaw, and let your belly out.

5. Float in a heated swimming pool. If you have access to a warm pool and a mask and snorkel, try this: Swim around in the pool for a few minutes to adapt to the temperature of the water. When you're ready to experiment, lie face down on the water, breathe in and out through the snorkel in your mouth, and flail your arms and legs for about a minute or two. Then let everything go limp. Take five deep cleansing breaths, sucking air in through the snorkel and blowing out through the snorkel. Feel your body bob on the water, getting light as your lungs inflate and sinking slightly as you empty out the air. You may feel more comfortable doing this exercise with a partner, taking turns watching over each other in the water.

6. Let your mind drift for a few moments. Every so often during your day, make sure you take a minute to look at the sky, breathe deeply, and watch the clouds. Watch fish in an aquarium. Go to a pretty spot in nature and watch the light move through the trees or the wind move the grass. At night take some time to look for the moon and stars and to breathe the night air. Rock in a rocking chair, lie in a hammock, swing on a swing, or hang on a chinning bar. Let go. Let yourself be.

Chapter 6

Pain Relief:
Turning Pain Into Pleasure

*How to first soothe, then release, resolve,
and acquire wisdom from pain*

. . . .

Smilingly, out of my pain,
I have woven a little song . . .

—*Aline Kilmer*

Pain relief is a very powerful, very fundamental pleasure. Any kind of pain demands your attention, contracts and clogs up your energy, and keeps your world very narrow. At its worst, you can only lay in bed, weak, trying to distract yourself. When blessed relief finally comes, what a great joy it is. Whether it's a physical healing, like getting over the flu or healing a pulled back muscle, or emotional, like expecting bad news and getting good news instead—the ending of discomfort of any kind makes you feel energetic, expansive, and wonderful.

However, even in this very basic of pleasures, we can still hold ourselves back. Some people just don't know how to comfort themselves or take comforting from others—maybe no one ever comforted them—so they don't open themselves up very much for kind strokes. Other people reject offers for TLC because they don't trust that it can come with no strings attached. Still others appear to have an infinite need for comforting, yet whatever you give them is never enough—obviously the comfort is just not getting through.

If we're not good at easing our pains through the intrinsic pleasures that most naturally soothe us, more than likely we'll depend on drugs and alcohol to spell relief. Don't get me wrong, I'm all for painkillers. When I get a headache, I don't hesitate to reach for an aspirin. But there's a difference between acute pain that can be medicated with minimal side effects and chronic pain that takes stronger and stronger doses of potentially lethal chemicals. Alcohol is a painkiller and a great problem for people who don't know about more enduring, more life-affirming ways to soothe their pain.

Another factor that may prevent us from getting genuine pain relief is that people who are adrenaline junkies—who rely on anger and fear as a source of energy to motivate them—are usually pain junkies as well. They depend on their discomfort and bad feelings to drive them. Usually, they feel a lot more secure putting out familiar old fires that they can continually rekindle than enjoying the unknown and the expansiveness of feeling pretty good for an extended period of time. A woman, half-jokingly, once told me, "I find I'm only happy when I'm miserable." Then, completely seriously, she added, "I wouldn't know what to do with myself if everything was going well."

If you hold on to pain and don't permit yourself true pain-release, there are a number of ways you may be trying to exact a modicum of pleasure from your pain. One rather limiting sort of pleasure is to get gratification from playing victim. People who think of themselves as victims tend to believe that they're in pain because of what somebody else has done to them or continues to do. If only the other person were different, then they themselves would be fine.

People who have a deep sense of identity as a victim can never really give up their dissatisfactions because they would have to give up their image of themselves. They would have to see themselves as fully capable of grappling with their problems and resolving them, or they would have to accept things, and even enjoy them, for exactly the way they are. This they don't want to do. So while people who play the martyr may manage to squeeze a few drops of pleasure from a bad situation, a major drawback of playing victim is that to maintain the meager pleasures of sacrifice you have to stay stuck in your problem forever.

Some people also have a kind of masochistic love of pain. It's not so much that they get sexual pleasure from their troubles. Rather, they tend to romanticize pain, as though their suffering bestows importance on the details of their lives. These people are not exactly willing to give up their anxiety and fear, their smoldering resentments, guilt, or shame, because if they did, deep down inside they believe that doing so would somehow diminish them.

I have met quite a number of people who believe that if they're not driven by dissatisfaction, they won't have the edge that makes them perform at their best. Unfortunately, people who rely on negative emotions to motivate them can make themselves ill from the continuous stress. One muckraking journalist told me that he knew his constant indignation and hostile manner were damaging to his health, but he was afraid that without it he would lose his fighting spirit and would become complacent about the injustice in the world.

To anyone who is concerned that a life without pain would be superficial, meaningless, indolent, and dull, let me reassure you: Pain is never that far away. Give up one pain and another lurks just around the next corner. Pain is a natural part of life. Whether its origin is physical, like stubbing a toe, or emotional, like a heartache, we will all encounter hurt as we go through life. In fact, pain is actually very helpful, often alerting us to something that requires attention. If we're willing to deal with it, we can rectify a bad situation and get to a good place with it again.

Extremists that we are, however, if we're not pain junkies we tend to be the complete opposite: pain-phobic. If we're not romanticizing pain and using it to turn our ordinary lives into epics, we'll do anything to avoid it. Pain-phobics deny bad feelings and go numb to their inner sensations. Some people take a pill with their orange juice in the morning to dull their edges all day long. Avoiding pain as a way of life, however, can also become a serious liability. Being an "avoider" absolutely guarantees that whatever is wrong will persist, because denial enables us to put up with the conditions that continue to do us harm.

Getting Unstuck from Pain

A young married couple came to see me in a state of crisis, seriously considering splitting up. Patrick and Marla didn't look at each other as they sat on opposite sides of the couch and addressed all of their grievances to me. Marla was angry that Patrick didn't give her son by a former marriage enough attention. She was hurt that he spent so much time at work and so little with her. She was annoyed that he talked down to her and was always trying to teach her something. On the contrary, Patrick said, it was she who was always trying to teach him how to do things. Nothing he ever did was good enough; she was the one who was critical and withholding, and he was avoiding her because he was afraid to be around her.

When we went into their backgrounds what came out was that as kids, neither one of them had been showered with much loving acceptance. Each had an absentee father: Hers was a successful businessman who was never around, and his was a passive man who deferred the parenting to his wife.

Patrick had been born with a foot defect requiring several childhood operations, which made his mother overly controlling and protective of him. Marla's mother, on the other hand, was rather timid; she complained but she never did anything about her dissatisfactions. Marla vowed never to let herself be taken advantage of like her mother had been. In a sense, each had spent a childhood being trained for the position they now held with one another. Patrick had learned to hide from a woman who tried to get too close; Marla had learned to be angry and resentful of a man who wasn't there. But while he had learned to avoid pain from his avoiding father; she, using her ineffectual mother as a negative role model, she was determined to be fiercely confrontive.

Finally, I had heard enough of their harsh words toward one another. They were both very verbal and, since each had already been in a lot of therapy, they could easily go on and on being very articulate about all their hurt and disappointment. Besides, they had covered this ground with one another many times over and were very well ensconced at an impasse.

I told them that I had had enough of their talking to me. I wanted to hear them talk to one another, and I specifically was interested in what was good about their relationship. I asked them to take a few deep breaths, since they were both holding themselves very tightly, and to share with one another what they most loved and appreciated about the other.

This they most decidedly did not wish to do. Marla said there was hardly anything about him she loved these days. Patrick said he wouldn't feel comfortable if she said anything loving to him because he knew it would be false anyway. If nothing else, her contempt for him was honest, and he appreciated that. I took his comment as an acknowledgment of sorts and considered us off to a good start. I also told them that if they couldn't come up with some more positives for staying together, I didn't think I could help them. For one thing, they needed at least a few good feelings together to justify the effort of going into and getting through their pain. Besides, I said, I myself needed a sense of what was good about this relationship to suggest that it would be worth working on.

Marla considered that I had a good point and decided to indulge me by telling Patrick what she had once loved most about him—that he could make her laugh, how kind he had been to her son when they first got together, and his little surprises. She began to warm to the task and managed to toss in a few current appreciations when suddenly, Patrick lurched forward, buried his head in his hands, and began to sob convulsively. Marla was practically airborne as she leaped to his side and threw her arms around him to comfort him. I was stunned. I had never seen this exercise work so well. Needless to say, I was thrilled.

Patrick sobbed about how sad it was that they had such a sweet love and that it had come to this and how he could hear the love in her voice for the first time in months. Then Marla started to cry and to tell him how lonely she had been and how much she missed him. He took his face out of his hands and looked at her with red swollen eyes, then declared that he still loved her and that she was everything to him. She smiled back and said she still loved him too. So that's how their first session ended. Now that we all knew there was something worth saving, we could get to work saving it.

This story highlights two primary sources of nourishment that most effectively can soothe pain and bring relief.

Affectionate Touch and Reassuring Words

One of our greatest joys in life is to have our pain soothed. A frightened infant is comforted by the warmth of human contact; a person rocking and holding him, making sweet sounds of love and protection.

Whether the pain is physical or emotional, if we're really hurting, it reaches into our deepest layers where, no matter how old we are chronologically, we are all still very young children. Male and female alike, when we're in pain, all we really want is for someone big and strong to hold us and stroke us and tell us that everything is going to be okay. Comforting touch and soft reassuring sounds are the most naturally healing antidotes to pain.

Affectionate human touch is an essential nutrient for surviving and thriving during our earliest years and continues throughout our life span to have tremendous healing power. Without warm physical contact, a newborn's chances to survive and grow are minimal. We now know that when infants in orphanages waste away, it is largely because they were not picked up and held.

But the value of touching to infants and children may be beyond anything we've even imagined. Jean Leidloff, an American writer on expedition in South America, was so impressed with how consistently happy the Indian guides were on her trip that she decided to go back to the Amazon several times to study them, particularly with regard to how they raised their children. There seemed to be a complete absence of unhappiness among these gentle people; they enjoyed their work, and though they were smaller and less muscular than their white employers, they were able to carry heavier loads and for longer distances. They seemed to enjoy the challenges of their task and laughed and joked their way across difficult terrain.

What Liedloff discovered when she started to study these Indians was that their infants, until they began crawling, were held constantly in the arms of their parents, or anyone else who was around, all day long. Based on these observations and supported by a wealth of clinical research on "maternal deprivation," Liedloff concluded that the lack of safety, comfort, and affection that is common in our own culture shows that most of us are probably victims of early touch deprivation.

More recent studies on premature infants—when weight is a crucial variable in a baby's chances for survival—also highlight the value of touching. In an important series of experiments, preemies who were massaged by a staff of volunteers, three times a day for ten days, weighed almost 50 percent more than babies who were not massaged. Stroked infants turned out to be more alert and responsive, calmer and less irritable, had better metabolism, and tended to leave the hospital six days earlier than their unstroked counterparts.

In fact, the love you received a long time ago as a child continues to this day to keep your battery charged. In one long-term study that began in 1951, the mothers of four hundred children of kindergarten age were asked details of how they and their husbands spent time with their child. In 1987, ninety-four of the children from the original study, now adults in their early forties, were tracked down and questioned about their current life. The results showed that adults whose mothers and fathers were warm and physically affectionate tended to have happy marriages, good friends, and satisfying work, while those with cold, strict, or distant parents tended to be depressed and lacked a sense of emotional well-being.

Physical affection was a more critical factor than whether they came from a poor or wealthy family, or whether their parents were divorced or stayed together. Imagine that! The most significant determinant predicting happiness was whether or not their parents had been loving to them thirty-five to forty years earlier.

Warm physical contact with others never loses its potency to nourish and sustain us. Comforting touch has been shown to be capable of dramatically slowing the heartbeat of someone who has been traumatized. Deep massage, when used to treat a group of chronically anxious patients, was able to markedly reduce their sense of distress, their heart rate and muscle tension, and the likelihood that they would require medication. It may even be the case that one reason married people live longer than single people is that they have more access to the life force transmitted by loving touch.

But if you, like me, didn't get that loving warmth as a child, it doesn't mean that as adults we're doomed to a life of unhappiness. Folks with warm parents certainly have had an advantage in that they had positive role models, people who cherished them and modeled for them nurturing ways of being. The rest of us have to learn, as adults, how to give and receive comfort.

If we didn't get comforting early on, it doesn't usually come naturally to us. We have to learn how to comfort the people we love when they're in pain, rather than torture them. We have to learn how to accept affection and reassurance when we're down, from the people who want to be there for us. Most importantly, we need to learn how to comfort and reassure ourselves. We most certainly don't want to be giving ourselves a hard time when times are hard, but that's often what we do. Kids who grow up on a low-warmth diet have to relearn this most basic of pleasures of comforting and taking comfort, when they are adults.

Initially, Marla and Patrick were not very good at comforting one another. When I looked at their pinched faces and sunken chests, I saw two little kids in agony, dealing with it the only way they knew how, and it was driving them further and further apart. Marla said she wanted him closer, yet her endless complaining pushed him away. He said he wanted her off his back, yet his ignoring her kept her defiantly in his face. They were punishing each other, and the pain made them continue to be defensive with one another. By getting them to speak kind words, it soothed some of their pain and revealed the genuine love and goodwill, which was just underneath the surface.

The Pleasure of Pain Release

When Patrick threw his face into his hands and sobbed, he was releasing months and months of anguish, which had cramped his heart and gut and choked him up. The hurt, guilt, and sadness had never gone away because it was never productively dealt with. Neither of them knew what to do with all that disappointment, misunderstanding, and especially, frustrating incompetence to resolve it. Pain in many ways is stuck energy, and an unhappy person becomes like a pressure cooker ready to blow. It feels good to finally let it all out, especially if you know how to channel that release so that not only does it not do damage but so it also does some good.

Patrick's blowout did a lot of good. He had learned as a child not to be a "cry baby" about all the pain he experienced with his foot, and he had carried over his stoicism in his relationship with Marla, feeling as though he had to hide his grief from her. In fact, letting it out not only released him from enormous heartache, but it also showed Marla that he did love her, which she was seriously beginning to doubt. Only then had she felt safe enough to cry and unload some of the hurt and anguish in her heart. Holding and saying nice words to each other, and crying and breathing into their pain, allowed them both to feel their love. Underneath the tight chest each wore for protection like a medieval armored breastplate, was the genuine caring and tenderness that had brought them together in the first place.

We tend to think of pain as physical if there's injury to or illness in the body, or emotional if it's one's feelings that are hurt. But in truth, we usually feel both together. Most physical pain has emotional components because the most natural thing in the world is to get upset or scared when we think we might be sick or injured. Emotional pain is always physical—it's always felt somewhere in the body. When the heart is heavy with disappointment or the gut is tight with guilt, the pain is no less physical than if we're having chest spasms or stomach flu.

All painful emotion needs to be expressed to be relieved. If you feel hurt, disappointed, or sad, internal pressure builds up and makes you want to cry. Patrick had obviously been holding on to a lot of hurt and sadness for it finally to break through in such a torrent of tears. But if you're fearful or anxious, you'll feel more like screaming for help. You can almost hear the scream in the typically high-pitched tone of voice of some chronically anxious people. If you feel guilty or ashamed, you feel like groaning as you beat up on yourself. If you feel insulted, angry, or incensed, you'll want to bellow in rage.

If you don't express yourself—literally expel the feeling out of your body—you're likely to de-press yourself, pushing your emotions down and feeling burdened. If you stockpile your feelings, the pressure will build, and eventually, one little off-handed remark from someone and you'll become a Mt. Vesuvius. On the other hand, just blowing off steam continuously, wherever and whenever you want doesn't work either. We can't just blurt out anything that feels good for the moment because we can do a lot of damage—and sometimes the pain of cruel words can last a lifetime.

What often helps the most is learning how to express the pain in a way that doesn't harm anyone. You can write angry letters, then rip them up later, or hit a stack of pillows with a baseball bat, or rant and rage in the privacy of your own room, or take a long run to cool off. Then when you've calmed down, you may be able to address the painful issue with more patience and intelligence.

The Pleasure of Resolving a Painful Issue

Today many therapists feel that, in the past, we may have put too much emphasis on painful expression. We encouraged clients to ventilate their hurt and anger—in fantasy or in support groups—toward the people past or present who had offended them. We thought the way for people to let go of the past was to cry or rage about the offenses done to them that they had never let go of. What we found was that without some kind of satisfying understanding about the issue, the pain never went away. The emotional outburst merely discharged enough of the over-the-top torment so that a person could live with the low-grade distress until it boiled over once again.

While it can be a relief to just scream and rail when you're alone about what's bothering you, that's not enough. You also have to come to terms with your pain in some kind of productive and empowering way. Ideally, you want to learn from your pain and to make something worthwhile of the experience.

If the first level pleasures of pain relief come with affectionate touch, soothing words, and releasing pent-up emotion, second level and more satisfying pleasures come with pain resolution and with having a clearer understanding of the larger picture. For example, say you have a heartfelt realization that, though your parents did things that hurt you, they really didn't mean to harm you—they just didn't know how else to be. That insight may enable you to forgive them their ineptitude. In doing so, you release the hurt that keeps you feeling like a victim, allowing you to be more trusting in love.

When Marla and Patrick stopped denouncing and began stroking each other, they saw that what each of them had been doing had brought out the worst in the other. Marla's in-your-face disapproval sent Patrick far away, and Patrick's disappearing acts made Marla badger him when he deigned to come around. Seeing how they were both bungling it, started them on a long, and actually very delightful, path toward learning how to handle their differences better.

In music, a chord is said to be resolved, when it moves from a dissonant to a consonant tone. The same is true emotionally. You feel resolved when whatever friction and discord you feel with a person or an issue can be worked out to your satisfaction to achieve a greater sense of inner peace and harmony.

Pain's Most Joyous Pleasure: Turning Grief into Wisdom

Pain is a natural part of life. It's a signal demanding our attention and alerting us to something within that needs to be addressed. If we go through all these processes—of feeling and facing the pain rather than avoiding it; of taking sustenance from reassurance and from comforting human contact to carry us through; of safely releasing the agony that distorts our thinking and makes us act hatefully; and of ultimately arriving at some kind of peaceful resolution—if we can do all that, we can achieve some of the greatest pleasures that pain can bestow upon us—the third level pleasure of growing wiser as we get older.

Pain is a great teacher, if you're paying attention in class. The saying that the only thing sorrier than a fool is an old fool is true. People who don't derive lessons from the vagaries of life as they go along arrive at the end of their days dumber than when they started. At least as infants they had all their instincts intact. Old fools usually have been so out of touch with their depth and authenticity that they can't trust even their own perceptions anymore.

Wisdom is about seeing the bigger picture while, at the same time, not making more of things than they really need to be. Wisdom comes from a willingness to grapple with complicated issues, eventually reaching a place of inner clarity and a solid sense of genuine knowing.

The wisdom gained by learning from painful experience is one of the genuine rewards of maturity.

The experiments that follow are all about exploring for yourself the intricacies involved in the very satisfying pleasures of pain relief, pain release, and resolution.

Personal Experiments

. . . .

1. Either in writing or in conversation with a friend, seriously ask yourself this question: "Am I willing to give up my self-inflicted pain?" The search for the answer is not to be taken lightly. Some pain is unavoidable. We've all had physical ailments or emotional crises we've had to endure, and no doubt, in the hopefully long course of our lives, we will continue to encounter pain. But do we multiply our level of distress by the inept way we react to it?

Honestly answer these questions: Do I suffer more than I have to? Do I double my pain by refusing to face issues and talk about them? Do I hang onto my dissatisfactions to get attention or sympathy that I honestly don't know how to get any other way? Do I have trouble accepting comfort or a problem allowing myself to be encouraged and inspired by kind words and warm hugs? Do I nag at myself, judge myself harshly, criticize others, scare myself when I'm sick, worry about the future, regret the past, and expect the worst?

On the bright side, am I ready to give up resentment and anger as motivating forces in how I act? And most importantly: Who do I know who's wise who can be a role model for me?

2. Practice breath control periodically throughout the day to relieve and release pain. Since all pain is physical, the best way to deal with any unpleasant feeling is to breathe into those areas of the body that are tight and contracted.

Start by taking a few slow and deep cleansing breaths. Remember that each breath starts with a long inhale through the nose, first filling your belly, then moving up as your rib cage widens, and finally lifting your chest and upper back as you reach the top of your inhale. Then blow out through slightly puckered lips and make your exhale twice as long as your inhale. Notice that first the chest falls, then the ribcage narrows, and finally the belly flattens and pulls in as the used air in the lungs is pushed out.

With your eyes closed, take inventory of any tightness or unpleasant emotion or sensation anywhere in the body and see if you can encourage your breath into that area, feeling it expand with each inhale and blowing out the tension with every exhale.

3. Practice venting your feelings in a safe way. When you have some privacy, take a few cleansing breaths but instead of simply blowing out, vocalize the long exhale. As you breathe out, chant, moan, groan, or even whine or whimper, if that's what fits the feeling. Try making a deep bass sound in such a way that you can feel the tone vibrating your tense chest and throat muscles. Keep the sound going until you run out of air. Try varying the pitch from high to very deep and see which feels best.

If your sounds bring up tears, let yourself have a good cry. If your sounds bring up rage, you may feel like growling and pounding on your sofa or going to the gym and working out on a punching bag. See if you can discharge your emotion and bring yourself to a place of greater relaxation and calm.

4. Stretch for a minute or two at a time, every few hours, or as often as you can remember. You can't stretch your capacity for pleasure without stretching your body. The more uptight and self-denying you are, the more your body contracts and you experience pain. Not keeping the body open and stretched out may, in fact, be a major factor contributing to the typical phenomenon of people getting smaller as they get older.

It's not enough to do a few stretches once or twice a week. To keep the muscles supple and flexible you have to work out the kinks every single day, several times a day, even for just a few minutes at a time.

Here's a simple stretching routine that will take you about five minutes and that you can do right now, just sitting wherever you are. It will help you relax in the four critical areas where we carry so much of our tension: the neck and shoulders, the jaw, the chest, and diaphragm. Take a deep cleansing breath; let your head fall back as your chin points to the ceiling and blow your tension up and out. Then inhale as you let your head fall forward, with your chin against your chest, and blow down. Now inhale as you bring your head up so that your chin is parallel with the floor and look as far over your right shoulder as you can and blow out. Then inhale as you look as far over your left shoulder as you can, and blow out. Now looking straight ahead, inhale, and let your right ear move toward your right shoulder. Feel the stretch on the left side of your neck. Rest your right hand for a few moments on the left side of your head to stretch your neck even more. Blow out. Keep looking straight ahead, inhale, and let your left ear move toward your left shoulder. Feel the stretch on the right side of your neck. Rest your left hand for a few moments on the right side of your head for a longer neck stretch. Blow out.

Inhale as you interlace your fingers and place them behind your head. Let your head drop forward and let the weight of your hands stretch the back of your neck. Blow out the tension as you move your neck from side to side.

Slacken your jaw and lift your shoulders toward your ears; drop them gently a few times. Then make circles rolling your shoulders and elbows first forward three times and then back three times. Remember to inhale all the way to the top of your chest and to blow all the way out in long controlled exhales.

Let your breath loosen your diaphragm and abdomen. Encourage a yawn. Then bend forward at the waist and drop your head between your knees, with your arms over your head and your hands dangling near your feet. Let the weight of your head stretch your back naturally. Hang there for a few seconds and feel the release all up and down your spine. Sit up, lightly shake your arms and legs, then wiggle your fingers and toes. Breathe deeply.

Stretching on your feet is also a wonderful way to release tension. Bring your feet parallel to one another about shoulder-width apart and make sure you have your weight evenly distributed on the balls and heels of your feet. Lift your arms over your head and hold your right wrist in your left hand. Take a deep inhale and, as you blow out, lift your right arm higher and gently pull your waist out of your hips, elongating the whole right side. Now do the opposite side, holding your left wrist in your right hand. Gently pull up and out and elongate the whole left side of your body. Feel the breath expand all the way down to your waist.

Hunkering is a great way to release tension in the small of the back, a place where most of us feel a great deal of stress. Separate your feet to about two-feet wide and squat. Try to keep the heel of each foot on the ground and not just your toes. If you can't keep your heels flat, put a book under your heels that's the right elevation to allow your heels to relax. Once you're squatting, hold that position and support yourself by hugging your knees or by holding on to the leg of a couch or desk. Inhale and exhale, releasing the tension in the back, hips, and pelvis.

5. Enjoy massage as therapy. When muscles are tight, they grip the bones and organs underneath them, and it feels wonderful to have someone knead your muscles and encourage them to let go. If you have an intimate partner, you may find it adds enormously to your physical connection if you trade massages, possibly using fragrant oils to make your hands slide more easily and sensuously on the skin.

You may also find that scheduling a massage periodically with a skilled massage therapist helps you keep your body generally more toned and at the same time infinitely more relaxed. Particularly if you don't get a daily dose of good touching, hugging, or stroking, it might make a big difference in your life if you were to schedule a massage for yourself on a regular basis.

6. Try using pleasure aids to give yourself a massage. Pleasure aids are gadgets to be used for self-massage not only when no one else is around to rub your tight muscles, but to cultivate the capacity to be self-sufficient and able to nurture yourself. They allow you to work out your own tension and can be helpful in releasing painful spasms.

Try lying on the ground, on a tennis ball, with the ball at just the right point in your back so that the weight of your body on the ball massages a sore spot. You might also enjoy a "ma roller," a wooden spool made to roll down your back in much the same way you might use the tennis ball but so constructed that in rolling on it you get to massage the muscles on either side of your spine from your shoulder to the small of your back. You might also experiment with using a vibrator on your tense muscles, propping it up and leaning into it so you don't have to strain to hold it up.

Native Hawaiians have a stick, known as a *lomi kua,* made from the polished branch of a guava tree that is about an inch in diameter, two feet long, and shaped like a V with one arm longer than the other. If you hold the longer branch of the V with both hands, you can press the smooth, round tip of the shorter branch into a sore muscle in the back. Then pushing up on the longer branch enables the shorter branch to penetrate into the muscle like a deep massage. In that way you can pleasurably work out a knot in your own back. You may be able to find a *lomi kua* stick on the mainland at a bookstore or health food store.

Also worth looking for are Bongers. Here a rubber ball the size of a small fist is attached to a flat flexible metal handle about the length of a drumstick (the musical kind). You get two to a package and you can gently beat on any of your sore muscles like a drummer beating a drum. Or like a gorilla in a display of territoriality, you can gently and rhythmically pound at the tightness in your chest.

7. Practice asking for comfort and reassurance. When you're worried or feeling upset, ask someone dear to you to hold and comfort you. You can even tell them the exact words you need to hear to make yourself feel better—not everyone instinctively knows what you need to hear that will be comforting. Just don't ask anyone to misrepresent their true feelings to reassure you because that's just inviting betrayal. But if you give them something more basic—like "There, there, everything is going to be okay."—you'll be amazed how, even though you told them what to say, you'll still feel an enormous sense of relief. Breathe deeply, relax into the comfort, and let yourself be nurtured and strengthened by the emotional support.

8. Practice giving comfort and reassurance to others. Sometimes the best way to learn how to receive comfort is to give it. See if you tend to be stingy with your warmth and caring, just giving a few quick pats on the back and walking away. Or, see if you tend to tell people who come to you in pain how they ought to handle their problems, rather than simply give comfort. A person in pain wants soothing reassurance not solutions, and if you offer solutions, very likely, they will feel resentful and cheated of any real warmth. If someone comes to you for comfort, you might even ask them to tell you what you could do or say that would be most consoling to them.

9. Practice giving yourself comfort and reassurance. Some people give themselves a terribly hard time when things aren't going well. But we need to remember that we can generate a lot more energy toward rectifying a difficult situation if we can be sympathetic and kind with ourselves. Instead of thinking the worst about whatever it is that is troubling you, see if you can call up a more optimistic side of yourself. If you're expecting things to turn out badly, see if you can give equal time to imagining how things could possibly turn out well.

10. Either in writing or in conversation with a friend, ask yourself, "What grief have I endured that has made me wiser?" Think about something unhappy or unfortunate that happened to you and ask yourself what lessons you have learned from that sad situation. If indeed the painful event has made you wiser, there will be no touch of bitterness, resentment, self-pity, or resignation. Wisdom allows you to observe the event with a sense of detachment and to be grateful for having come through it, in the end, a better person.

Chapter 7

The Elemental Pleasures: Play, Laughter, Movement, and Sounding Out

....

How to lighten up

. . . .

Angels can fly because
they take themselves lightly.

—*C. K. Chesterton*

You probably know some people you can take in only small doses because they have a tendency to be heavy. For one thing, they just look heavy—with their sour pusses and disgruntled body language, they're not pleasant to see. For another, they complain a lot, about the people they're closest to, or about what's wrong with their lives, and they're not above finding fault with you. It makes you want to say, "For heaven's sake, lighten up! You're seeing things in the worst possible light. Look at how miserable it makes you; it makes me miserable just being with you."

But then again, how would you react if someone you cared about said that to you when you were being heavy? Would you be thankful or would you resent them? Or might you let them help you out of your funk? Lightening up is about being buoyant, having a good time, and taking things less seriously. These are the elemental pleasures—the basic building blocks that foster levity. They are: playing, laughing, moving energetically, and being vocally expressive.

Play

To play is to engage in an activity just for the fun of it, just for the excitement and stimulation of it. When you're playing, you're fully absorbed in what you are doing, right here and right now—and anything you do in a playful spirit, even if it's work, puts you into a pleasurable flow. You enjoy what you're doing, and it's the sheer joy of it that keeps you going.

People who make a living being creative know that you have to tackle a project in the spirit of play to enlist the imagination and get in touch with your originality. Then your writing, drawing, or whatever you do to express your artistry feels like it's coming through you, surprising and delighting even you. Bringing your creativity to what you do for a living blurs the distinction between work and play.

The only hitch to enlisting your inner artist to work for you is that your inner critic usually tags along, casting aspersions on the value of what you are creating. These two guys are joined at the hip—invite one and you get both. If you're playing and enjoying yourself as a way of priming the pump for ideas, the critic says you're wasting time and not accomplishing anything. If you're sketching something in your notebook, the critic says you're not good at this and shouldn't even be trying. However, if you manage to dismiss the negative chatterings of this undermining part of yourself, you may end up with a product, an idea, or a direction that turns you on. And of course, whatever turns you on very likely will turn on others.

When artists suffer, it's primarily because of the emotional obstacle course their own inner critic makes them run. But if they trust the creative process and come through it, some say the high is better than sex.

Play doesn't have to be creative, however, it can be just plain fun. Indeed, when it comes to leisure, our most favorite playtimes seem to be when we're not doing anything very special at all—just playing with the kids, chatting with a neighbor, or reading a book under a tree.

What kind of play makes us happiest has even been put to a scientific test. Dr. Csikszentmihalyi, at the University of Chicago, devised a procedure to test what people are actually doing when they are feeling happiest. Subjects in the study wore a beeper that was programmed to go off at random intervals eight times a day. They also carried a rating booklet in which they were to indicate, at every signal, what they were doing and with whom, and how happy or sad they were at the moment. What was found was that when people were enjoying leisure, they were happiest, not during special times playing with lavish toys, but when they were engaged in simple pleasures like hanging out with friends, working in the garden, or making something with their hands.

Never Underestimate the Value of Play

The first time I saw Annie I could see that she was a very unhappy young woman. Though she was tall and thin, with long brown hair and pleasant enough facial features, she was too tense to be considered attractive. Her brow was knit, her eyes squinted, and she carried herself stiffly. She sat on the couch with her hands folded and looked at the wall behind me as she talked. She was probably almost fifteen years younger than me, but I felt like a spunky kid next to her.

Annie told me she worried about everything and never made a move without second-guessing herself. Actually, if she were to think things over only twice that would have been fine. She belabored every task and made herself think through all the potential hazards of every situation so that nothing she did was ever spontaneous. She just didn't trust herself to do the right thing.

It was no surprise to me to find out that her parents were as gloomy as she was. The only person in her family who was any different was her younger sister, her only sibling, who had thrown caution to the wind at an early age and left home at seventeen. Unfortunately, she ran into some hard times and developed a drug problem, reinforcing in Annie and her parents that this is a hostile world and you can never be careful enough.

Annie was lonely. She had few friends and rarely dated. She worked as an account executive at a big advertising agency and felt as isolated at work as she was when she was off. Her life sounded bleak. She made good money but she hardly ever went anywhere to enjoy herself. She told me she had come for therapy wanting to understand more about why she was this way and to see if there was any hope for her to lead a normal life, with a husband and children and a nice home. I sensed she rather doubted it and had come to me to prove her worst suspicions.

I found Annie difficult to work with at first because she was hard to warm up to. She thought making small talk at the beginning of our sessions was a waste of precious time. Therapy was too expensive for that, she said. She wanted to get right into what new worries this day had brought. I would occasionally remind her about the value of chitchat in building warmth and rapport, and how her ability to be friendly with me might help her strike up some warm friendships with others. She was impatient but she begrudgingly acknowledged she could use a few pointers in that department.

Annie and I worked together a long time. Her greater satisfaction with her life today has to do with her own determination to change and with a variety of different aspects of her explorations with me: what we talked about, her willingness to practice breath control, and her developing trust in having a more relaxed encounter with the world. But she leaped a major hurdle when she became willing to experiment with being playful.

Annie mentioned one day that she had looked through the catalogue of a local community college and noticed a few courses she thought might be interesting. One that she mentioned took me by surprise: mask making. She said she had always been fascinated by masks but had never taken an art class and didn't think she would be comfortable in a messy kind of environment. I felt like we had struck gold.

I suggested to Annie that she immediately sign up for the course. I told her she seemed to have lost her ability to play at a very young age and that this class might help get it back. She mulled it over and finally said that she didn't know if she could commit to a full five weeks, but she would enroll and at least go a few times.

That class became a turning point for Annie. She got her hands dirty for the first time in her life and lost herself in what she called "blessedly mindless activity" crafting *papier maché* masks and painting them fanciful colors. She met some nice people including a man she dated for a while. For the first time in the six months I knew her, she cracked a joke with me, and it was genuinely funny. It was ironic how making actual masks that she could hold in her hands had enabled her to drop the frozen look that masked her own real face. I was astonished at how pretty Annie actually turned out to be.

As Annie's story shows, play is not the frivolous nonsense it is usually thought to be, just a circumscribed little region of your life where you escape from the world of serious business and responsibilities into idle games and fantasies. In genuine play there is vitality, excitement, enthusiasm, and an enormous store of creativity to tap into. Just like kids playing house and practicing to be adults or kittens pouncing on dried leaves gearing up to be mousers, play can be the fuel that drives us to discover new talents, to energetically rehearse valuable skills before they really matter, and to just revel in being alive.

Laughter

A good belly laugh is one of life's greatest physical pleasures. Your whole body shakes and vibrates, and your breathing rhythms are profoundly altered. Deep inhales occur reflexively and exhales are often loudly vocalized. Whether its a high-pitched tee-hee-hee-hee, or a deep ha-ha-ha-ha, or a scream, or a howl, your entire body is actively engaged in energetically expressing glee.

We're all aware that a good laugh can induce a state of relaxation and well-being. The fact that we can sometimes wet our pants laughing gives personal evidence of how laughter can loosen the grip of all the muscles of the body. But it has also been demonstrated in the laboratory. Mirthful laughter not only reduces muscle tension but can result in a substantial decrease in resting heart rate and blood pressure.

Hearty laughter can also energize us. Enjoying a good laugh is a state of physiological arousal that boosts oxygen–carbon dioxide exchange. Laughing increases muscular activity, which in turn stimulates the cardiovascular system. When you laugh, stress hormones in the blood such as adrenaline, epinephrine, and norepinephrine decrease. Laughter even enhances your immune response by releasing endorphins and other neurotransmitters and raising your count of disease fighting T-cells in the blood.

Some people say that, more than anything else, sharing the same sense of humor is what drew them to their spouses. Not uncommonly, couples who get along well say that they often share a good laugh together and that being able to look at the funny side of a situation has helped them through tough times. Cracking a joke or saying something silly in the midst of stress reminds you that things probably aren't as dismal as they look.

Even in the middle of a disagreement, it can help if someone says something that highlights the absurdity of what is going on. But be careful. Put-down humor in the midst of hostility is rarely amusing and could earn you a fat lip. Only genuinely good-natured humor, with both people laughing at themselves, can end a fight.

Laughter is so good for us that it has become a subject for serious study and has even been given a scientific name: gelotology. Research gelotologists have provided definitive proof that, when it comes to enjoying a long and healthy life, those who laugh, last.

Energetic Movement

Several years ago, I bought a birthday present for my husband at a big department store and took it to their gift wrapping department in an out-of-the-way corner on the top floor of the building. I brought my package, examined the sample gift boxes and bows hanging on the back wall in assorted colored papers, and chose one. Then, there was nothing more for me to do but sit down on the hard wooden bench and wait next to a teenage couple who looked as bored as I felt. I had no book, no newspaper, and there was nothing there to even look at. All I could do now was sit and daydream as I stared at the dingy walls around me.

After a few minutes, a mother came up with a package to wrap, her three children tagging along beside her. They were beautiful kids, the eldest was a little girl about six, the two boys around three and four. The children began to play by running along an empty corridor near the gift-wrapping booth, chasing and tickling one another and giggling excitedly. They were so cute to watch that the young couple and I became transfixed. But the mother became annoyed. She ran over to the corridor, yelled at the girl for not having more sense, slapped the bigger boy on his bottom, and looked cross as she shook the youngest.

The teenagers turned away, looking bored again and even more antsy to get out of there. I sighed and got back into my waiting mode, but as I watched the kids hold themselves in, I got interested again.

The smallest child snickered into his hands and tried to hide his laughter. The bigger boy squirmed as he sat in his chair, probably because his bottom stung. The girl stood by her mother, her arms folded across her chest, making faces at the boys. I was glad to see that their little spirits had not been dampened by their mother's lesson regarding how to behave themselves in public. But I couldn't help but wonder, what would have been the harm to let them play in a barren little cubicle where they really weren't bothering anyone and couldn't possibly do any damage to themselves?

Swiss psychiatrist Alice Miller, in a brilliant study of the traditional childrearing practices of Western culture from the last four centuries to the present, showed how what has been considered "good upbringing" for hundreds of years actually has targeted a child's natural exuberance for life. Miller presented a multitude of examples from eighteenth-, nineteenth-, and twentieth-century European childrearing manuals, most of which were written by German doctors or clergy, where spankings, beatings, and humiliation were advocated specifically to suppress curiosity, physical energy and excitement, and all strong emotions.

Miller went even further to examine the political implications of how a society raises its young. Through case studies, she was able to show how stern disciplinary practices during childhood could be responsible for what enabled so many Germans as adults to embrace Nazism. Every child needs a parent who is empathic rather than controlling. To Miller, the typically rigid upbringing for German children, which prized obedience over other qualities, set them up to become passive in the face of cruel authority and to blindly obey grotesque orders for mass murder from those they saw to be in charge.

Few of us today have been subjected to the kind of spirit-dampening authoritarianism advocated by nineteenth-century moralists, but many of our grandparents and our parents were exposed to it and used less extreme but, nonetheless, still cruel tendencies in their childrearing practices. Those of us raised on the punishment ethos who were spanked or chastised as children for having too much energy have learned to mistrust spontaneity and to associate genuine expressiveness with danger.

The tendency to suppress a child's vitality by inhibiting his or her physical activity exists even today. Critics of drugs programs for hyperactive children in grade schools have suggested that some children diagnosed as hyperactive and placed on drugs at school may be within the range of normality but too energetic for the parents' or teacher's comfort.

The Benefits of Enjoying Movement

The rewards for vigorous activity—what we usually call physical exercise—have been well documented over the years. Make a commitment to at least thirty minutes of cardiovascular activity three times a week, and you not only add years to your life, but they're good years at that. You have more energy and stamina, your heart is strengthened and made more efficient, and you have better circulation, lower blood pressure, better metabolism, and better resistance to cancer and other potentially life-threatening illnesses.

All these medical test statistics translate into good feelings for you—you feel healthy, alert, glad to be alive, eager to face the day, and it does a world of good for your spirits. Working out regularly, in whatever way turns you on the most, puts you in a better mood, gives you more self-confidence, reduces depression and anxiety, and enhances the capacity to handle stress and to enjoy challenge.

But unless you find an activity that you can take pleasure from, it's very unlikely you will be able to maintain the discipline. The people I know, who joined a gym or health club and ended up letting their membership lapse after going three or four times, never discovered what it was that makes other people so joyously addicted.

There are lots of ways to get a cardiovascular energy fix. Play at sports, ride a bike, run, swim, power walk, hike, go dancing, climb stairs, or make love very enthusiastically. To be cardiovascular, just be sure that whatever it is you're doing, you're doing it energetically: Your heart is pumping, your breathing is faster and deeper than usual, you're sweating (unless you're swimming), and you have a good rhythm going.

You can also enhance your vitality and sense of well-being by doing meditative or deliberate movements such as yoga, tai chi, or chi gung, or by doing stretches like the ones I suggest in Chapter 6.

But if you have difficulty discovering the pleasures of movement on your own, you may want to consider a form of therapy that focuses on movement. The Alexander Technique, Feldenkrais work, and dance therapy are three well-developed bodywork technologies for helping people relearn how to move in a more relaxed and more pleasurable fashion. The Alexander Technique has focused on developing sensory awareness of the sensations of movement in the body, especially between the head, neck, and back, so that body alignment improves naturally, and physical activity feels freer, lighter, and more satisfying.

Feldenkrais methods also focus on bringing greater pleasure to body movements. These exercises involve practicing small, unfamiliar patterns of movement to bring awareness to unconscious, self-limiting motor habits and to regain the pleasures of balance, vitality, and spontaneity in movement. Dance therapy often encourages people to find their "authentic" movements, actions that most lyrically or symbolically express their current feelings or life situations.

With each modality, the task is always to gain greater kinesthetic awareness of how the body feels, to move and to develop a greater capacity to take pleasure from spontaneous, expressive activity.

Physical Mastery

Another way to get pleasure from physical activity is to set a goal for yourself, to achieve skill or mastery at something like dancing or athletics, and then to watch yourself improve over time with practice. Learning to swim well has been that kind of teaching for me.

I've always both loved and been terrified by the water. I have a vague memory of having been pulled from the Atlantic Ocean at four or five and rolled over a barrel until I regurgitated water. My father, who in my vision is anxiously watching over my shoulder, swears it never happened. I also have memories of many summers at

Washington Baths, a beach club in Coney Island, where from age eight through my early teens, I would have to screw up my courage anew each season to jump into the deep end of the pool. Once in, I'd kick off the bottom, surface, and then splash and struggle my way over to the steps at the shallow end. Then, with my heart pounding, I'd climb out and do it all over again.

Many years later, when I was living in San Francisco and suffering from low back pain, I joined a health club with a pool and worked out by doing laps several times a week. My swimming hadn't improved much over the years, and one day as I was splashing up and down the pool, I noticed an elderly man watching with great interest as I made my way down to the end where he was standing. When I got near him, he shook his head at me and clucked disapprovingly, "You work so hard, but you don't get anywhere."

At first, I was terribly offended and embarrassed. But I couldn't deny that he was right, and it wasn't just about my swimming either. He didn't know it, but he was talking about my life. At that moment I vowed that I was going to learn to glide and work my way through the water effortlessly and skillfully until "going far easily" would become my new metaphor for life. I started to take my swimming more seriously and began to practice relaxing and moving more gracefully and rhythmically through the water.

One of my life's greatest moments was the summer on the big island of Hawaii when I swam out from Kealakakua Bay with my husband and a small group of friends to try to catch up with a school of dolphins that were spotted about three-quarters of a mile offshore. To say that my heart beat wildly at first is to put it mildly. When I could no longer see the ocean floor through my face mask and it turned dark beneath me, my heart really pounded. On several occasions, I had to stop to readjust my snorkel, and I would lose sight of my friends. I felt like a cork bobbing in the open sea. But I kept swimming, reminding myself to breathe slowly and to maintain the ease I had cultivated in the swimming pool. The effort turned out to be very worthwhile.

Eventually, we did catch up with the dolphins, or perhaps it was they who caught up with us. They surprised us by coming upon us from behind. In what seemed like a procession in slow motion, they passed about ten feet below us, in twos and threes, babies and young close to their mothers. We were transfixed as the parade of huge gray animals slowly and deliberately presented themselves to us underwater. When the whole school had completely passed below us, they turned back and started to play with us. This time, they swam every which way, examining us with the same apparent interest and spiritedness that we had for them.

After a few minutes of sheer delight, they all disappeared only to reappear about fifty feet away, and this time leaping into the air. They were doing tricks for us! They would burst from the sea, do corkscrew spirals and triple back flips, then elegantly plunge from their heights back into the water. We were being graced with an incredible display of interspecies generosity. Without a doubt, these naturally playful creatures from the wild were performing for us.

At this point, we had our masks off and were cheering them on, screaming "aah" and "ooh" as though we were watching fireworks on the fourth of July. And then, suddenly, the show was over. They were gone. We laughed and hugged each other, and very satisfied, started our long swim back to shore.

Since that time, my swimming has taken on a distinct new character. I have known courage in the water. I was afraid but I made it. I breathed, I relaxed, I told myself I could do it, and I did it. Somehow, that experience has had a remarkable effect on how my body feels when I swim now. I'm lighter in the water; I feel more like I'm flying in air than maneuvering through a denser medium. I coast between strokes, and my movements give me a longer glide. But most especially, my body apparently knows something now it didn't know before. In my heart and in my bones, I now know I won't sink—not in the water and not in life.

Sounding Out

When my friends and I were excitedly watching the dolphins' gymnastics, it was the most natural thing in the world for us to be whooping and cheering them on. One of the most exquisite moments of that whole experience was all the joyous hooting and hollering that spontaneously erupted from us while we were watching their dazzling farewell.

Jubilant shrieks are to pleasure what crying is to pain. Expressing a feeling through sound, whether it's joy or sorrow, goes beyond simply expressing yourself verbally and rationally. Alexander Lowen, the originator of a body psychotherapy known as Bioenergetics, has said that in order for any emotion to be released cathartically, it has to move through the throat in sound.

In other words, weeping silent tears will not release sadness. That's just emotion leaking out, and coming out that way won't really afford much relief. For grieving to be truly therapeutic, a person who is crying needs to make sobbing sounds. That's what having a good cry is all about. The importance of exercising the vocal cords in releasing tension and painful emotion is also why chanting certain sounds and rhythms can be effective in healing practices, especially for dealing with frustration and anger.

In fact, expressing joy can be just as releasing and relaxing as getting out negative feelings; perhaps even more so, since saying "yay!" is usually a lot more energizing than saying "nay." Cheerful people hum or whistle as they move through their day. Are they whistling because they're feeling cheerful or feeling cheerful because they whistle? Probably, it can go either way.

Moan in ecstasy when you're being rubbed at just the right spot on your shoulders, or when you're biting into a tender morsel of food, or sipping a delicate wine, or smelling a gardenia, and the experience is all the more exquisite precisely because you let out a sound of appreciation.

The same is true for sex. One of the biggest complaints I hear from people who are not sexually satisfied with their partner is that he or she makes no sound during sex, not even at orgasm. Women tend to interpret silent orgasms in a man as his holding back emotionally from her because he won't let go and be real with her. Men usually read it somewhat differently, that she is not holding back from him emotionally but physically, and that's because she is afraid of sex.

Whether there is a gender difference or not with regard to the meaning behind silent orgasms is interesting speculation. It's probably all of the above for both sexes—they are holding themselves back both emotionally and physically, and probably not just from their partners but from themselves as well. But no matter how you interpret it, the experience of the partner who makes barely a gurgle during lovemaking can be very frustrating for a lusty lover who yearns to hear sounds of enjoyment. There is the sense that if the partner were to make sounds and get into the whole experience more, the sex would be better for both of them.

Other than having the good fortune of a sex life full of hearty grunts and melodious moans, there are many other ways to express pleasure vocally that can enhance your daily life. Singing can be a particularly satisfying form of self-expression, especially when you can really belt it out. Sing in the shower or in your car with a familiar tape and already your day has started off on a pleasant note. Poetry can be sensuous to recite, not just because of the rhythm of the meter but also because of the sensation of each syllable as it trips off your tongue and echoes in your ear. Read a favorite verse to a friend and it just might make you feel closer. Let out exuberant whoops of appreciation as you applaud a musician at a concert or club, and you may enjoy the performance even more. Hum your delight when someone hugs you, and the hug may feel even warmer. Without a doubt, all pleasures can be intensified through making joyful sounds.

Personal Experiments

. . . .

Here are a few ways to explore playfulness; each requires no more than five to ten minutes of your time. If you are willing to give it longer than that, even better.

Play and Creativity

1. Breath life into your artist. Build in a few minutes at a time during your day to check in with your spontaneous creativity. First focus your energy with breath control. Take three cleansing breaths—long inhales through your nose all the way to the top of your chest, and then blow out through slightly puckered lips all the way down to the very bottom of your exhale. Check in with your body. See if there is any tension, emotion, or discomfort, and if so, breathe and stretch for a few moments into those tight areas to loosen up. Now, doodle on a note pad or write a quick poem—just to keep your creative wheels greased. You may wish to give yourself even more opportunity for artistic expression and devote a whole day to writing, painting, or making music.

2. Draw a picture of yourself as you are at this very moment. Use a pencil, a pen, crayons, or felt-tip markers and lined or unlined paper—just grab whatever is handy. The picture can be symbolic: Let your hand move automatically, shaping figures on your paper or swirling what seem like the most appropriate colors. The picture can be literal: Draw yourself surrounded by the most important people in your current life, or draw yourself alone wherever you are right now. Then just study what you have committed to paper and see what it tells you about your present moment. Did you enjoy what you did? Would you enjoy taking ten minutes more?

3. Write a few paragraphs on the following theme: "If I had the courage to do it, I would . . ." Your little essay could be symbolic or literal, fiction or fact. You might tell yourself a little story and make it funny, poignant, sad, or inspirational.

What's most important is to get your critic out of the process. Critics are spoilsports. Nothing inhibits creative expression more than holding yourself up to some fixed standard of excellence that essentially eliminates the possibility of surprise and genuine innovation.

As Jack Kerouac said about writing, "First thought, best thought." Just talk to yourself and write down what you hear as fast as you can, as though you were taking dictation. Or allow an image to come up in your mind's eye and simply describe it on paper. Don't read what you're writing as you write it. Don't erase anything; just add your afterthoughts the way you would if you were talking to a friend. When you are finished, walk away from it for at least ten minutes. Then come back and read it out loud. How does it sound? How does it feel "tripping off the tongue" and out of your mouth? How do you feel about what you've written? Now, if you want to smooth it out so it trips off the tongue better, you're allowed.

4. A special exercise for procrastinators: Say you need to get something done at work that you've been postponing because you either hate doing it or, underneath it all, you just don't feel you're going to do a good enough job. It's that damn inner critic again! Here's a way to increase the possibility of completing a dreaded chore: Approach it as an opportunity to be playful.

Take a few cleansing breaths, a few deep sighs, and tell yourself to "have fun with it." Then do just that, even if it means making a fleet of paper airplanes out of your work and launching them across the room. Whatever you do, no matter how silly it starts out, can unexpectedly materialize into something very fine. Then you've ended up with something pragmatic that has some real potential and you won't even know where it came from—except that, miraculously, it came from you.

5. A special exercise for lovers: Take yourselves out on a date where each one of you is playing a particularly wonderful and fun-loving alter-ego. It could be Sophia and Marcello, Natasha and Boris, Fifi and Pierre, or Sadie and Clem. Play, laugh, entertain each other, and be romantically provocative. If you get into a disagreement, see if you can lighten up and fight like your whimsical alter-egos.

6. Find your own means of artistic expression. Write a poem, tell a joke, dance to a tune on the radio, sing with attitude to a friend, play house with a child, make a present for a sick neighbor, draw your own greeting card for a relative, or play at romance with your lover/spouse.

Laughter

7. Support your favorite comedians: Rent or buy their video or audiotapes. When Norman Cousins discovered he had a bad heart, he apparently was able to laugh his way to wellness by renting Marx Brothers videos. He died in his nineties having added a good fifteen years to his life by lightening up. Whose humor does it for you? Have their tapes on hand when you could use a few laughs.

8. Create a folder of favorite cartoons. Read some of the comics in your daily newspaper. Anytime a cartoon tickles your funny bone, cut it out and save it. Stick them onto sheets of typing paper, make copies, and send them to your friends and relatives in your correspondence. Cut out cartoons your lover/ spouse might particularly enjoy and leave them on his or her desk or pillow.

9. The laughing meditation. Here's a good exercise promoted by a Dutch physician originally to help chronic pain patients and then, because it worked so well, to inspire attendees at medical congresses and conventions.

Experiment with this exercise in the morning. Start with a few cleansing breaths, then some yawning and some stretching. Then smile and start to giggle a little, slowly and with a relaxed throat; build up to a hearty belly laugh. Focus your complete attention on how it feels to be laughing and see if you can let go and allow yourself to be genuinely amused. After a few minutes, stop laughing, let your body be still, and notice your breath without controlling it in any way. See if you feel lighter and more energized.

Movement

10. Take up several physical activities you enjoy and practice them regularly, so that you do something active at least three times a week. Branch out so that it's not the same thing you always do for fun. Go bowling or folk dancing, take a step class or a dance workshop; try Pilates, weight lifting, swimming, hiking, or walking; play softball, basketball, handball, tennis, or golf. You might also practice yoga, tai chi, aikido, tae kwan do, or karate. Get more active.

11. Choose a physical discipline to develop your mastery. Whatever you select, set yourself a goal of becoming progressively better at it. Take a class or get a personal trainer for a while just to learn more about how to be skillful at your chosen activity. Then practice on your own by setting little goals for yourself and watching yourself progress. Even if you go for weeks without any noticeable changes, if you stay at it, without a doubt, you will become more skilled and you will feel good about what you have managed to accomplish.

Sounding Out

12. Express yourself. Sing in the shower or in your car. Get together with some friends and sing old songs together; if one of them has a piano, meet at his or her house. Attend a sporting event where you and your friends can root loudly for your team(s). Read tender poetry to your lover. Practice saying short, sweet, simple declarative sentences such as, "You're great!" "What fun!" "I feel good!"

Now that we have explored the most fundamental pleasures, we can move into the psychological pleasures of the mind and the emotions. However, to fully enjoy more complex pleasures, we need to incorporate the basics at the very core of every pleasure: that of letting go and just being, of releasing pain, and of engaging our capacity to be light-hearted, to play, laugh, move our body, and make sounds.

PART THREE

The Psychological Pleasures

Chapter 8

Mental Pleasures:
Mind Matters

. . . .

How to think good thoughts

. . . .

Reality! What a concept!

—*Robin Williams*

Most of us need a lot of mental stimulation to feel awake and alive. In childhood, some of our biggest turn-ons come from acting on curiosity. Young children enjoy being inquisitive, investigating a situation with a completely fresh mind, gaining new information, refining skills, solving puzzles, having insights, and making discoveries.

By the time we reach adulthood, however, a lot of the fun can go out of thinking. We've been taught how to think and what to think, and although we may like to see ourselves as intellectually independent, we're all subject to patterns of thought that we're not often aware of at all. We can adopt rigid ways of making sense of things and hold on to a "my mind is made up, don't confuse me with the facts" philosophy. We can get stuck in limited areas of interest and not venture into unfamiliar territories of learning—like technologically challenged people who can't program their VCR and wouldn't consider learning to use a computer. We can also bore ourselves to tears—particularly if the same old voices keep haggling it out in our heads.

People who require more mental stimulation than they allow themselves in positive, enjoyable ways can fall into a habit of getting their mental titillation from the mind games and melodramas they can fashion out of their lives. For people tortured by their own thoughts, the hardest thing to give up is their dependency on the adrenaline triggered by living one's life as a passion play.

The fear of boredom is also one of the most common reasons I hear from people who abuse drugs, particularly alcohol and cocaine, for not wanting to give up their addiction They're afraid that without their favorite intoxicant, life would be too boring. The fact is that it will be—unless they actively cultivate new avenues of interest to be curious about, learn new skills, and discover new recesses of their mind without relying on drugs to get there.

The task for all of us, to stay mentally alert and positive, is to learn how to use an expansive mind to generate pleasures that can nurture and inspire our lives.

Pleasures of Mind

There are many ways to enjoy the life of the mind. Reading, learning new skills, and solving conundrums of all kinds can be very satisfying activities. Aesthetic appreciation provides other pleasures, such as enjoying a play or opera, and it can stimulate a mental sense of beauty, balance, symmetry, or irony. There are also the pleasures of a quiet mind, perhaps during a meditation or a walk in a garden, when for a short while, there are no thoughts and we feel at peace. We'll examine aesthetics as a sensual pleasure in Chapter 10, and a quiet mind as a spiritual pleasure in Chapter 12.

The two types of mental pleasures we'll explore here are those based in reality and those based in fantasy—what we imagine in daydreams and night dreams. When your mind is stimulated in expansive ways in both of these areas, it can have a profound effect on the quality of your life.

Happiness Depends on Thinking Good Thoughts

How you interpret the events in your life can determine whether you are happy or depressed, energetic or drained. In fact, whether you realize your dreams or not ultimately may be more a factor of how you explain the disappointments and losses in your life to yourself than the fact that bad things happened to you.

Dr. Martin E. P. Seligman, professor of psychology at the University of Pennsylvania and a researcher for more than thirty years on the psychology of motivation and success, has found overwhelming evidence to show that pessimism and optimism are not just about whether you think the glass is half empty or half full. They are truly self-fulfilling prophecies. People with pessimistic habits of thinking are more likely to interpret mere setbacks as disasters, to become depressed, and to give up more easily than people who tend to be more optimistic. In fact, experiments have shown that optimists not only do much better in school, at work, and in sports but that, when they run for office, they're more likely to win. Overall, optimists have also been found to be healthier, to age better, and to live longer than pessimists.

Seligman found that the difference between pessimistic and optimistic thinking patterns is related to how people explain to themselves what has happened to them and how they think it will affect them in the future. Confronted with a painful situation, pessimists are more likely to think the bad event is going to be permanent—that it will last forever; that it is pervasive—that it will impact all aspects of their life; and that it is personal—that it's all their fault, and if they were smarter, more attractive, more talented, taller, shorter, younger, slimmer, or more lovable, this terrible thing would not have happened.

Optimists have a markedly different "explanatory style." They are more likely to understand the bad situation as temporary, limited in its effect, and unrelated to their worthiness or capacity to do well. In one study, the optimists maintained their performance advantage even though they may have been unrealistic in their expectations, seeing things through rose-colored glasses, while the pessimists actually were seeing things more accurately. Optimists in a state of denial are more likely to overcome a difficult situation than pessimists who are seeing the situation more clearly. Can there be any doubt that this is due to the greater vitality available to someone who is energized by his or her hope, faith, and dreams, and inspired to action?

Melancholy Baby

The first time I met Risa, an attractive, petite woman in her middle thirties with big brown sad eyes, she told me that she "felt like she was on a slow train to nowhere." She wore her short dark hair in a blunt cut, a print dress that showed off her trim figure, and sat with her hands folded on her lap, like a schoolgirl.

Speaking softly, Risa went on to say that she had a good job at an insurance agency but felt she'd risen in her company as far as she could go. She had never been married and yearned for a relationship but rarely dated, and though she had been in a few intimate relationships, none lasted longer than six months. Her friendships, on the other hand, were more lasting, and she had several good friends, both male and female, with whom she enjoyed going to gallery openings, singles events, and concerts. But she felt like the years were passing, and she was terrified that she would end up a dried-up old lady, having wasted her life.

I wondered out loud how someone as attractive, gentle, and eager for a relationship as she could be without any real love interests. Risa shrugged her shoulders and shook her head blankly. Her friends liked her. She knew she had plenty to offer. It was just that nobody was taking her up on it. Then I asked her about work—what she felt would be the next step for her—but she said she didn't want to stay in insurance. It was only a job she fell into, and she didn't particularly care to excel at it. She just didn't know what else she might want to do.

Risa was an only child who had lost her mother in a freak car accident at age thirteen and had maintained a close loving relationship with her father. But as she spoke of her father, I could hear that the two of them encouraged in each other a fatalistic outlook, what I called "you never know what terrible tragedy tomorrow will bring, so try hard to make the most of what you have today." Risa laughed when she heard me formulate her life's philosophy so succinctly. She had thought their way of thinking was very positive considering the sad turn of their family events. It may not have looked like pessimism on the surface. But bitter accommodation, to my mind, is not exactly a positive point of view.

On the outside, Risa had developed a calm, peaceful manner, but inside she suffered from a low-grade depression that was like a chronic infection. In truth, she had never fully grieved the loss of her mother because she was too busy ministering to her father's needs, reassuring him and taking over her mother's role of nurturing him.

She developed a sweetly reserved demeanor. But she had no spirit of playful challenge. She took no creative risks at work and became shy around dynamic men.

As Risa worked with me to more fully grieve her mother's death, she began to see the thought patterns that kept her spirits down. She had a voice inside her that tended to undermine the possibilities that came her way, work-wise and with men. In fact, when anything did excite her, not uncommonly, she'd warn herself that something bad could come of this, and her surge of energy would quickly turn into agitation or nervousness.

Inner Narratives and Dialogues

All day long we talk to ourselves in our heads, only a minute portion of which is ever uttered aloud. We narrate the events of our lives as they're happening, and the spin we give them depends to a large extent on whether we have adopted a positive or negative style of explaining things.

As Australian therapists Michael White and David Epston have shown, we weave these narratives together and make sense of it all by making a story out of it—a kind of running autobiography that has a beginning in the past, a middle in the present, and an end somewhere in the future. Everything that happens we explain to ourselves, and to the people we confide in, in a way that fits in with the larger story.

Yet, unless we speak the story out loud, it's hard to be aware of all the different themes of the story we're telling ourselves. Many of us find that we may not even know what we think about something until we hear ourselves talk about it to others. It's only when we express ourselves to a friend or therapist, or write down our observations in a journal that we can begin to examine our thoughts.

It's also hard to be aware of all the stories we tell ourselves because there's usually a cacophony of voices talking to us—often all at once. It's like being tuned into the radio between stations and picking up five talk show hosts each presenting a different reading of the same event.

Inside, we're not the singular, consistent personality that we try to project on the outside. Opposing voices battle inside us: the prude and the tease, the people-pleaser and the rebel, the spiritual seeker and the vindictive one, the fearful one and the brave one. Usually, one of them is stronger, and we act on that one while the other side nags from the bleachers. Sometimes we yearn to act on an insistent inner voice that we try to ignore but find we can't. When we do finally act on it, friends and family may tell us we're not being ourselves; but actually we are, it's just a part of ourselves they hadn't yet met.

Some voices may talk sweetly to us and make us feel good—like the encouraging part of ourselves that I call the "inner ally." This is the voice that is like a good parent who comforts us when we're hurt and cheers us on when we've had a setback. Unfortunately, this can be a weak voice and in some people, nonexistent.

Some voices are frightening and make our hearts race—like the "misfortune teller" who is always reading the future and telling us how bad it's going to be. Two of the most important inner voices to be cognizant of, in that they can be our constant companions, are the "inner critic" and the "inner victim." These two voices usually dialogue with one another. While one side puts us down and finds fault with whatever we're doing, the other side sustains the brunt of the attack and feels insecure, or at worst, tormented. A bad bout of a critic/victim dialogue can drain your energy and make you feel depressed and full of self-pity, anxious and spinning your wheels, or angry and looking for a fight.

These internal dialogues—whether we're conscious of them or not—determine our emotions and stress levels more than what's actually going on around us. In fact, it is particularly when we are not consciously aware of these voices, that they can most affect our emotional and physiological reactions.

Abraham Lincoln once said, "Most people are about as happy as they make up their minds to be." The fact is that you can think positively or you can think negatively. If you think negatively you will trigger adrenaline and are likely to get anxious and obsessive, thinking the same thoughts over and over, and doubting yourself. You might make yourself paranoid, continually interpreting the events of your life suspiciously and trying to read the "signs." You might weigh every interaction with another person in terms of your performance, trying to figure out what you're supposed to do next.

Or you can adopt a running commentary that serves you better; one that lifts your spirits and gives you something positive to do about it all. You can narrate your day's activities as interesting, challenging, fun, or fruitful. You can praise your progress and encourage yourself on. How you choose to talk to yourself will determine your mood and affect your health and immunity. How you talk to yourself will influence how you talk to others—especially your nearest and dearest, whom we tend to mistreat in the same ways we mistreat ourselves. How you talk to yourself will usually determine whether you take risks and have a rich life or play it safe and quit too easily.

Truth Is Not Necessarily True; Reality Is Not Necessarily Real

No matter how logical we are, our thinking doesn't necessarily provide us with an accurate reflection of the truth. We may think there is an objective reality. We may believe that one of those voices inside has the right explanation while the other voices are wrong—and that all we need to do is figure out which is which. The fact is, as soon as objective reality begins to make sense, that's a sign that it's already subjective.

The famous Heisenberg Principle of Uncertainty applies just as much to observing our inner lives as it does to observing planets orbiting the sun or an electron orbiting the nucleus of an atom: The observer changes the thing observed. What we're looking for apparently determines what we find, whether we're talking about an astronomer studying the stars or an ordinary person searching his or her soul. We can't know what is really happening, because we are seeing it all through the lens of our old stories, customary explanations, and habitual inner dialogues.

Mental set not only determines what you look for but also how you remember what you encounter. Studies in the field of memory have repeatedly demonstrated that your mental set will not only influence your first impression of an event, but over time, your memory will change to accommodate your mental set. People in one study were flashed pictures of ambiguous figures and then asked to draw a picture of what they saw. Half the group was given one set of descriptive labels for the figures, the other half a different set of labels. For example, one figure was labeled a crescent moon to half the subjects, the other half was told the same figure was a kidney bean. When they were asked to draw a picture of exactly what they saw, those who were told it was a crescent moon drew the figure to look more like a crescent, while the kidney bean group drew it to look more kidney-shaped.

Some time later the subjects were asked to draw the figure again, and in most cases, the figures became even more crescentlike or more kidneylike, depending on how the figure had been labeled. Their memories were not static freeze-frame accounts of the past, but over time, actively evolved to conform to their experimentally induced bias.

I refer to this experiment when I'm working with a couple who are describing a fight they had, and each partner has a very different memory of what actually took place. After the second or third go-around, when each is trying to convince the other that he or she is right and the other is wrong, I remind them that there is no way to remember a situation accurately. Their mental sets going into the fight laid down different memory traces of what actually took place; thinking it over later only made those memory traces evolve even further in the direction of their bias.

I advise couples who try to resolve their quarrels by figuring out what "really" happened to give it up. I tell them that you can never work it out by going backward. You can only go forward from this moment on. What do you want to do about it now? What agreements can you make with each other for the next time, when the same situation comes up again? Which it will.

The stories we weave over time about our lives, the internal voices we listen to, and the meaning we attach to it all are habits of thought. "Reality" is an interpretation we make of what happens to us that sets us up to act in ways consistent with our expectations—for good or bad. That's why, if we don't like our reality, we can construct a new one by telling ourselves a better story, one that lays out a potentially more gratifying design for action.

Questioning Old Stories

When Risa and I started to look at her current life, she told me that she and her father usually had dinner together three times a week. I asked her if she enjoyed seeing her father as often as she did, and at first she said yes. But later she admitted that there were all sorts of events or classes she didn't permit herself to go to because it would take her away from him. She also said she didn't have as much time as she would have liked to be alone in her own apartment. But she felt guilty even just thinking about spending less time with her father because he really depended on the times they spent together. When I asked her what he had to say about it, she said that to protect his feelings she had never raised the issue and never would.

I suggested to her that what she called a daughter's devotion might also be seen as putting him down, underestimating her father, and not giving him any credit for being a resilient person. She was offended at first but said she was willing to consider the possibility that he was not as needy as she thought. One evening, when she and her dad were cleaning up after dinner at his house, she told him what we had talked about. He said that he felt it was she and not he who needed to be in constant contact, and that he was concerned that she had become too dependent on him as an adult.

Risa couldn't believe her ears. For almost twenty years, she and her father had been operating from opposite storylines. Her dad said that he felt she needed him there for her several times a week. He said he hadn't dated as much as he would have liked because he didn't want her to be hurt. And he did feel that she was overly solicitous of his feelings and that there were times he felt she treated him like a baby. Risa left his house in shock, went home, and proceeded to "cry her eyes out." All those years wasted, she later told me, on conjecture and misunderstanding.

Actually, I told Risa, maybe she and her dad had both interpreted the situation according to their own needs and that not talking about it enabled them both to hold on to their misunderstandings. It wasn't a question of who had read the situation more accurately. Maybe they were both too scared to venture out and each made the other an excuse for staying close to home. In any event, it was time for both of them to see their lives in a new light.

Envisioning a Pleasurable Reality

One of my least favorite sentiments is when people say "Well, this has been wonderful, but now we have to get back to real life." I hate to hear "good times" contrasted with "reality." There are many different possible realities. How we explain things creates one kind of reality, while another explanation of the same event creates a totally different reality—like Risa and her father, each believing they were accommodating the other's greater wounds.

If reality is something we construct with our mental habits, why not exercise some skill in being expansive with our thoughts and constructing reality the way we want it? Why not interpret events in the best possible light? It's certainly the most logical position to take given all the data demonstrating that the right spin can propel us with enthusiasm down a productive path of possibilities and opportunities.

Positive thinking is nothing more than promoting good feelings and energetic activity by making sense of the world in the most creative and personally appealing way. Thought generates action. An exciting thought can launch you like a human cannonball so you hit the ground running. On the other hand, a depressing thought just sinks you deeper in the mud.

But a warning—not everybody appreciates you when you are a positive thinker. My husband, laughingly, has accused me of being able to find something good in a train wreck. A dear friend, and a therapist herself, once admonished me in an exasperated tone of voice, "Oh come on, not everything that happens to us is good."

I don't believe everything that happens to us is good. Train wrecks are not good things. But once something bad happens, we can be

dragged under by how bad it was, or we can look for the good
make of it. As the saying goes, "Shit happens." But shit also makes
garden grow.

Prevent train wrecks, by all means. However, once you've been
derailed, what can you learn from it? What new knowledge do you
have that you didn't have before? How can you grow as a person
from this? How can you prevent it in the future?

One of the most important tools in constructing a more positive
reality involves being able to generate a positive vision for the future.
Seeing that picture in your mind's eye connects you with your sense
of purpose and can empower you to achieve real goals. Having a
vision of where you want to go in life is like having a blueprint for
building a house. If the only blueprint you have is one you don't like,
you're going to end up with a house you don't like either. If you like
the blueprint, you'll like the house.

Besides, as I often tell worry warts, "You may not live long
enough for your worst fantasies to come true." For most of us, that's
an oddly reassuring thought.

We all need to be aware of any tendency we may have to run bad
movies in our head and to recognize that we do have a choice about
what we think. But we don't want to fight the tendency to make bad
pictures, or even to suppress those tendencies because that just sets
up resistance and tension in the body. It's not productive to fight ourselves—we just end up spending a lot of energy to stay paralyzed.

See the bad in things, if that's your tendency. Just be sure to give
equal time to making good pictures too. Especially, breathe and relax
into those good pictures.

There are lots of ways to enjoy your thinking mind. You can welcome learning. You can investigate situations thoroughly, ask honest
questions, and challenge yourself to stay open-minded longer without opting too soon for the most obvious conclusions. You can practice making a case for a more positive interpretation of the data. You
can choose to make good pictures and inspire yourself. And you can
entertain your ambivalence, dilemmas, and mysteries with a lighter
heart—until you achieve a measure of clarity, an insight, or that rare
mental orgasm known as epiphany.

the Power of Imagination

, the misfortune-telling side of ourselves runs
orst case scenarios, which are nothing more than
von't happen. Yet, if you consider that thinking is
ehearsing for action, it doesn't make much sense to
continu... se our worst fantasies. Research has shown that the pictures we make in our mind's eye actually stimulate the brain to trigger specific muscles to contract. When we think negative thoughts, our brain is subtly directing us to act in ways consistent with those thoughts.

In one classic set of experiments, electrodes were placed all over the bodies of test subjects and connected to a polygraph printout. When subjects were asked to imagine hitting a nail with a hammer, the same muscles in the arm that would be involved with hitting a hammer in true life were stimulated to fire through fantasy. When they were asked to imagine running, their leg muscles began to fire. It's not too much of a leap, then, to suppose that thinking bad thoughts is more likely to trigger avoidance or damage-control type of activity rather than any kind of fresh, forward movement.

I once watched a television special on dangerous sports that showed a group of athletes careening down a mountain highway, flat on their backs on luges with wheels. They whizzed by at more than seventy miles an hour, their heads perilously close to the concrete. When one of them was later questioned as to the most significant factor in maintaining control, he replied without hesitation, "Don't look at where you don't want to go! If you do, within seconds, you'll crash into it." There's a lesson in there for all of us. It certainly makes a good argument for habitual worst-casers to, at least, give equal time to spinning best case scenarios.

Enjoyable daydreams are the clearest reflections of our truest preferences and most heartfelt desires. The Casper Milquetoast who dreams of standing up to his boss and asking for a raise or the personal assistant who fantasizes on her coffee break about writing a screenplay and winning an Oscar are simply mentally rehearsing the actions their life-affirming nature is urging them to take.

Daydreams are a pleasurable and valuable source of creativity. Albert Einstein claimed to have discovered the theory of relativity by picturing himself in a daydream riding a ray of light that curved through space. Sculptors, poets, musicians, mathematicians, and pioneers in every field of science have reported that much of their inspiration for new projects and discoveries have come through the spontaneous visual imagery that presented itself while they were out walking, swimming, driving, taking a bath, listening to music, or lying in bed, especially just before falling asleep or upon awakening.

The imagination also is, apparently, an enormous source of healing energy. Survivors of concentration camps, war prisons, or hostage situations where people have endured long ordeals of degradation, confinement, and horrendous living conditions repeatedly credit their survival to their ability to keep their imaginations pleasurably stimulated.

Those in captivity who recall positive memories, play imaginative mind games, and set elaborate goals for themselves in the future aren't as damaged by the experience as they might otherwise be. Terry Anderson, a hostage of a terrorist group for nearly seven years, built a dairy farm in his head and worked out the economics—how to staff it, how many cows and acres it would take, the changing prices of milk—as an exercise to keep himself alert and alive.

Victor Frankl, the inspirational psychiatrist who suffered three agonizing years at Auschwitz and other camps, described the powerful role that having a rich inner life played in his survival. He didn't know what had become of his wife and family, but he visited with them in his mind every chance he had. And even though they were apart, his relationship with his wife continued to develop, as he spent many hours mentally engaged in whole conversations with her or in lovemaking. He certainly knew about many disastrous events he could have replayed in his head or worried about happening to him and his beloved wife. But to survive, he gave himself hope, love, and, at least in his mind, something and someone to live for.

Night Dreams

Dreams are usually understood to represent significant symbolic messages from as yet undiscovered inner regions of the mind. Freud called dreams "the royal road to the unconscious," and most forms of psychotherapy accept the value of studying dreams for clues to feelings, desires, and motivations a client may not have as yet totally owned or acknowledged. But there's a vast resource in dreams that few forms of therapy have yet to tap.

While most people feel somewhat in control of the images that appear to them during their daytime reveries, few people feel that they have any control over the images that appear to them in their dreams at night. Yet a fascinating series of experiments run at the Stanford University Sleep Research Center suggests that some people are capable of "lucid dreaming"—becoming conscious in their dreams while remaining asleep and of directing their dream self in deliberate and desired ways.

Psychologist Stephen LaBerge, working with subjects who can fulfill a previously agreed upon task during a dream, such as counting, singing, or viewing their hands—while remaining asleep—has made some valuable discoveries. Dreams in general, and lucid dreams in particular, have a perceptual vividness and a level of brain wave activity that corresponds more to waking perception than to imagery associated with either imagination or memory. In a sense then, night dreams are more real to us than daydreams. In daydreams we know we're fantasizing, but unless we have a moment of lucidity, we usually don't know we're dreaming when we're asleep.

These findings suggest new possibilities beyond the traditional model that sees dreams merely as opportunities to decode dark urges and primitive forces. You may be able to encourage yourself to become conscious in a dream without waking, confronting issues and making positive choices with issues that are difficult for you in your waking life. Empowering yourself in your dreams can carry over to your effort to strengthen desirable attributes when you are awake.

Here's an example of how one woman in therapy worked on a recurrent dream in a way that gave her self-confidence and positive motivation in her waking life. Leslie, at age twenty-eight, was a determined young woman, married for two years to a man she loved and working at a good job with plenty of promise. But she was troubled about her inability to control her eating at night. Because her looks were important to her, she got up at five every morning to work out at the gym. She went from there to the office and worked a full day, came home late, then, essentially, ate until she went to bed. Her over-control in the morning reinforced her being out of control at night and vice versa—blowing it at night, then punishing herself by being on her best behavior all day long.

Our work in therapy focused on Leslie's extremism, from hypercharged to too stuffed to move. She knew some of her habits came from her struggle as a child, the eldest of three daughters of an alcoholic mother and a stern father. For as long as she could remember, she felt that if she couldn't keep everything in control she'd feel helpless.

Over the months, Leslie got to know the tough cop in her mind who barked orders at her during the day, but who usually took the night off. That's when the overeater would appear, pig out, and collapse. Much of our work together, and her homework during the week, involved learning how to find a more moderate path of discipline, one that she could more pleasurably relax into.

But it was the dream work that had the most dramatic effects. Leslie came in one day and told me that only a few nights earlier, she had had her recurring dream. She described it like this: "I'm walking down a dark street at night, and I notice an evil looking stranger following me. I'm afraid, but I sense that if I let on that I know he's there, he'll attack. So I walk briskly, not looking back, and I hope my pretense will bring me to a safe harbor. At some point, however, my stalker, with a menacing grin, starts to slowly close in on me. I then face the evil presence, and I try to scream for help. But nothing comes out. My mouth is frozen in terror, and all I can muster are some thin whimpers and muffled groans. The stalker moves in, openly mocking me and laughing at my futility. I feel helpless, and I wake up in a panic."

In my office, I asked her to create a dialogue, out loud, between Leslie-of-the-dream and the evil presence, taking the roles of each. Evil presence turned out to be not just the potential violence in the world at large but also her own resentment at her difficult childhood and a deep cynicism that not everything works out in the end. Then, I asked her to redream it all again, only this time to see if she could let herself scream. This she did with such a force that my next-door neighbors started banging on my office door to make sure we were okay. At that point, she developed a falling-over case of the giggles, which turned out to be very infectious for me. The session ended with both of us howling in laughter.

Less than a week later, Leslie had the dream again, but this time, she told me, she whimpered for a few seconds and then let out a scream that blasted her husband out of bed and onto his feet. She awoke with her heart racing but ecstatic. Her husband told her he was sure her scream had taken a few years off his life, but he thought it was probably a psychological milestone for her and for that he was happy.

Over time, her dream continued to evolve. Once, she dreamed she turned and confronted the evil presence, asking him what he wanted from her. He stammered and didn't seem to know what to say. In her last dream of the sort, he followed her home to where she was having a party, and she invited him to meet everybody. They found out he wasn't such a bad guy, after all—just someone from a bad neighborhood (like herself), who acted mean but really wasn't. It's been a few years now, and Leslie is feeling more in charge of her life and at the same time more relaxed, especially when it comes to food.

We don't have to accept the imagery in our dreams if we find ourselves waking up with images we don't like. If dreams are a reflection of our deepest feelings, we may also be able to impact our deepest feelings by sending more positive imagery to our less defended minds in our dream states. Try it for yourself. If you are awakened by a bad dream, let yourself go back to sleep and redo the ending of the dream more to your liking. Even if you can't sleep, lie in bed and imagine a new way to take charge and reverse the bad outcome. Turn it around into something you can feel good about. It's like a post-hypnotic suggestion delivered to an open and relaxed mind, only in this case, you're also the hypnotist, developing your own ability to positively re-program yourself.

Personal Experiments

. . . .

1. Practice breath control before each of these experiments. Take a few cleansing breaths to break your mental set and to stimulate a more relaxed and more alert mind. Check your body for tightness and emotion, and breathe into and, for a few moments, stretch out any areas that feel tense. Take some deep sighs through an open mouth whenever you feel some emotions coming up, and let yourself really feel them.

2. Change a few old stories. What would you say are the three most difficult times in your life? Now, taking each period separately, ask yourself, "what value have I actually derived from that experience?" "How has it veered me into a worthwhile direction?" "How has it deepened me as a person?" See if you can reinterpret these events as positive influences, or potentially so.

Be particularly aware if it is difficult for you to acknowledge that you got something good from something bad, as though that acknowledgment would either be sacrilegious or too forgiving of those who have hurt you.

3. Practice positive thinking by turning a problem into an opportunity. This is a good exercise to do with a friend, though it can also be done in writing. Think about something that is happening in your life right now that you consider to be a problem. First, detail all the salient issues and tell your friend or write down your problem.

If you are with a friend, ask her to merely listen to you and to resist the tendency to want to give you advice. When you finish talking or writing, take a few deep breaths and retell or rewrite the situation, only this time describe each of the issues, again in detail, not as a problem but in terms of what opportunities or challenges it provides you. Give yourself permission to have fun with it and to make up silly sounding opportunities or challenges. You may find, on second thought, that they're not so silly after all.

If you find yourself resisting and drawing a blank, ask yourself, "How does it serve me to stick with my negative way of viewing this?" and "What do I feel I would have to give up to adopt a more productive view?"

4. Practice changing your inner dialogues. Take a few deep breaths and choose a personal issue you feel some conflict about. You can do this aloud to nobody in particular but yourself. You can have a friend there as a witness, or you can write it as a dialogue between two characters inside you, like the protagonist and antagonist of a play.

Close your eyes and take one character's side in the issue and completely immerse yourself in that point of view. Present your case by talking out loud to the other side. Let half of you be performer and the other be the audience. Don't censor and listen to what you say. Then switch sides and become fully committed to the opposite point of view.

One side could be your inner critic and the other side your victim; or one side could be your serious side and the other the joker. In each case, see which side gives you the most energy or which feels more familiar.

When you run out of new things to say, see if you can push into new territory and expand the point of view of each. Can the critic be less rigid and punishing while still maintaining standards of excellence? Can the victim stay sensitive and deep and make choices that overcome and integrate bad times as valuable life experiences?

Just as a convenient fiction, imagine that you have a guiding spirit that lives inside you. What would this "inner ally" say to you? How would you like that spirit to guide and support you?

5. Explore your daydreams and your imagination. Find a place to be alone without the television or radio on, with no other distractions. Lie back and relax, take some deep breaths, and look around you. As you look around, invite an image to present itself to you in your mind's eye; imagine something wonderful. Perhaps you've won something you've wanted for a long time, such as someone's affections or generosity, an acknowledgment of some kind, or vindication where you feel you have been judged harshly. You may keep your eyes open or closed, just as long as you stay awake and alert.

See if you can make the image in your mind even more vivid and detailed—fill in more colors and add details to the scene. Every so often take some deep sighing breaths, inhale and exhale through an open mouth, and let yourself relax. Let your mind wander where it wants to go, and let yourself be entertained by the movie in your mind.

6. Experiment with lucid dreaming. If you have a recurring dream, one where the settings may change but the predicament you find yourself in remains very much the same, get together with a friend or group of friends to do a dream circle. Any one or all of you may wish to present a dream.

If you are alone with one friend, take a few deep cleansing breaths and, with your eyes closed, relate your latest dream as though you are watching a movie only you can see. Make it more immediate and vivid by describing it in the present tense as though you are not just redreaming it but reliving it. Imagine that your dream represents a piece of your current life and has an insight for you—if only you break the code and discover how.

Once you have told the dream all the way through, take a few deep breaths, check for tension or emotion, and relax. Now create a dialogue between two of the most involving characters in the dream. You can assume these dream-selves represent not just you and someone else, but also two opposing parts of yourself. What would you like to say that you're not saying? How would you like to see this dream re-creation end differently from the way the night dream ends?

If there were a kind of existential message to you from your dream, like the moral of a parable or like the caption of a photograph in a newspaper, what do you imagine your deeper nature is trying to tell you? See if you can say it simply in one sentence. For example, a person who was constantly running for planes and trains in her dreams because she would get lost on the way to airports and stations described the moral of her dreams to be: "Get the directions before you start the trip, and you're more likely to reach your destination." The message she got from that was that she was flying too much by the seat of her pants, and she needed a better plan to get where she wanted to go in her life.

Like a post-hypnotic suggestion made to a person in a state of complete relaxation, take a few deep sighs and ask your dream-self to perform in a particular way the next time you have this kind of dream. Request of the dream-maker inside you a repeat performance of this type of dream very soon.

You may also experiment with lucid dreaming by giving yourself a pre-sleep suggestion to include a particular image in whatever you dream this night. The image may be of you counting, running, playing with a ball, or visiting with a particular friend. Sit up in bed, and with your eyes closed picture a pleasant image that you would like to appear to you at some time during your sleep. Take a few deep cleansing breaths and relax while you hold the image for a few moments. Keep doing this exercise until it works for you.

If you find yourself waking up in the morning and coming out of a dream where you don't like the ending, go back to sleep for a few minutes to change the ending. Redream it the way you would like it to end. When you feel satisfied about how you turned things around in your dream, let yourself reawaken.

Chapter 9

Emotional Pleasures: Variations on a Theme of Love

. . . .

How to feel good feelings

. . . .

Self-acceptance in its transformative sense . . .
is difficult, exacting, subtle; we cannot do this work alone.
We need help. Can two people living together as man and
woman, united by the bonds of affection, attraction, physical or
emotional type, common interests, or sexual passion . . . help each
other to know themselves as two-natured beings who contain the
seeds of mysterious possible unity? I think such help is possible
between two people. This help is love.

—Jacob Needleman

Joyce, an energetic woman in her early thirties with shoulder-length curly blond hair and hazel eyes, was trying to decide whether she should give up Jeff, a man she had been dating for a year who was warm and loving and someone she had been considering marrying. She had recently met Brad, a moody, self-centered man, but someone to whom she felt very drawn. In my office, she weighed their respective attributes. Jeff enjoyed hiking like she did, and together they played a mean game of doubles in tennis. Brad kept to himself, but he was a talented songwriter, and she felt she might be able to help promote his work.

Something critical was missing for me from her calculations, and the more Joyce talked, the more I became aware of its absence. When I finally asked her the question that was uppermost in my mind—namely, do you love either one of them?—-she stared at me dumb struck, as though I had suddenly lapsed into Swahili. When she responded, it was in a tone mixed with irony and despair, "I don't think I know what love is. I think I know a lot more about sex than I do about love."

Joyce is not alone in her confusion about love. How much do we really know about something that's supposed to "make the world go 'round?" Everyone wants love. We want to fall in love, to be in love, to be loved, and to keep love alive in a relationship. The concept of love is central to our moral code: to love our neighbor as ourselves. Yet how many of us fully comprehend and feel fulfilled in what everyone would agree is the supreme pleasure of the heart?

A few nights after that session with Joyce, I was scheduled to do a small group on relationships. There were about twenty-five people sitting around in a circle in the room, mostly in their thirties and forties, and I decided to do an informal survey of what people think about love, just off the top of their heads.

I started the evening asking them, "What is love? Do you have love now? Would you like more of it?" One intense-looking young man with a beard sitting right across from me said, "I've never had the love I need, and I don't think I ever will." A perky woman to my left, a bit older, said, "I just finished a special project at work that I loved doing, and it was a complete success. I'm exuberant and I'd like this feeling to last because it makes me believe I can do anything. Isn't this a kind of love?" Another woman to my right offered, "I'm very close to several women friends. I get a lot of love and support from them, and we're really there for each other. I'd like to have that with a man." A young man a few seats down volunteered that he feels fortunate to have so much love in his life. He loves his wife—he turns and smiles at the woman next to him and takes her hand—and their little girl; he also loves his parents though he would like them to be more accepting of him. "But," he adds, "I'd like my wife and me to be in love the way we were before we were married, when we would get excited just thinking about each other." The woman next to him nods her head, then adds, "I like the passion, but it's the closeness that makes me feel love. Honest sharing is what love is to me."

Each of these people was focusing on a different aspect of love. The sullen young man who spoke first was describing love as a need and was alluding to the fact that he felt love-deprived. The successful business woman was describing the emotion of love: her heart was full of excitement, satisfaction, and pride in her work, a form of self-love. The woman who followed spoke about the bond of love, the strong feeling of connection between people who care deeply about one another, like between parents and children, between siblings and between friends. The man who spoke next referred to the bond in his connection with his wife, child, and parents, but he was particularly concerned with how to maintain passion in a long-term love relationship. The woman who spoke last was referring to the quality of intimacy and a particular kind of interaction.

I'll add one other kind of love that bears exploring—the kind alluded to especially by the yearnings for passion and intimacy of the married couple. It's the urge to find true love—the kind that's shared between people who are emotionally and physically intimate—and perhaps most importantly, to be able to hold on to it.

The truth is, we crave love in all these areas, and we're at our best in life when we have it all. Without a doubt, to be fulfilled in love is to be blessed. Yet, when love is hard to find or doesn't last, the temptation is always to blame the situation, our lover, or just women or men in general. But we need to bear in mind that whenever there is a lack of fulfillment in any aspect of love, it may actually have more to do with our own pleasure-anxiety than with bad luck or a partner's limitations.

Chronic fear or anger can armor the chest and keep it tight. Under these conditions, when loving feelings make the heart swell, there can be a discomfort with the expansive sensations, triggering anxiety. As the heart starts to close down in response to fear, the mind gives the denial of love a voice—finding fault with everything. To whatever degree any of us may have learned to deny ourselves our full bounty of love, with awareness and courage, it's possible to open the heart more and to hone the capacity to know and share the pleasures of love. We do that by becoming more familiar with all the different qualities of love, especially with regard to how these qualities manifest in ourselves.

Love As a Need

Love is a nutrient as basic as mother's milk. We've talked about the studies showing how critical touching and physical affection are to an infant and young child. Other research, seeking to address the selfishness and narcissism that seems rampant in our culture, has focused on what appears to be a critical period in child development. These studies have shown that, up until the age of about two and a half, a young child needs to feel very special, as if he or she were the most important person in the world. If these "narcissistic" needs are met and the child feels loved and accepted in his uniqueness, he will have a truer sense of himself as a person and feel greater empathy with others. But if these early needs are not met and the child has to hide his true self to be loved, he is likely to turn out confused about his true feelings, self-centered because he is always needy for approval, and less able to understand and empathize with the feelings of others.

Those of us who haven't been held, touched, cradled, cooed over, and approved of for the first few years of our lives are not going to feel as secure as those who have. If the need for physical affection and emotional approval are not fulfilled, the emptiness may never go away. Some people try to fill their longings for love by becoming rich and powerful, or through food, drugs, or constantly nurturing others. There is no amount of fame or fortune, however, no compensatory activity, that can ever fill the hole left by the absence of authentic love.

Fortunately, there is hope for all of us. Studies show that the missing experiences of childhood can be made up at any age. Our best chance for love and happiness, for those of us who were love-deprived as children, is to find someone who is physically affectionate and loving. Ideally, this person is not only giving but also someone who can teach us how to graciously accept love and return it, something the love-deprived don't ordinarily learn from their parents.

The sullen young man with the beard, in the small group that I mentioned earlier, actually had the good fortune to find such a woman. Peter had been raised by parents who simply weren't there for him. He can't remember either one of them ever hugging him or any of his siblings—two older brothers and a younger sister—or expressing any real concern that wasn't said in an angry tone of voice. When Peter started to date Carol, however he was amazed at how warm and loving she could be.

On several occasions, Peter was ready to back out of the relationship because of miscommunications or what he read as Carol being demanding. But he also acknowledged that he might be backpedaling because this was the closest he had ever been with anyone, and he wasn't entirely comfortable with the feeling. So while he was very clear that Carol had her limitations—a bad temper and a seemingly insatiable need to discuss their relationship—Peter also had a keen awareness that this was the first time he had ever been with anyone who could warm his heart with just a smile.

When I met Carol, I immediately liked her. She was friendly, made good eye contact, and seemed genuinely interested in Peter's point of view, even when they disagreed. She acknowledged that she did have a bigger appetite for verbally hashing things out than he did, but she respected their differences and was willing to ease up on what he called the "relationship chronicles."

While Peter didn't need verbal reassurance as much as Carol did, what he did need, and was particularly appreciative of, was all the time they spent just lying in each other's arms, chatting or being silent together. He had never received that kind of physical affection from anyone before, and he sopped it up. It was as though he had been running on a low battery all his life, and Carol's love charged him with energy. Peter told Carol he was very grateful that, because of her, he could feel his love for her in his heart—really feel it. And because she wasn't critical of him for his ineptitude at love, but kind and caring, he felt that she had also helped him learn how to love.

Peter's awareness of love as a physical feeling was a particularly important insight for him and is not something that comes easily for most people. Often we have a mixture of feelings when we love someone which include anxieties, disappointments, or resentments, and the feelings of love are buried underneath. Yet being able to tune in to the physical sensation of love—the warm energy that radiates from the chest and makes us feel expansive—is critical for anyone who wants to be motivated to act out of love or to share that emotion with someone else.

Love As an Emotion

When I ask people in therapy what they're feeling, usually they have no trouble describing their emotional pain. They may say they're feeling angry, resentful, anxious, ashamed, guilty, or depressed. If they're feeling good, however, they may say only that they're fine or even that they're not feeling anything at all as though only painful feelings count.

It has become clear to me that few people really understand what we mean by positive emotion. I can hardly bear it when I read a respected author who writes that love is not an emotion but an exercise of will, a selfless act of nurturing another's growth that has nothing to do with feeling. Promoting a singular notion of love as duty or self-sacrifice only confirms the commitment-phobic person's worst expectations.

I don't think this is a misunderstanding only about the emotion of love. I think there's a lack of familiarity with what we mean by emotion in general. Many people were raised in homes where emotions were hidden and disallowed. Others found their true feelings invalidated, where parents insisted that their children shouldn't feel what they felt or want what they wanted. Some of us were raised in families where a beating was called an act of love. Anyone growing up that way is likely to be confused about their feelings, to lose their inner compass, and to suffer from a kind of "emotional dyslexia"—an inability to clearly identify or articulate what they feel.

The ability to be aware of one's genuine feelings and to be guided by them, however, has been found to be a critical factor enabling people to thrive in life. Based on a host of psychological studies, Dr. Daniel Goleman has made a good case for "emotional intelligence"—the valuable ability to be informed by one's feelings in thinking clearly and acting wisely.

We may want to believe that we can figure things out solely through logic by taking a cold, hard look at the facts; but to Goleman, that kind of thinking is hyper-rational. Our emotional experiences sharpen memory, hone intuition, and generate empathy for others—all valuable assets that foster good choices. He shows that people with a high IQ but little ability to read their own or others' emotions in a situation may actually do less well in business and relationships than people with a lower IQ but a greater awareness of their own and others' feelings.

Research also shows that one of the most critical skills in emotional intelligence is the ability to tune into the visceral signals of feelings as they are happening. People with the ability to monitor the sensations in their body from moment to moment can learn how to manage their moods, marshal their emotions in the service of their goals, and have satisfying, constructive interactions with other people. In doing so, they're likely to be rewarded with pleasurable feelings in the chest, of a relaxed, warm, and open heart.

The Sensation of Emotion: True Feelings, Loving and Otherwise

Any genuine emotion can be felt as a sensation somewhere in your body. If you say you're feeling something, but you can't identify where in your body you're feeling it, either you're out of touch with your body, or it's not a feeling at all but a thought. We do that kind of thing all the time—for example, say we're afraid of something when we're not really afraid of it anymore. We're just repeating a familiar story, an old way of thinking about ourselves, that's no longer true.

On the other hand, when your emotion is genuine, you can feel it in your body, particularly in the emotional center between the face and the pelvis. All emotions activate you to do something or express yourself. If, because of your family training, you don't allow yourself to fully feel what you're feeling, you'll resist that spurt of energy by deadening that area of your torso.

We all learn to hold our feelings in by gripping the activated muscles and by breathing shallowly so as not to release the hold. If the withheld feeling is chronic, something we've been holding back for a long time, the sensation adapts to the constant tension and that area goes numb. But when we start to breathe deeply into the torso, enhancing its action and relaxing a bit, any withheld emotional energy will soon be felt as muscle tension in very specific areas, especially when there's a churning sensation underneath. In this way, we can feel where we're holding ourselves in, and, if we continue to breathe deeply and stretch the tight area with our inhales, the tension can begin to release.

From many years of breathing with people and asking them what they were feeling and where in their body they were feeling it, I've observed a remarkable consistency with where emotions lodge in our bodies. These observations are compatible with observations Wilhelm Reich made more than seventy years ago.

Tension in the jaw relates either to a determination to control emotions or—when the lips tighten to bare the teeth and the shoulders and back are up—to anger. A lump in the throat is often a sign of sadness. When the throat feels dry or gripped, it's often the feeling of fear. Sadness, hurt, and disappointment are often felt as a heaviness laying on the chest, while anxiety is often experienced as a tight band around the chest. Guilt and obligation often appear as a knot in the gut or diaphragm. Shame may be felt as a clutching in the genitals and/or anus.

Since all of these emotions consist of an activation of energy that is resisted and held in place by a contraction, they are not pleasant. They involve muscular isometrics and mental conflict. Resistance affects our thinking. We become self-critical and pessimistic, which only makes us feel worse. Painful though the feelings may be, when we allow ourselves to feel them and permit ourselves expression, the energy trapped as tension is released; our bodies feel expansive, as though we've been let free.

Love, however, is the most expansive, most pleasurable feeling we can have. Love is always felt as a warmth, a lightness, and openness in the chest. Sometimes the loving heart beats faster; activated by both adrenaline and endorphins, we feel absolutely fantastic, excited, and open. At other times the heart feels completely relaxed, warm, and cozy. The emphasis is on the parasympathetic side of the nervous system; it's not as passionate a kind of love, but it's still very satisfying. When there's love in the heart, we feel like we're beaming. Love energy always signals safety, well-being, and vitality.

All positive emotions are variations of love. Anytime we feel any loving feelings—such as appreciation, gratitude, pride, hope, faith, devotion, and even that unfairly maligned feeling, infatuation—it's enormously gratifying. Anytime we act out of love—being generous, courageous, or compassionate—genuinely feeling that emotion propelling us, it's the most powerful incentive there is. We feel drawn to what we like or love, and we feel good about ourselves. The heart radiates energy. We feel uplifted. At the highest end of the range of positive emotions—third level emotional pleasures—we have our occasional bursts of enchantment, rapture, jubilation, exultation, and bliss.

Love Heals

It's a scientific fact: Feeling the emotion of love is healthy. PNI research is abundant with data showing how feeling loved, thinking about a loved one, feeling appreciative, acting charitable, and having friends raises immune factors in the blood and contributes to a longer and healthier life.

In one study, investigating the effects of the emotional states of compassion and anger on the immune system, researchers at the Institute for HeartMath in Boulder Creek, California, tested their subjects' saliva for immunoglobulin, an increase of which is associated with lower incidence of disease. They found that when subjects intentionally focused on feelings of compassion toward someone for five minutes, it profoundly enhanced immune factors in their saliva. Subjects who focused on feelings of anger for five minutes not only had significantly inhibited immunity, but in some cases the decrease lasted for as many as five hours after the five-minute emotional experience.

This same group of researchers has also demonstrated that sincere feelings of love and appreciation cause heart rhythms to have a smooth, regular pattern. Having rhythmic heart beats not only contributes to the health of the heart, but also keeps the nervous system in balance. Loving and caring, maintaining hope, and having faith and compassion are not just ways of feeling and acting, they are like food for the heart. A homeopathic doctor I know has a sign on his wall that reads, "A merry heart doeth like a medicine."

Love As a Bond

When someone has accompanied you through different milestones in your life, sharing love while building history together, a bond is forged that feels etched in your physiology. A bond is a deep emotional connection with a person whom you consider to be family, regardless of whether you are connected by blood or friendship. When called upon, such people are there for you and you're there for them.

A bond is the only true commitment. Too much emphasis these days is placed on whether or not someone is willing to make a commitment. You can make a pledge or a promise to be there for someone. You can take vows in a chapel. But as Samuel Goldwyn once said, "An oral contract isn't worth the paper it's written on." It's not the spoken commitment that counts, and, nowadays, the piece of paper we call a marriage license isn't worth much either. The only thing that keeps people together is building an enduring bond.

Why would anyone want to resist sharing a bond with another human being? Probably, one of the biggest fears setting up resistance is that sharing a bond with someone opens you up to pain. If you never love anyone deeply, you will definitely never have to feel the profound tragedy of losing him or her. There's no denying it—we do lose people we love all the time. They may leave us or they may die. Even if you're lucky enough to end up in a long and loving marriage, one of you is likely to survive the other. But death is a fact of life, whether you come to the end having enjoyed a deep and loving connection with someone or not.

Another reason people sometimes hold back from feeling love is that expansive feelings in the chest can feel frightening to people with pleasure-anxiety. If they have a habit of resisting excitement, loving feelings can cause them to tighten up and find something to criticize in the potential loved one. It would certainly be a sad state of affairs if someone rejected love because they couldn't tolerate feeling that good, but it happens all the time.

One other kind of fear associated with sharing a loving bond that needs to be addressed is if you believe you have to prove your love by renouncing your own personal needs. Proving is not loving. Proving is about performance; it's what you do on the outside. Loving is about experience; it's about feeling something inside your heart. When people feel obligated to those they love, the knot in their gut can blot out the loving feelings, thinning the bond rather than strengthening it.

On the other hand, when you feel love in your heart and are motivated to give from those genuine feelings, giving is a tremendous pleasure. Lovers enjoy giving each other gifts and special treats, dressing to please the other, and being kind and supportive—not because it's required but because it feels good to express caring. A woman checks with her partner before accepting an invitation for both of them, not because she has to, but because it's respectful to do so. A man who desires another woman, who chooses not to act on it, does so not because his partner would raise the roof if she found out, but because he feels good being true to her.

Perhaps, in fact, it's not that we give to another because we love him, but rather, we love him because we give to him. Antoine de Saint Exupéry, the French writer and aviator, expresses this sentiment in the fable, *The Little Prince*. He describes the moment of discovery when the little prince realizes what makes his one rose on his little asteroid so special, when she is, in fact, no different from the fields and fields of identical roses he finds on earth. The little prince, thanks to the guidance of the fox, suddenly understands that what makes his rose unique is that he cared for her—he watered and sheltered her and killed caterpillars for her. "Because it is she that I have listened to, when she grumbled, or boasted, or even sometimes when she said nothing." Now that the little prince understands, the fox tells him a very simple secret. "It is only with the heart that one can see rightly; what is essential is invisible to the eye . . . It is the time you have wasted for your rose that makes your rose so important."

Passion: Falling in Love

Falling in love is one of life's most intense pleasures. You feel utterly charmed by someone whom you experience as a singularly spectacular human being. You want to talk about that person to all your friends, and when you do you can't stop smiling. You're excited just by anticipating your next meeting.

I can actually remember the very moment that I fell in love with the man who was to become my husband. For me, our first few weeks of dating were relatively lukewarm. He seemed already somewhat smitten, and I wasn't entirely comfortable with that (my lingering pleasure-anxiety, no doubt). But one particular Saturday we had a great day together, riding around on our bicycles all day and singing corny old songs to each other like "Daisy, Daisy, give me your answer do" and "Red River Valley." Later that evening we went out for dinner. As I leaned up against the wall at the crowded restaurant where we were waiting for a table, he bent toward me with a big smile and warm eyes and kissed my nose. There was something about that simple gesture—maybe it had to do with how lovingly he looked at me— but it was the culmination of all the warm tenderness I had felt from this man since the day I met him. I simply melted. My knees buckled, a soft moan escaped from my throat, and I grabbed a button on my jacket—for support I guess—and yanked it clear off. Shocked, I opened my hand and we both gaped at the telltale button lying in the center of my palm. Then he threw back his head and roared with laughter. He clearly understood what had just happened.

When you first fall in love with someone, your heart leaps when you think about him or her. You feel all lit up.

The fact is, biochemically, you really do light up. Michael Leibowitz, a psychiatrist who has done extensive research on the physiology of love, has shown that the initial stages of love can induce the strongest arousal of the limbic system—the part of the brain known as the pleasure center. This kind of love, it turns out, is an even more powerful stimulant than amphetamine drugs or manic emotional states.

Research has shown that infatuation, characterized primarily by feelings of strong attraction, triggers a powerful neurotransmitter known as phenylethylamine or PEA. PEA revs up the brain and causes feelings of exhilaration, elation, and euphoria. PEA is why lovers can lie together for hours, their arms entwined, without losing interest. They can dance until three and make love until the sun comes up, because they are literally high on love.

However, the research evidence is overwhelming that this level of excitement, considered to be the infatuation stage, usually lasts only somewhere between three days to a maximum of two and a half years. If the lovers make it past the attraction stage and form an attachment, the chemistry changes not just between them, but inside each one of them. The brain chemicals that predominate now are the endorphins, calming the mind, producing a sense of safety and a decrease in anxiety. Infatuation, as it turns out, is like being on natural speed, while achieving a loving bond is more like being on tranquilizers. The dilemma is that while feeling bonded is reassuring and comforting, the infatuation stage of a love relationship is a lot more exciting.

Passion in the early stages of a love affair usually relates to feeling like you have found the king or queen of your dreams, the one human being who perfectly completes you. At some point, however, the myth of perfection is blown—naturally. It turns out that what's perfect for you isn't necessarily perfect for your lover. So the bliss of illusion inevitably gives way to the despair of disillusion. If you're looking for Shangri-La, and you find your feet firmly planted back at your own front door, you may just decide to move on in search of your next few months or so of magic. If you do stick around, but you and your partner cause each other grief, it may be that the two of you are actually unconsciously colluding on a negative way to maintain passion in your relationship.

Negative Passion: Generating Destructive Intensity in a Relationship by "Playing Uproar"

A critical element in sustaining passionate love is often that, while there are strong feelings drawing the lovers together, there are also equally strong forces keeping them apart. Passion thrives on just the right mix of longing and yearning, of forced separations and obstacles to overcome. When lovers are unavailable to one another, separated either by physical distance or by circumstance, their unfulfilled craving becomes a potent force raising the intensity of their feelings. All the great lovers of myth were kept tragically separated. Romeo and Juliet, Lancelot and Guinevere, and Tristan and Isolde didn't exactly set up housekeeping. There's something about opposing forces pulling you apart that naturally, organically, and magically intensifies the magnetism between you.

Modern star-crossed lovers can have heated phone calls where they whisper their undying love for one another in a way that just wouldn't carry the same impact on the living room couch—particularly if they own it together. And if they're having a clandestine love affair and can meet only in secret, the fear of getting caught and the element of risk and danger adds adrenaline that fans the flames of their desire.

But some people hooked on romantic passion do commit to one another, and while they may not have ready-made circumstances keeping them apart, still they may generate intensity in their relationship, unconsciously, through creating melodrama. I've watched many couples stir up passion in their relationships by "playing uproar."

Two people play uproar by creating an emotional scene and displaying intensely negative feelings toward one another. They may rage and yell at each other, bang doors, and say disgusting things they regret afterward. They may threaten to leave, then throw themselves on the furniture sobbing or begging for forgiveness. For added intensity, they may do it all in front of other people. The conflict first separates them, then ratchets up their passion, and ultimately acts as an aphrodisiac as they fall into each other's arms, aching to make love.

I've seen couples keep a relationship going for years that just oozed with the pathos of testing each other, of provocative, cutting remarks that would escalate into biting recriminations until someone bled emotionally. Then, at some point, the scene would turn into tearful reaffirmations of their undying devotion to one another. Unfortunately, these kinds of scenarios take more energy than they give back and ultimately cannibalize what's good about the relationship in order to feed a "jones" for histrionics. Making trouble may keep the passion going for a while, but if time doesn't mellow the soap opera, a couple can get washed up playing the same sudsy scenes.

The big question is this: Can you maintain passionate love in an ongoing relationship without all this *sturm und drang?* The honest answer is, it's not easy.

If a relationship makes it past the illusion stage, recovers from the disillusionment stage, and you do get along well, it can easily settle into that mature kind of love that is comfortable but nothing that raises the pulse or quickens the heartbeat. The fact remains, however, that if the thrill is gone, it will be missed. Everyone knows there are ways to keep some romance going in a long-term relationship— romantic dates, maybe a night in a hotel away from the kids, or some sexy underwear. But this is only a superficial approach to a very complex issue.

There is a way, however, to generate real passion in a long-term relationship that runs a lot deeper. But to do so we have to redefine what we mean by intimacy.

What Is Intimacy, Really?

Our traditional ways of understanding intimacy have a big effect on why men and women in a relationship have so much difficulty communicating with one another. If we regard intimacy as sharing weaknesses and vulnerabilities, we can see that women will be more positively disposed to such an exchange than would men. Women have been taught to think of their vulnerabilities and weaknesses as attractive; it's feminine to be sensitive, to shed tears, to lose at chess. With this kind of fragility built into the job description, intimacy is "ego-syntonic" for women—in harmony with how they've learned to be female.

But showing weakness is "ego-dystonic" for men. It's antithetical to our cultural standards of manhood and what it means to be a male. Men have been encouraged from the time they were babes in diapers to be strong, to keep a stiff upper lip, to not show weakness, and to win, win, win! That means that women will be more attracted to the standard notion of what's called intimate communication because it fits women's gender role programming far better than it does traditional male programming. In fact, in many ways they're polar opposites.

Whether or not you think men and women should be conditioned this way is a social issue. When it comes to your being able to have a successful and happy love relationship, however, it's completely immaterial. The conditioning is already wired into our circuitry. We all have to deal with the way things are. Does this mean that most men with traditional upbringing are destined to remain more limited than women in being intimate? Yes—if we hold on to old models of intimate sharing. But there's another way to understand intimacy that may actually level the playing field and enable men to be as capable as women.

Intimacy As Self-Disclosure

In our traditional understanding of it, intimacy is self-disclosure. You're supposed to be honest about your weaknesses and to tell the truth about yourself. But in fact, you can be completely honest with another person, without necessarily telling him or her the truth. You may think you're exposing the true you, but you may simply be repeating an old story you've been telling yourself for years. You're being honest, but when what you share is a reflection of something you believe and not something you feel, it's not a true reflection of the real you.

Self-disclosure also smacks of confession and then having to explain yourself. You may be able to generate a plausible theory for why you felt or did something. But it's not a deep inner truth in the same way as when you feel that truth in your body—as a physical sensation.

Intimacy as Self-Discovery in Another's Presence

A more positive and productive way of understanding intimacy is as a process of self-revelation, that is, discovering yourself in the presence of the other.

Self-revelation involves just being with another person and discovering your feelings in the moment. It's sweet surrender on an emotional level, when you feel so at ease and accepted by the other that merely being in his or her presence puts you in touch with deeper layers of yourself.

This kind of intimacy is a process in which you are both present-centered. You explore issues together, not by explaining yourself but by examining the sensations in your body in the moment they occur, and describing them to your partner along with any thoughts, images, and memories that spontaneously come to mind. There's a match, a congruency, between what's going on inside of you, experientially, and what you show on your face and body or verbally express.

This kind of intimacy requires the courage to connect with your truths, the skill to read your insides, and the ability to describe and communicate your present experience to your partner. Because you want the other to be able to hear you, it helps to describe your feelings clearly and without blame. Self-revelation is what provides insight in therapy, though in therapy, by necessity, it's usually a one-sided unfolding. In a loving relationship, both partners can become better acquainted with their own true selves, along with the true self of the other. The key to this kind of intimacy is that you're describing your experience without trying to explain or justify it.

Obviously, if your partner likes to play uproar and reacts in anger or hysteria to hearing your truth, that kind of reaction will inhibit true intimacy in the relationship and not encourage authenticity and self-revelation. There's no getting around it—uproar limits every aspect of a relationship. On the other hand, if you're both willing to rock the boat in a constructive fashion and to breathe into your feelings and to discover your truths in the presence of one another, this way of communicating can bring you a lot closer and deeper with one another.

Admittedly, it's not easy, especially when you're out of practice. It can take real focus and a lot of deep breaths to treat your clashes as opportunities for mutual self-discovery rather than to find fault and place blame. But with practice, this kind of intimacy is vastly more stimulating, very bonding, and neither gender has the edge in terms of skill. It's as challenging for women as it is for men.

In the Personal Experiments section of this chapter, you'll have an opportunity to experiment with this present-centered process of intimacy.

Positive Passion: Intimate Individualists

We've all heard the saying that when people marry, two become one. The question is, if they do, which one of them do they become? To maintain the illusion of complete harmony, they would both have to suppress their distinct qualities. Without a respect for their differences, there is often a loss of the dynamic that brought them together in the first place.

Among the couples I know who are happiest, where there is both a bond and an apparent spark of passion, there is a minimum of uproar. What keeps their passion alive is their individuality.

They may share a life together, but they are each very much their own person, with their own work or interests that keep them involved. They may have friends in common, but they also have friends of their own. They may keep individual bank accounts and occasionally take separate vacations. Periodically, they may travel alone on business or to visit family, missing one another and enjoying sexy phone calls and romantic reunions.

There is also a willingness among these people to rock the boat with one another rather than stifle themselves for the sake of keeping the peace. This is different from playing uproar in that they're not generating emotional intensity by stirring up drama. Rather, they're willing to confront difficulties with courage, challenging themselves to articulate what they want in a loving, nonpunishing way so the other person can best hear it. They encourage the other to grow rather than blame and chastise them for their limitations, and they're open to discovering their truths in one another's presence. As it turns out, respect for one another, ability to be open to honest feedback given lovingly, and shared opportunities for self-discovery have been known to be great aphrodisiacs.

The fact is male-female relations are undergoing profound changes, not just in our personal lives but in our society. Riane Eisler considers that we are in the second phase of an ongoing sexual revolution where our yearning for fulfilling connection is spawning the emergence of a new partnership-oriented way of relating. Eisler points to an unprecedented social movement today with large numbers of women and men consciously and deliberately wanting to unlearn old-style ways of relating that perpetuate the war between the sexes. There are more opportunities now than ever before—through men's groups and women's groups, couples' counseling, workshops, and books like this one—for people wanting to overcome the stale habits that foster power struggles and to relearn how to love in more caring and empathic ways, as partners and equals.

The Evocative Relationship: Bringing out the Best in Each Other

The lesson to be learned in keeping long-term relationships pleasurably passionate seems to be that what maintains ardor is the right balance of closeness and privacy. It is far more stimulating to be with someone who has interests you can learn from and who periodically has to be wooed and won again than to be with someone willing to lop off parts of him- or herself to keep the peace. For the contemporary man or woman, a more spacious kind of relationship may ultimately have more staying power.

I think of this as an evocative way to generate passion, rather than the provocative way that people use when they play uproar to create passion. Uproar locks you into a power struggle as you try to affect each other by manipulation and punishment. We've seen how destructive the punishment ethos can be when it comes to having a loving relationship.

When you're evocative, rather than focusing on and punishing each other for what you don't like or love, you appreciate and stroke in one another what you do like and love. You nourish each other to be the best you can be, and you become powerful partners in contributing to each other's growth as a person.

True Love

True love is not just about being true to another. The most fulfilling love is when you are also true to yourself. You are open to discovering yourself in the presence of the other precisely because you want to be loved for who you truly are, not for who you can pretend to be.

Most of us have a sense that sharing true love makes life more meaningful. Jacob Needleman, the American writer, suggests that the key quality enabling people to sustain a long and satisfying relationship is that, together, they are involved in discovering and creating meaning in their lives. They provide support and encouragement for each other's personal growth, and what makes the relationship flourish is that they do it together.

To have passion in your relationship, you need to have passion in your life, and that usually depends on your willingness to put effort into activity that is meaningful to you. When life partners can feel love in their hearts, help each other grow as people, and support each other's meaningful enterprise, they have much to be grateful for. They are actively nourishing one of life's greatest pleasures: true love.

Personal Experiments

. . . .

1. Are you getting the love you need? If yes, great. If not, how can you put more love into your life through deepening your friendships and family ties? If you have a partner, talk about how you can create more loving feelings together. Don't complain, but give direction instead. See if you can ask for what you want in a way that makes your partner happy to give it to you.

2. Practice breath control and taking your emotional inventory. All emotions can be subjectively experienced somewhere in the body. To become more skilled at reading your authentic feelings, learn to identify your emotions by noticing first where in your body you feel them. Then observe what thoughts or dialogues you are running in your head and the images flashing before your mind's eye. Finally, see what urges you may have to express or act on your feelings—like wanting to run, cry, hug, or laugh.

With your eyes closed, take three cleansing breaths—breathing in through the nose to the top of your chest and blowing out through slightly puckered lips until you run out of air. Take one or two deep sighs, and then check in with your body. See if there is any tension, tightness, or excitement anywhere in your emotional center—that area between your head and your pelvis. Wherever you feel a contraction, especially when there's a churning underneath, it's likely to be part of an emotional response.

Check your eyes for worry or tears; your jaw for control or anger; your throat for fear or sadness; your chest for hurt, disappointment, or anxiety; and your diaphragm for guilt or obligation. Or you may notice expansive feelings in your chest such as love, pride, gratitude, and hope. Check how your feelings affect the rest of your body.

If you feel sad but your grief seems stuck inside of you and you want to bring up your tears, try the charging breath. Take five to ten quick sighs through an open mouth, and then stop and feel what you're feeling. If the tears come, great. Enjoy them. If not, try the charging breath one more time, and if the tears still don't come, let it be and try again another time after you have done some of the other experiments.

What thoughts or images are being triggered by your emotions? What do your feelings motivate you to do? Share your observations with an intimate partner or write them down in your notebook.

3. Practice this visualization on love. Take three cleansing breaths and get a picture in your mind's eye of someone you feel grateful toward, someone with whom you share a loving bond. Keep the person's image in your mind's eye and see if you can feel your chest open and relax and your heart grow warm. Recall specific instances when this person did you a kindness or remember special qualities of him or her that you most cherish. Do this visualization every time you feel tense, angry, depressed, or scared, and let your loving sensations calm and comfort you.

4. Practice intimacy as self-revelation. The object of this exercise is to explore the process of self-discovery in the presence of the other. The key to doing it properly is to stay in the present, as much as possible, observing your moment-by-moment experience. Report to your partner your awareness of the sensations in your body, the images or memories coming to mind, or the inner dialogues going on in your head. Talk about what these inner experiences do to you.

Choose a personal issue which you have some feelings about that you are both interested in discussing. You may have agreed to something you would like to renegotiate. You may be concerned about something that has happened. You may want to talk about something that's about to happen that needs to be addressed.

Start with each of you taking some deep cleansing breaths, checking your body for tightness or excitement, and simply report to one another what you observe in your own body. Maybe your chest is tight and you're feeling scared. Or, you've got a knot in your gut and you feel like you're on overload. Maybe your heart is light and full of love.

When you tackle the issue you've chosen to address, stay as close as you can to present experience without trying to justify or explain yourself. If you don't like what your partner is telling you, say how it makes you feel, but resist the urge to play uproar or to punish him or her for feeling or saying it. See if you can look for new thoughts and feelings, rather than go over the same territory you've been over before. What's important is to both talk and listen, not just give information to your partner, but also hear what your partner has to say. See if you can learn something new about both of you.

5. If you have a mate, ask yourself how you have held back from being completely true to yourself in this relationship. Even if you don't feel comfortable sharing your truth with your partner, at least be clear about it with yourself. Write a letter to your mate, which you may or may not give to him or her, and share some of your deepest feelings that you have held back. How has your withholding kept your relationship lukewarm? Do you have the courage to tell your truth?

6. Inspire your mate with your love and practice bringing out the best in him or her. Share with your mate what you love most about him or her. Be clear about your gratitude, your understanding, your empathy for their travails, and your pride in their accomplishments.

We're now ready to explore reaching our fullest potential for pleasure. In the next chapter we'll see how expanding our capacity to delight in what we see, hear, smell, taste, and touch not only makes us more sensuous but can also help us develop some very special skills.

PART FOUR

Realizing Your Full Pleasure Potential

Chapter 10

Sensual Pleasures:
Sense and Sense Ability

. . . .

Becoming more sensuous

. . . .

If we had a keen vision and feeling of all ordinary
human life, it would be like hearing the grass grow and
the squirrel's heart beat, and we should die of that roar
which lies on the other side of silence.

—*George Eliot*

Our senses are where the world registers on us. Everything we know of our surroundings comes from how the brain reacts to and interprets stimuli as they impinge upon our body. Special organs act as sensory receptors to receive the information: eyes take in photons of light, ears garner sound waves, fingers and skin discern textures and temperature, the nose draws in aromatic molecules, and the mouth and tongue respond to what is licked, sucked, nibbled, and chewed.

There's a big difference, however, between sensory and sensual experience. Sensory goes along with data. We get sensory information from what's around us, as well as from inside our body; internal sense organs known as proprioceptors let us know when we need water or are tense, in pain, or satisfied. To be sensual, on the other hand, is to linger over the stimulation, to be drawn by its beauty, and to focus on it not for data but for delight.

When something is highly sensual, we think of it as sensuous. Such experiences are often intensely engaging and can arouse emotion. We can feel moved by the heady aroma of jasmine in bloom on a balmy night; the swirling vibrancy of colors in a Monet painting of waterlilies; the sweet green fragrance of freshly mown grass in late August; the last twinkling stars fading on a desert horizon at sunrise as a peach-colored sky turns to blue; or the wrinkly soft skin of a newborn's hand.

The best thing about sensual pleasure is that it awakens us to the present moment. When we stop to gaze out a window and delight in the play of sunlight on a tree or are shaken from an intense reverie by the song of a bird, we're savoring what is happening right now. The vividness of the experience takes us out of our heads where we can get lost in our fictions and moves us into our bodies where we feel more fully alive.

Sensory Brown-Out

Regrettably, we don't usually leave time for dawdling over how good something feels or smells, continually overlooking possibilities for sensual pleasure that are all around us. There may even be sound reasons for shutting down, especially in the city, where there's a good deal of information we'd just as soon avoid. Toxic chemicals in the air don't smell so good, and we'd rather not look at the homeless person on the sidewalk and see the sadness and fear in his eyes.

Yet, when we close our senses to pain we are also restricting our potential for pleasure. Our sensory system is geared to respond to change in our environment. We adapt rather quickly to constancy in our visual field, to droning sounds, to an unwavering touch, and to an overly familiar scent or flavor. Anything constant ceases to stimulate us, and we turn off to it. One of the great values of sensual pleasure is that it reignites the senses, once again tuning us in to the world around us.

Trained to Narrow the Field of Delight

As babies and young children we're very sensual. We're fascinated by all there is to look at around us. We like sweet tastes and all kinds of new smells. We like falling asleep stroking a teddy bear's belly, comforted by a parent's song.

But we learn very early on that it's not appropriate to openly enjoy sensual pleasure. Adults usually become uncomfortable with a child's display of sensuousness. As a result, sensuality gets split into two realms: infantile and sexual, with nothing in between. We learn to not let ourselves get overstimulated.

One woman, who came for therapy to explore her lack of sexual interest in her husband, remembered being shamed by her mother for her sensuality when she was in the third grade. Mary Lou and her best girlfriend, Abbie, used to sit at desks that were side by side, and sometimes during class they would tickle each other's legs under their desks, very slowly and lightly. One day, the teacher caught them and wrote a cautioning letter to both sets of parents.

Mary Lou's mother was appalled and told her daughter that she was too old to be playing with Abbie in that way and that if she didn't stop she would grow up "twisted." Mary Lou thought her mother had overreacted, but she let Abbie know that they couldn't play that way anymore.

This seems like an innocuous event, and Mary Lou herself felt her mother was being prudish. But she traces her discomfort with sensual experience back to that time. Perhaps her memory encapsulates a whole assortment of experiences in which her mother, perhaps others in her family, and certainly her school, cracked down on her sensuous nature.

Not too long after that incident, Mary Lou began to overeat and has had concerns about her weight ever since. She now recognizes that food has been the only outlet she has allowed for her sensuousness. When we began to talk about cultivating sensuality in other areas of her life, she felt her whole body tense up. She could spend hours preparing homemade pasta and elaborate sauces; she could bake bread and braid the dough into intricate designs; and she enjoyed making meat patties and crab cakes and handling all kinds of food. But just thinking about taking a bath in candlelight or of her husband and her massaging each other's body with oil made her feel restless. She had the patience to wait for bread to rise but not to sensually awaken and enjoy her body.

Sensuality's Special Benefits

Becoming more sensually attentive makes us more receptive to all the other pleasures we've already looked at. When we surrender to our senses, it's easier to let go and just be; sensual enjoyment encourages pain release. Sensuality very naturally lightens us up and fosters playfulness, gets us out of our overemphasis on thinking, and helps relax and regulate the heart. As we shall see, a heightened sensual attunement has a highly intensifying effect on sexual pleasure, and with the greater perceptiveness afforded by sensuality, we can even become more in contact with our spiritual nature.

But sensual development has another major bonus as well. Developing our sensual enjoyment may enable us to become more intuitive, perhaps even to the point of becoming more responsive to what seems like psychic levels of awareness.

Enhanced Sensuality Sharpens Intuition

Having a greater appreciation for sensual pleasure encourages a greater overall awareness. The more we train ourselves to consciously let the eyes linger for a moment on the flowers in a garden, or to stay focused on a piece of music, or to relish the feel of a friendly cat's furry coat, the more fully alive we become to the world around us.

However, there are also levels of sensory stimulation that, while they are below our threshold of conscious awareness, are well within our threshold of physiological response. This means our bodies are reacting to subtle stimuli all the time: something that moved in the corner of the eye, a smell carried on the wind, or a sound over the left shoulder. These events may be too subtle to register a conscious thought, but they can still trigger a memory or cause the heart to cramp and the breath to shorten. We may get an urge to act in a partic- ular way, though we don't know why. We say it's just a hunch.

Yet, researchers are now discovering that intuition is a genuine phenomenon in which people respond to real information they don't know they have. Premonitions, solutions to difficult problems that appear spontaneously when you're not thinking about them, or a sense of rightness about a particular route that takes you to your des- tination without a map may all be accounted for as a responsiveness to nonrational, but nonetheless real, sensory experience.

There's plenty of evidence that we're operating on this level all the time. Writer Diane Ackerman in her thorough exploration of the senses reported on a number of studies on subliminal stimulation, showing that people can react emotionally to a stimulus even though they are unaware of it. In one experiment, a librarian lightly touched students' hands half the time as she was checking out their books. The other half the time, she did nothing special. The students were followed outside by a researcher and asked to rate the library services and their life in general. None who had been touched knew it, but they all reported greater satisfaction with the library and their lives than those who hadn't been touched.

Perhaps, if we hone our ability to consciously enjoy our senses more, we may become even more intuitive in picking up on subtle cues. In fact, there's even evidence that the more open you are to sensuous experience the more highly developed you can become in ESP. Research evidence suggests that people who seem to have ESP are responding not to extrasensory information but rather to subtle sensory data that actually comes through ordinary sensory channels.

Jenny Randles, the author of over five books on the paranormal, UFOs, and other mysterious phenomena, has proposed that clairvoyance, telepathy, precognition, and other psychic events may simply be highly sensitive perceptions to subliminal stimulation involving nothing more than the ordinary five senses. For example, a man who smelled a fire in his home a week before it happened, may have somehow gotten a hunch of the future danger. The hunch may have come from emotional cues too subtle for him to consciously identify. But his brain may have responded by sending him a message about the potential danger in the form of a hallucination of a burning smell that no one else could detect.

Perhaps a more accurate description of psychic ability is that it isn't extrasensory, something beyond our ordinary five senses, but rather *ultra*sensory. Just as ultraviolet is at the extreme end of the light spectrum—invisible but still capable of stimulating the eye and doing it damage—this kind of stimulation occurs at the furthest edge of the spectrum of our ordinary senses. Ultrasensory perception picks up subtle data from all the sensory receptors everywhere in the body and signals a sensory response. But while the original stimulus is real though subtle, our amplified reaction is actually mentally induced, occurring nowhere in the real world other than in our own imagination.

It is very possible that the more deliberately sensual we are—the more we enjoy our eyes, ears, nose, mouth and tongue, skin and fingers—the more tuned our sense organs can become, and the more informed and aware we can be, even at the most subtle levels.

The Real Sixth Sense: Phantom Sensing

We're all very much aware of the phenomenon of imagination—the ability of the mind to conjure up images and to "see" pictures and movies in our head. Visualizations of this sort can be considered a "phantom sense" in that what we "see" isn't really there—it's a mental representation of a visual stimulus.

In fact, each of the other senses has an inner, phantom counterpart. When we picture ourselves walking along the beach, we can also hear the seagulls overhead. We can feel the wind, smell the sea air, and taste the saltwater. The vividness of the imagery is enhanced by mental hearing, mental feeling, mental tasting, and mental smelling.

We use our phantom senses all the time. Thinking utilizes phantom hearing, mentally listening to the inner dialogues that instruct our actions throughout our waking day. We can also "hear" a melody, a repetitive refrain that sometimes we can't seem to shake for days. Inner sensing involves phantom touch, a gut feeling that something is right or wrong. Phantom taste is used every time we go to a restaurant and choose between alternatives on a menu—imagining first how the steak in green peppercorn sauce will taste, then the poached salmon, and making our choice from how the dishes "tasted" internally. As we have just seen, too, subtle cues may stimulate the phantom senses, signaling danger by conjuring up the smell of fire or perhaps a vivid mental image of a car crash.

Most of the time, we're oblivious to our phantom senses and how much, unconsciously, we rely on them. As we explore ways to enjoy greater sensual pleasure in each of the ordinary five senses, we'll also look at becoming more attuned to how our phantom senses affect us and to the very valuable role they play in increasing our overall capacity for pleasure.

Sight

Poets and philosophers have long speculated on what it is about eyeing nature that contributes to such a peacefulness of spirit. It could be watching waves crashing onshore, giving chase to sandpipers who race back as the tide recedes; it could be staring into a fire, transfixed by dancing flames and glowing logs spitting sparks of ash; it could be contemplating puffy white clouds drifting across a valley, casting shadows on a plain below.

All of these experiences have a similar quality—they allow us to bear passive witness to a timeless moment in an unceasing flow. Our eyes have been captured and held fast by nature's beauty, fascinated by its constant movement and shifting patterns of light, colors, and shapes. Within seconds we feel hypnotically lulled by its rhythms to become a part of, and in harmony with, nature.

Pleasurable visuals can heal. A host of studies have shown that rich natural visual stimulation can make people friendlier and happier, lessen pain, ease sadness or fear, and reduce stress—beyond anything urban scenes and drab walls can do. Recall the surgery patients who recovered quicker when they had hospital rooms that faced a view of trees rather than a brick wall. In another study, patients with hypertension and under stress were asked to gaze for twenty minutes into an aquarium filled with colorful plants and tropical fish. Not only did watching the fish often lower their blood pressure to normal, but these patients remained calmer even under renewed stress.

You can also become more cognizant of the visual beauty around you. You can take greater care to bring items into your personal space that will provide a pleasing spot for your eyes to rest. You can put up photos of beloved family members or inspiring people whose qualities you admire. You can bring flowers home, or you can decorate a workplace with some colors or designs that will keep your eyes restfully stimulated. You can especially remind yourself, every so often, to relinquish your mental images for a few moments, look around, and relish what you see.

Phantom Seeing

The eyes are as much the organs for inner sight and insight, as they are for outer sight. We've already looked at the intimate connection between how you think and your visual imagery. We've seen how optimism is about making good mental pictures and how your imagination actually commands your muscles to act in ways consistent with whatever you picture. Clearly, holding positive visual images and having a positive vision of the future can energize you to move in productive directions.

Hearing

No doubt you derive a great deal of pleasure from sound—from music, the laughter of someone you love, or a wind chime ringing softly in the breeze. Perhaps you can also recall some sensuous sounds you really treasure: the murmuring of pines in a mountain windstorm; the tinkling of a gentle brook skipping over stones; the soft rolling thunder of a distant electrical storm across a prairie; the angelic harmony of voices in a children's choir; or the familiar "hi there" of an old friend unexpectedly telephoning long distance. Sound is very precious to us, and hearing is one of our most vital senses.

Music has been shown to have a particularly healing effect on the human body. Singing causes the pupils to dilate—a parasympathetic response—and endorphin levels to rise. Listening or playing music affects breathing rhythms, lowers blood pressure, and reduces the level of stress hormones in the blood. Music has been successfully used as therapy to treat everything from headaches to severe burns and has been effective with premature babies, autistic children, and comatose and brain-damaged patients.

Music can soothe and calm you, or it can energize you and motivate your workout at the gym. Music is emotionally evocative. A marching cadence can fire nationalism; bluesy rhythms can make you feel sexy; and certain drumbeats just seem to make your pelvis rock instinctively. Chanting is a form of meditation that enables you to focus your mind without words.

Tuning Out

As with the other senses, hearing undergoes a form of sensory adaptation. We shut off to constant, moderate auditory stimulation of any kind, relegating it to the category of "noise." A ticking clock recedes into the background because we cease to attend to it. The person who drones on without making eye contact, not really expecting or demanding to be heard, can easily be drowned out by our own thoughts. And when those inner thoughts are a constant monologue of disaster, a person may close off the desire to even hear themselves—what we usually call denial.

People also stop themselves from hearing because they don't want to listen. To listen also means to obey—like when a parent says, "That child simply won't listen." As a result, some people may sacrifice their ability to hear because they don't want to conform to what is being asked of them. Tuning out can cause a temporary deafness, like when your mind wanders, or it can lead to a permanent bad habit of inattention—and eventually maybe even actual hearing loss.

People who don't know how to say "no" clearly, or who don't feel entitled to say it, may simply tune you out if they think you're trying to tell them what to do. A man I know almost lost his fiancée that way. Danny and Laurie were an attractive couple in their early thirties who had started a small business together. During business hours, Danny seemed interested in what Laurie had to say. But after hours, it seemed to Laurie that he would automatically nod and mumble "yes" as she talked, but then it would turn out he had agreed to plans he had no memory of making. Laurie felt she didn't want to be in a marriage with someone whose mind wandered every time she spoke.

It turned out that Danny didn't feel like he had the right to say, "Laurie, I'm not available to talk right now." He felt like he was supposed to be available all the time, and he didn't feel comfortable saying no to anything she asked of him. So instead of dealing with a potential area of conflict by saying how he actually felt, he simply stopped listening, claiming ignorance later on.

Laurie's contribution to their difficulties was that she didn't listen either and was much better at talking. In fact, often she gave too much information and was hard to follow; I too found myself losing interest in her windy explanations. Laurie needed to be concise and Danny had to realize he could listen without having to do as he was told. Especially, he needed to know he was entitled to ask for silent, restful times with Laurie without conversation.

Inner Sound and Phantom Hearing

Certain qualities of sound also describe attributes of mental, emotional, and spiritual well-being. We say that a person who has a deep compassion or empathy *resonates* with others and that a peaceful spirit reflects an inner *harmony*. In physics, resonance is when the sound made in one body produces a similar vibration in another body. In music, harmony is when different tones in a chord combine to create a pleasing sound. There seems to be a profound connection between physical sound and our psychological soundness.

Health and happiness depend on our ability to listen to our inner voices, to sense inner dissonance, and to resolve it in the direction of what "rings" true. One of the more vital inner voices we need to listen to is the counterpoint to the inner critic—the inner ally. The ally is the voice of comforting, encouragment, and inspiration. You know you've found your ally when it's a real pleasure listening to yourself think.

Smelling

The bouquet of wet grass in the air after a morning rain; the yeasty sweet mixtures of breads, cakes, and cookies in a neighborhood bakery; the crisp woodsy tar of a burning log; the telltale whiff of perspiration and personality in your tee shirt that determines if it can sustain another wearing—these are four of the thousands upon thousands of unique odors that we as human beings can detect.

Smell biologically connects us with our reptilian ancestry. The nose is directly wired to the oldest and deepest part of the brain, the rhinencephalon, literally the "nose brain," located inside the limbic system. Because the sense of smell is not wired closely with parts of the brain associated with language and logic, odors do not lend themselves to easy description. Rather, odors are evocative of feelings, moods, memories, and desires. Even if you haven't smelled something for twenty years, smelling it again can instantaneously trigger a strong visceral feeling of familiarity and emotion—what might happen if you were to catch the scent of a perfume your mother wore when you were little.

The Nose Knows

The smelling sense is fed by every inhale. But since most of us tend to be shallow breathers, we don't make use of our sense of smell to the degree we might. We downplay its importance and rely more on sight and hearing—the more analytical, rational senses. As a result, we probably don't consciously "sniff things out" enough. Potentially valuable information is in the air all the time, like such basic information as the smell of poisonous fumes or of food that's gone bad.

However, that doesn't mean that we aren't picking up the information below the level of conscious awareness. It's very likely that we are constantly responding to scent information without registering the source as a scent. Since smell is not directly wired to language but to imagery and feeling, a few airborne molecules up the nose may be quite enough for our brains to react with a visual image of a past event, such as the face of a loved one or an enemy or a shift in mood from light to heavy without ever realizing that what caused the change was something we inhaled.

The Inner Nose and Phantom Smell

The inherent wisdom of the English language suggests that the nose is more than just an organ for the likes of roses and fresh laundry. It's no accident that we have terms like *to sniff around and find out* or *to have a nose for news.* The nose seems to be central in detecting information on an instinctive, nonlinear level.

Enhancing the sensual responsiveness of your nose will not only further develop your sensuality but can actually improve your skills of detection and discrimination. Taking deep breaths facilitates smell and may have a hidden benefit of encouraging you to "smell out" situations more carefully.

Aromatic Influences

Smells actually influence us a lot more than we think. New research has shown that fragrances are so arousing that some can even act as stimulants improving alertness on the job. For example, lemon and peppermint scents can stimulate performance on a routine task and reduce the rate of error by as much as 54 percent. Scent also affects mood. One whiff of spiced apple scent reduces tension by slowing down the breath, lowering heart rate and blood pressure, and relaxing the muscles.

Modern research, however, is only confirming what has been known for centuries: the validity of an ancient practice of herbal medicine now known as aromatherapy. More widely practiced in Europe and Asia than in America, aromatherapy is the use of essential oils distilled from flowers and herbs to be used in baths, during massage, or in special vaporizers as a way of reducing anxiety, depression, lassitude, and increasing a sense of well-being. For example, lavender, bergamot, and chamomile might be recommended for relaxation, rose essence to lift the spirits, and pine and eucalyptus to feel invigorated.

Some researchers have speculated that scents may operate by activating neurotransmitters, and as such, they may even have a direct effect on immunity. We know certain smells. such as chemical odors, pollutants in smog or gasoline, or buildings that circulate stale air, can make us feel queasy and sick; it makes sense that other odors would affect our health more positively. Some experiments are being done on terminally ill patients; they are pairing certain odors with vital medications that have toxic side effects. After a number of pairings of the odor with the necessary medicine, the odor itself may have the capacity to perform the same healing effect as the medicine—without any of its negative side effects.

Sex and Smell

Smell is not only arousing emotionally but sexually too. Napoleon is said to have written Josephine asking her not to bathe in the two weeks they were to be apart so that he could enjoy her natural aromas when he returned. Today's fastidious nose might not quite relish a two-week body ripening, even in France. Still, chemical signals given off during sexual excitement may have a far greater effect on human beings, particularly in close quarters, than ever before imagined.

Sex is quite literally in the air. A female moth ready for mating will release molecules into the air that can bring male moths from miles away. It's possible that the same sort of molecules, known as pheromones, released by human males and females, have a similar, though not quite so compelling, effect on our own sexual responsivity. These chemicals work very much like hormones except they are released by one individual yet effect the physiology and behavior of another.

How responsive are human beings to such chemical communication? Apparently, quite a bit. While pheromones in humans are perhaps not as commanding as in other animals, research in the last few years has indicated that there really is a chemistry between people. The smell sense, conscious or not, can draw people together as lovers and potential mates, and it can synchronize our internal body rhythms.

On the other hand, certain other types of odors may repel. There's some evidence that different emotions may give off different odors— anxiety, for example, may give off an unpleasant musty smell in a person's sweat. We are clearly repelled by some people or drawn toward others virtually by the nose. No doubt subliminal odor information of all sorts is a subtle yet real form of communication existing between humans.

Taste

Taste is the least refined of all our senses. Humans can perceive only four basic tastes: salty, sour, sweet, and bitter. By some estimates, 80 percent of what we experience as taste, as in a delightful dinner or a fine wine, is actually aroma. In fact, smelling food before eating it is a good practice because doing so not only enhances the flavor of the food but it also stimulates the salivary response, which aids in digestion.

There's also a lot more to tasting than just flavor and smell. Taste is a complex sense that involves temperature sensations of hot and cold, like a steaming cup of tea or a pineapple sorbet; textures of dry and crunchy like potato chips; or moist and smooth like applesauce. Taste can also stimulate a pain response, as it does with spicy foods like jalapeño peppers, hot curries, and horseradish—bursts of sheer pleasure for aficionados but agonizing torture for the more tender-tongued.

Certain taste preferences actually reflect ways in which we self-medicate in response to our emotions. Research has shown that different foods may trigger the production of neurotransmitters, those chemical signals between different parts of the brain that affect mood, alertness, and motivation. If you crave a candy bar, it may be that what you're seeking are the endorphins released by the sugar, which contribute to a feeling of euphoria. On the other hand, if you feel stressed, you may gravitate toward certain foods that are high in carbohydrates and considered "comfort foods." Pasta, bread, potatoes, and other starches have been found to raise the level of serotonin in the blood, a chemical capable of calming anxiety.

Taste also has a lot more significance than merely the tongue's response to chicken soup. Because different foods are associated with maternal love and care, family celebrations, social gatherings, reward for hard work and compensation for disappointment, taste is particularly linked to emotional and symbolic factors. People who overeat often feel emotionally undernourished and fill their longing with sweets and carbohydrates.

The Psychology of Taste and Phantom Chewing

Less often examined are the factors connected with tasting that relate to making good choices. When a person is said to have "good taste," that person is considered to be a good judge of quality, capable of discriminating between something fine and standard fare. Taste is also about another kind of discrimination—where you chew things over not just with regard to what you put in your mouth, but with respect to ideas as well.

It can be very valuable to reexamine the beliefs, attitudes, and personal habits that you were "fed" as a child, which you may have taken on as your own without questioning them. Young children become socialized by interjecting—literally swallowing whole their parents' ways of thinking and acting; but if you want to be an adult who thinks for him- or herself, you need to chew over what you've been fed.

Do you swallow other people's values and judgments without mulling things over? Can others get away with shoving their ideas down your throat? These are not merely accidents of speech but profound metaphors linking how we eat with how we take in and process information.

Our language draws other parallels between chewing and processing information. To chew something over is to consider it carefully. To ruminate however, is to obsess, to continually go over the exact same thoughts—similar to what a cow does. A cow is a ruminant and that means she chews her cud, continually bringing up undigested material that has been swallowed to chew again. To be gullible is to be easily fooled. The word *gullible* has at its roots the middle English word, *gull*, meaning to swallow. A gull is also a dupe, a dope, or a person easily cheated or tricked.

You don't want to ruminate obsessively. But you do need to chew over what others are trying to feed you—enough to examine your own beliefs, attitudes, and values without merely swallowing things on someone else's authority.

Touch

Sensuality is almost synonymous with touch. Usually, however, it makes people think of pleasures only possible during intimate times, when being stroked or caressing a lover. However, there's a world of simple pleasures available through sensual touch, which, when included in your everyday life, can hone your ability to reach greater heights of pleasure during special times.

Touch is actually three senses in one: receptive touch, active touch, and sensing. Receptive touch is aroused when something makes contact with your skin—a breeze on your bare arm, someone's leg leaning on yours, or a soft terry bathrobe on your body after a shower. Touch receptors embedded in the skin respond to a wide spectrum of sensation defined by opposites of temperature (warmer and colder), of texture (rougher and smoother), of vibration (faster and slower), and especially of pressure (lighter and heavier). Hairless parts of the body, such as the nipples and soles of the feet, respond only to very light pressure, while hairier sections respond to anything that moves the hair.

Active touch is involved when you examine something with your hands and fingertips, focusing on its contours and textures—like squeezing a peach to test for ripeness or running silk fabric through your fingers. Active touch receptors, located in the hands and fingers, respond to cold, warmth, pain, and constant deep pressure.

Sensing has to do with being responsive to internal sensation. Kinesthetically, you can sense up from down and be aware of the position of your arms and legs because internal touch receptors—proprioceptors, that are imbedded in the muscles, tendons, and joints—keep us oriented in space. Sensing is also about feeling hungry, happy, loving, angry, or sexually excited. Proprioceptors in the linings of the stomach, intestines, bladder, and other internal organs signal pain or need, emotions, pleasure, and well-being.

Empathic touch is one of the essential building blocks of pleasure. Yet it's not uncommon for people to lament the lack of touching in their families as they were growing up. Several crosscultural studies have shown that adults in the United States and Great Britain exchange far fewer caring touches with their children, and they touch other adults far less often, than people from other cultures. This was true whether the studies focused on the number of times adults in playgrounds were seen to soothe and comfort their children through touch or on the number of touches shared by couples sitting in a cafe. Americans and British consistently scored substantially lower than Russians, French, or Greeks.

The fact is, we connect most strongly with the people who touch us, and the more we stroke and cuddle each other, the warmer and more bonded we feel.

Healing Touch

Of all the senses, touch has the greatest power to heal illness. More and more scientific evidence is accumulating to indicate that the hands are a potent source of restorative energy.

Lewis Thomas, a physician/philosopher with an interesting medical perspective on the human condition, has suggested that while the invention of the stethoscope has provided doctors with an invaluable tool for listening in on a person's internal organs and enabling more accurate diagnoses, something valuable was also lost through its use. Doctors used to listen to a patient's heartbeat and lungs by placing one ear on his or her chest or back. Thomas offers that this simple gesture of caring and concern replaced by the widespread use of all kinds of diagnostic instrumentation prevalent today has essentially eliminated this "most effective act of doctors": touching the patient.

However, what has typically been lost to traditional medicine is being made up for in nontraditional options for healing. Touch is considered a significant aspect of the effectiveness of such practices as chiropractic and osteopathy, the Alexander Technique, Feldenkrais work, massage, shiatsu, acupuncture and acupressure, Rolfing, polarity therapy, reflexology, and therapeutic touch.

Many body psychotherapists also touch their clients in a variety of different ways to help them become aware of areas of stuck energy and to uncover buried emotions. For example, a Reichian or bioenergetic therapist may massage certain pressure points in the jaw or eyes to assist emotional release, while a Gestalt therapist may simply place her hands, with the client's permission, on his or her upper chest to encourage breathing. Some somatic therapists hold their clients in yogic postures; a Hakomi therapist may help a client curl up into a ball, if that's a feeling the client expresses. Two other body psychotherapies that often include touch in the healing process are Integrated Body Psychotherapy and the Rubenfeld Synergy Method.

While no research has yet been done to investigate the scientific basis for the apparent healing potential of touch, it may have something to do with some special abilities of the skin and hands. The skin is the largest organ of the body and has three very special talents: it can renew, it can repair, and it can regenerate itself. No other organ in the body is as capable of restoring itself after damage or of replacing its lost parts.

The skin renews itself. Every patch of skin has cells at different stages of the life cycle. New cells at the very bottom layer of the skin are continually being born to replace older cells that push through the layers, to die and be sloughed off at the skin's surface. Death and rebirth is an ongoing capability of the skin.

Healthy skin repairs itself. When cut, an enzyme is released that stimulates cell division and seamlessly joins the two edges of the wound together. Mending injury is a consistent attribute of the skin.

The skin is also regenerative. Medical science still has no way of growing new eyes or new livers, but researchers are capable of growing new skin in a laboratory in less than two hours. Doctors have been able to take small patches of skin from burn victims who have lost as much as 98 percent of their skin, culture these into sheets of fresh skin, and over a period of some months, graft these onto the body and recover its entire surface. The largest organ of the body can clone itself.

Hands also have some very special abilities. One of the lesser appreciated talents of the hands is that the hand can "see." Blind people know this because they use their hands to read, to examine a face, or to appreciate an item of clothing. A rarer skill pertains to the ability to pick up much more subtle information through the hands. Psychics call it "blind sight," when a person has the ability to pick up accurate premonitions and visual images about a situation through touch.

It may be that the special abilities of both the skin and hands are accessed when healers use their hands to detect areas of disturbance on a patient's body and to infuse it with restorative energy. For example, in one healing technique known as therapeutic touch, the practitioner passes her hands a few inches above the patient's body to sense the subtle energies emanating off the body. Then, in a fully focused frame of mind, sweeping her hands over the congested, undernourished areas, the healer attempts to move the energy out of the clogged places and to help the energy flow into the empty places. One study showed that ordinary people taught to concentrate and heal this way could actually generate a detectable drop in the anxiety of heart patients.

The effectiveness of all the healing methods that incorporate touch may have something to do with the hand's ability to read the body and to stimulate the skin's capacity to renew, repair, and regenerate itself. It may also be that touch has the power to invigorate not just the skin but our own overall capacity to renew, repair, and regenerate ourselves on a grander scale. Whatever it is, touch is clearly a vital nutrient for the skin. It makes sense to expect that when the largest organ of the body is nourished, the greater our overall capacity will be to mend and restore ourselves.

Feeling Good Inside

Pleasurable feelings can either be relaxed or energized, but they are always expansive. The heart is warm and relaxed, and inner vibrations are rhythmic and not jagged. There's no pressure or weight bearing down on your heart or crimping your muscles and inner organs. You feel light, energetic, and alive. Your body is saying, "All is well. Whatever you're doing, keep it up!"

One of life's supreme pleasures has to be the inner sense of rightness, enthusiasm, and enjoyment we call "feeling good" that involves all kinds of internal touch sensation. It's not even necessary that you feel no pain. In some cases, even when pain is chronic, a person may be capable of bracketing it off and focusing instead on what's pleasurable. To feel good inside means your emotional center—jaw, throat, heart, gut, and belly—is open and energized. You're humming like a finely tuned machine.

Being "in touch" with feelings is not just a figure of speech but very much a part of the tactile sense. As we have seen, there are touch receptors all over the inside viscera of the body that can respond to pressure, vibration, and pain. Internal touch receptors can also signal emotion, and, while some people think of their feelings more as mental experiences, those who are in touch with the physical nature of their feelings have far greater access to their own inner subjective truths.

Phantom Touch

Any time you have a fantasy about being touched or touching someone you are triggering a very special kind of inner sensing. Romantic or erotic novels stimulate phantom touch whenever you find yourself becoming aroused while reading a detailed description of how lovers touch one another. Any well-crafted story will use descriptions of how things feel to pull you deeper into the tale and give you a sense of immediacy. Any time you use imagery, whether it is for healing and charging the immune system or for practicing visualizations to stimulate optimal performance toward a goal, the ability to pleasurably arouse phantom touch is critical for increasing your sensual aliveness.

Aesthetics: Where Sensual, Mental, Emotional, and Spiritual Pleasures Meet

Having an appreciation for beauty in art and nature can be an enormous source of inner nourishment and replenishment. Beauty can stimulate the senses and the intellect, and, at its best, it can provide us with a sense of the divine. All the senses are involved in a heightened sensitivity to beauty. It can be evoked in the visual genius of an exhibit of Picasso drawings; it can be in the sound that arouses emotion through a poetry reading by Allen Ginsberg or in the jazz piano of Ahmad Jamal. It can even be in the aftertaste of a sip of a fine Bordeaux wine.

Your aesthetic appreciation can be stimulated by the pleasures of dance, theater, gourmet cooking, needlework, pottery, photography, walking in the woods, making jewelry, solving a mathematical equation, admiring a lover's face or body, reading a good novel, watching a brilliant film, or collecting driftwood and seashells on the beach. Aesthetic enjoyment can make you laugh or move you to tears. It doesn't even have to be classically beautiful to be beautiful. You can enjoy the aesthetic impact of a form of expression even though you feel shock, are repelled, or are made to feel guilty, like when hearing a masterful political speech or seeing a propaganda poster that has inspired a liberation movement.

Psychiatrist Victor Frankl, whose work highlights the critical importance of finding meaning in one's life, was strongly influenced by his years in Nazi concentration camps. Frankl observed that aesthetic pleasure was one of the few ways prisoners could find meaning in their meager existence. As a result of their deprivation, he noticed that his inner life and that of the other prisoners became more intense, and that they experienced beauty in art and nature as never before.

Frankl recounted a transfer of male prisoners from Auschwitz to another camp in Bavaria, when the men could behold the mountains of Salzberg in the glow of sunset through the barred windows of the prison carriage. He said it would be hard to describe the faces of those men who had given up all hope for life and liberty being carried away by the vision of nature's beauty. At the camps, despite their extreme exhaustion and desolate lives, prisoners wrote songs, poems, and plays and told jokes and organized an occasional cabaret with satirical skits and entertainment.

Here now is your opportunity to explore for yourself some new ways of experiencing pleasure through your senses. These simple experiments will enable you to cultivate a greater sensitivity to each of the different senses and, additionally, can foster the development of some very special capabilities.

Personal Experiments

. . . .

Sensuality is strongly enhanced by breath-control. Always begin these exercises by taking some deep cleansing breaths, inhaling through the nose, filling the chest all the way to the top without straining, and exhaling by blowing out slowly through slightly puckered lips until you run out of air. If you feel tense, take a few extra breaths, letting the breath enter and stretch the tight areas on the inhale, then imagine you are blowing the stress out on the exhale.

When you want to surrender more fully to sensual stimulation, sigh deeply with an open mouth.

Visual Sensuality

1. Getting an Eyeful. In a relaxed and experimental frame of mind, look around the area surrounding you and see what pleases you visually. You may see a print in a frame or a pretty view out your window. Look for vividness of color, a pattern of geometric shapes, lines converging and separating, a metallic sheen or patina, a play of light and shadows, and reflections of yourself or other objects mirrored off glass or glossy surfaces.

Then close your eyes and see what you can recall of what you just saw. What images or colors stand out for you? Open your eyes and compare the true image with what you imagined. Practice this experiment a few times and see if you can enhance your visual memory.

2. Visual Destressing. Take a few cleansing breaths and picture in your mind's eye one of the most beautiful natural scenes you've ever seen. It could be the view from a mountain top, along a stretch of isolated tropical beach, a lush garden, a stately forest, or a vast grassy plain. Let the image be animated by the movement of wind, friendly creatures, or the presence of a good friend or lover. Notice what you are feeling in your body. Take some deep breaths and let yourself be relaxed and replenished by the pleasure of your comforting scene. Conjure up this image anytime you're tense, to calm and relax yourself and continually add new sensual elements to keep it fresh and lively.

3. Envisioning with a Partner. Sit facing your partner. Each of you take a few deep sighs to relax; then study your partner's face for details. Look at how the hair frames the face. Look at the lines in the forehead, at how the brow may pinch. Study the look in his eyes; how she is holding her mouth or lips; or the emotion, if any, in his or her expression. Look for details, a mole or freckle you never noticed before, or the extent of a line or scar. Then close your eyes and see how much detail of your partner's face you can summon to memory.

When you think you have as good an image as you can retrieve, open your eyes, look at your partner once again, and see how much detail you left out. Close your eyes a third and last time and add your new reminders. In this way, see how detailed an image of your partner you can construct in your mind's eye. Pay attention to any spontaneous imagery that may come up for you as you are imagining your partner. When you are both finished, describe your experiences to each other.

Hearing Sensuality

1. Sound Sensitivity. Take few cleansing breaths, relax, and simply listen. (If you have the radio or TV on, turn it off.) See how many distinct sounds you can now hear. See if you can gauge the distance of the sounds. What sounds are closest to you? What are the most distant sounds you can become aware of? If you're indoors, open a window and see what more you now can hear. Can you hear any sounds of nature: the flutter of a breeze, birds chirping, a trickle of water, a dog barking, the buzz of a fly? Keep listening attentively for a few minutes and see if you can stretch your hearing sense.

Cup your hands tightly over your ears and see what internal sounds you can become aware of. Close your eyes, take a breath, and hold it. Listen to the roar of life within you. You may even be able to hear your heart beat.

2. Hearing with Your Mind's Ear. Stimulate your phantom hearing sense. See if you can remember a song your mother or father sang to you as a child. Can you hear your parent's voice in your mind's ear? Recall some favorite music from your childhood and see how vividly you can hear it in your imagination. Does it evoke any feeling? Where in your body can you feel it?

Recall some favorite sounds. Picture a fountain you've seen in your travels and see if you can hear the music of its waters. Picture a tree in the wind and see if you can hear the shimmer of its leaves. Picture a rainstorm outside, hear the claps of thunder, and listen to the sound of the rain hitting your roof and windows.

3. Sensual Hearing with a Partner. Sit facing your partner and take a few deep sighs. Look at your partner's face and think silently to yourself about what you most love and appreciate about this person. Give yourselves about three minutes to silently articulate your feelings. Then take turns sharing your appreciations out loud.

Pick out a few of your favorite poems and read to each other. Sing to one another. Listen to music by candlelight together. Bring your partner to a lovely spot in nature where it is quiet and peaceful. Sit and listen to the silence together.

Sensual Smell

1. Making Good Scents. Take a few cleansing breaths and sniff the air lightly as you inhale. See what smells you can become aware of right now. Allow your nostrils to become soft, relaxed, and open. Pick up a few items near you and see if their scent stirs any images or feelings. Find a memento and sniff it; see if it awakens any old memories. Take some quick little sniffs and then try some long, deep inhales that draw the air slowly. See if there's a difference in what you can discover in each of these two ways of sniffing.

For the next few days, become more aware of the body odor of the people you come in contact with during the day. Does their odor attract or repel you? Can you smell other people's emotions, such as their anxiety or enthusiasm?

2. Scent Memory. Imagine some scents that were significant to you as you were growing up. Can you recall how your mother smelled? Your father? Anyone else in your family? Do you have any scent memories related to food, holidays, objects you grew up with, rooms you spent time in? Recall foreign countries or unusual places you've visited and see if you can recapture, mentally, some of the unique smells from those trips.

Develop your scent imagery. Imagine taking a deep inhale of a creamy white gardenia. Picture it as vividly as you can and drink in the scent memory of the essence of gardenia. Now let that fade and picture and sniff a forest full of pine trees. Let your nasal passages open with the cooling air. Imagine some of your favorite fragrant objects and see if you can smell them right now. How do they make you feel?

3. Enhancing Sensuality of Smell with a Partner. Before doing this exercise, you and your partner will need to separately gather up some particularly appealing scents to surprise and share with one another—a delicately scented flower, a fruit, some herbs, sachets, cedar chips, a variety of tea bags, coffee beans, a fine soap, an exotic perfume, or an essential oil. Each of you can put your scents in a basket or dish and cover it with a cloth so your partner can't see them.

Sit facing one another and take a few deep cleansing breaths before you start. Then one person keeps his or her eyes closed while the other presents items one by one under the sniffer's nose. Allow a few moments between scents to clear the nose and see if you can each guess the smells being presented to you. See if the scent arouses any emotions or memories and share your observations with one another.

4. The Scratch and Sniff Lie Detector Game. Here's a great phantom smell game to play with a partner. Get a deck of cards and sit opposite one another laying out all fifty-two cards facedown in a sweep of the deck. Take a few deep cleansing breaths and decide who will go first. The first player chooses a card from the deck, studies it a few minutes, places it face down, and decides whether or not to tell the truth.

After deciding, he or she says "ready" and the other partner asks "What card did you choose?" The first player says which card out loud and either tells the truth or lies. Now, the other player has five minutes to decide if he or she is telling the truth. Whoever is guessing has to "sniff out" the situation. You can talk or ask questions. See what cues you rely on. Be sure to sniff your partner to deliberately attempt to bring in subliminal information. Are you getting any hunches that you're not sure where the cues are coming from? After you guess whether or not your partner was telling the truth, share any clues you were aware of. Then switch roles. This little game can help you build skills in reading each other's subtle cues, a vital skill for empathy.

Taste Sensuality

1. Enhancing Taste. Experiment with your next meal or with a little snack right now. Before you eat, take a few cleansing breaths, check your body for tension or emotion, and, if there is any, see if you can stretch and relax, blowing out some of your discomfort before you put any food into your mouth. Smell first, then take a bite of food, chewing it thoroughly and rolling the liquid around on your tongue before swallowing. What do you like about this food—the flavor, the texture, the temperature, and the familiarity or newness, or is there any symbolic attraction related to your childhood?

Take a few cleansing breaths and recall, in your imagination, the flavors of the items you just tasted.

Think about some of your favorite foods and see how vividly you can summon up your taste imagery. Picture some of the culinary highlights of the last two weeks and see if you can recapture the memory of how each first smelled and then tasted. You'll probably discover that you have no difficulty in conjuring up imagery strong enough to make you salivate right now.

Recall some of your favorite tastes from childhood. What kinds of lunches did your mother or father pack for you or did you get lunch at school? Can you call up the smell of the food and the taste memories of some of those lunches? See if any feelings are associated with some of those early food smells and tastes.

At your next meal, be aware of all the steps involved in tasting. Smell your food consciously before tasting. Be aware of your mouth watering before you start to eat. Bite into your food and be aware of the assertiveness in the acts of biting and chewing. Savor the food before you swallow it. Eat slowly so you can be fully aware of all the sensuous pleasures involved in conscious eating.

2. Enhancing the Sensuality of Taste with a Partner. Prepare a plate of three tasty tidbits to surprise your partner and ask him or her to do the same. Cover the plates so that neither one of you can see what the other is bringing, then sit in front of one another. Have a glass of water there for each of you. Decide who will be the first taster and wrap a blindfold, loosely but securely, around the taster's eyes.

Feed your partner by selecting a morsel of food, bring it slowly up toward her mouth, then stop as soon as she announces she can smell it. Allow the food to be sniffed, and when she's ready, bring it to her mouth so that she can slowly and deliberately, bite, taste, and chew it before swallowing it. Only then should she talk: guessing what the food was and describing the tastes aroused, the pictures that flashed in her mind's eye, how it felt to eat, and how it feels now having eaten it. Drink water between each taste to cleanse the palate. After three foods, the taste-giver reveals what the foods were. Then switch so that the taste-giver becomes the taster.

3. Stimulate Taste Memory. Share with your partner, in detail, a sensuous meal you once had. Describe how it looks laid out on the table in your mind's eye, how it smells, how it tastes in flavor, texture, and temperature, to bite into, to chew, and to swallow. See if you can get your partner's mouth to water and to have a vivid experience "tasting" this meal. Now your partner can share a favorite meal with you.

Sensuous Touch

1. Receptive Touch Awareness. Without shifting your posture, see what touch sensations you can become aware of right now as you are reading. Is there anything causing you pain or discomfort that you were unaware of until now? Is your clothing comfortable or is it too tight? Is your chair sticking you anywhere you hadn't noticed earlier? Is it soft or scratchy against your skin?

This evening as you get into bed at night, particularly make note of the sensations of temperature, pressure, texture, and pleasure on different parts of your body. What feels especially good, and what can you do to make it feel even better?

In your next shower, feel the sensation of the water streaming down your body, the smoothness of the soap on your skin, and the texture of your sponge or washcloth. Be aware of how you towel yourself dry. Can you do it somewhat more pleasurably?

Be more aware of the sensation of touch throughout your day: in how you touch yourself in the morning as you brush your teeth, comb your hair, and groom yourself for the day; in how your clothes feel on your body as you dress; outdoors, in the sensations of the wind in your hair and the changing temperatures on your face and body; and in how things feel as they make contact with your skin during your routine activities.

When you are being touched by others, be aware of how their touch affects you. What different temperatures, pressures, textures, and vibrations can you sense in the area of your body that is in contact with any part of their body? What feels good or doesn't feel good?

2. Active Touch Awareness. Take a few cleansing breaths and run your hand along the surface contours around you; feel the changes in temperature and texture, using your palm and fingertips, your wrist, and the back of your hand. Feel the difference in sensation between running your fingertips up and down and running them from side to side. See how easily you can detect the different shapes of things through your hands and fingers with your eyes closed. Now feel your face and throat, as well as your hands and arms, with palm, fingertips, wrist, and the back of your hand. What feels good about any of these sensations?

In your daily life, feel more consciously what you touch. Become more aware of the sensations on your hands and fingertips as you handle things during the course of your day. Be particularly aware of what feels good to the touch.

When you come in contact with others during the day, really touch them. When you shake hands with someone, feel the temperature, texture, and vibration of their hand in yours. When you embrace someone, put your palms flat on their back and see if you can feel his or her life energy.

3. Inner Touch Awareness: Sensing, Gut Feelings, and Intuition. Think of a decision you have to make soon between two or more alternatives. Take a few breaths and get a vivid picture of you choosing one of the alternatives, play out some anticipated consequences, and feel your bodily reaction. Now try another alternative and what you anticipate from making that choice. See which choice physically feels better.

Check in with yourself at different times throughout your day. If something doesn't feel right but you can't quite place what it is, see if you can find it by homing in on your gut feelings. Are you getting signals from your heart or gut? Be receptive to whatever images pop up in your mind's eye. If you feel good, reflect on what feeling good actually feels like.

Get a sense of the people you make contact with during the day by tuning into your own insides and feeling how their presence affects you. How does this physical response add information about your true feelings toward this person?

4. Guided Imagery. Here's an exercise to develop the phantom touch sense. See how vivid a re-creation of sensuous touch you can call up through your imagination and feel it in your body.

Imagine that you're on a beach on a beautiful tropical island. The sun is warm on your body but not too hot, and the bright blue sky is dotted with cooling white clouds. The surf is gentle, and the waves are softly lapping the shore. You have found a quiet beach where you can be alone, and you sit down. Take a deep inhale of hot humid air that smells of salt and fish and admire the scene before you—the expanse of blue-green ocean and deep blue sky, the white clouds and cawing sea birds overhead, and the miles and miles of uneven coastline to either side of you, lined with palms and other exotic trees.

Now begin to focus in on touch sensation. Feel the warm, gritty sand on the backs of your thighs as you sit. Feel your face and body damp with sweat. Kick off your rubber sandals and plunge your feet into the sand. Feel the pebbly heat between your toes and imagine you are fluttering and scratching your toes pleasantly from side to side along the coarse grain.

A soft breeze suddenly stirs up. Feel the short hairs at your hairline blowing backward, tickling your ears and neck. Feel the air wiping across your fore-head and the upper edges of your eyebrows, passing over the crown of your head, and mussing your hair. Now the air around you is still again. You feel peaceful and content, happy to be alive.

5. Enhancing Sensuous Touch with a Partner. Sit comfortably facing one another and within easy reach of each other's face. Decide who will start as the receptive partner and who will begin as the active one. Take a few deep sighs and relax.

You are both going to keep your eyes closed and your attention focused on touch sensation. The active partner is going to take five minutes to gently stroke and feel the face of the receptive partner. The passive partner is going to keep his eyes closed and focused on the pleasures of being touched, being alert both to the sensations aroused by the touching and any emotional feelings.

When you are the active one, start at the top of the head, and with your eyes closed, feel the hair, forehead, brows and brow ridge, eyelids and lashes, nose, cheekbones, lips, chin, and jaw of your partner. Feel for what feels smooth or rough, warm or cool, and hard or soft. Vary your pressure from firm to barely touching where there are "peach fuzz" hairs. Vary the direction of your stroke from up and down, to horizontal, to little circles and bigger ones. Use your fingers, the heel of your hand, the back of your hand, your wrist, and even your forearm. Then switch roles. Talk about it only after you have each done both roles.

6. Sensing Energy Fields. The receptive partner lies down on the floor while you, as the active partner, sit near his waist. Have his head point toward your left side and his feet toward your right. Both of you take a few cleansing breaths and focus your attention on your inner sensations. As the active one, you are going to be passing both your hands three to six inches above his body, moving very slowly from his head to his feet. See if you can detect any areas of warmth or coolness, or faster or slower vibration. Keep your eyes closed so that you can be particularly discerning of your own sensations. Be aware of any visual imagery that may spontaneously appear in your mind or any other phantom sense that may be stimulated.

Now, if it's okay with your partner, softly place your hands on his body and see if, with actual touch—lightly scanning his face, chest, and diaphragm—you can sense places where his body feels stuck or energetic. Talk about your experiences. Then switch roles, taking a few cleansing breaths before you start again.

7. Take time to appreciate the beauty of art and nature. Nourish your aesthetic spirit. Go to a museum or a gallery. Listen to a symphony. Draw a picture. Watch a cat lick herself. Admire the changing colors of the sky at sunrise, then at dusk. Look for constellations on a starry night. Read a poem. Write a poem to a lover or friend and read it aloud to him or her.

Chapter 11

Sexual Pleasures: Complete Fulfillment

....

Turning up the heat

. . . .

. . . Eventually, her desire died in her from sheer exhaustion.
All the tautness left her body. She became as soft as cotton . . .
For first time, the hunger that had been on the surface of her
skin like an irritation, retreated into a deeper part of her
body. It retreated and accumulated, and it became
a core of fire that waited to be exploded . . .

—*Anaïs Nin*

I'm in a big comfortable bed with a beautiful man—the man I would eventually marry. We're in love and just beginning to live together. Sunshine is streaming through the slatted blinds, the French doors in front of us open on a small Spanish-style balcony with a view down the canyon of chaparral and trees. This sunny Sunday morning has a special quality of sweetness. We've made breakfast together—French toast, fruit, and coffee—and brought it back into bed with us. We've eaten side by side propped up on pillows and under the comforter, reading the Sunday papers and hearing great music.

Later, with our breakfast dishes cleared from the bed, we lay in each other's arms listening to Beethoven's Choral Symphony. At a particularly lyrical coda, my lover turns toward me with a soft smile, looks deeply into my eyes, and kisses me with a gentleness that rocks me to my core. I swoon. My entire body spasms in waves of pleasure that ripple through every part of me.

Yet, instead of surrendering and letting myself be swept away, I feel a jolt of fear. I sit up and gasp for breath. He watches with concern as I recover myself. Then, when I have myself in tow, I swiftly cover it over and pull him back down to me with a veiling giggle and a kiss. He apparently thinks nothing more of it, and we resume lovemaking. But for me that jolt led to a startling revelation. It showed me that—to that intensity of feeling—I was afraid to let go. And as much as I liked to think of myself as a sexually liberated woman, I was not as free as I thought.

It doesn't have to be as obvious as a clutch back from the brink of nirvana to show you that you're afraid to surrender to sex. Perhaps just as you're getting really turned on, you suddenly flash on something you don't like about him or her, and you can't quite let go of that negative thought. Or maybe it isn't your mind that snaps you out of it but your body—a leg cramp, a stomach ache, or a heart flutter that worries you. Or out of the blue, you suddenly feel ticklish, and wherever your lover touches you, you act skittish and silly.

It can be as seemingly insignificant as that and still be significant. Anything that distracts you from your sexual focus and pulls your attention elsewhere is a sign of the number one limitation in enjoying sexual pleasure: pleasure-anxiety in sex. Sexual pleasure-anxiety is very likely nearly universal in our culture because, to some extent, we've all been trained in childhood to fear our sexual urges.

Why We Resist Sexual Pleasure

Much as we'd like to think otherwise, we're not that far removed from the nineteenth-century Victorian era—a time particularly characterized by its austere view of sex. Victorians believed in a strict code of behavior that actually aimed at limiting sexual pleasure. Virtuous women were expected to derive little pleasure from sex, while men were regarded as having an inordinate appetite that had to be tamed. Men were advised by their doctors to satisfy their needs with their wives in as short a time as possible to avoid draining their nervous system and to spare the good woman any drawn out unpleasantness.

Our grandparents and great grandparents were likely to have been raised in a Victorian atmosphere, and they in turn had a strong impact on the sexual attitudes of the mothers and fathers who raised us. A single man in his late thirties once told me that when his father was a little boy his mother locked him in a closet for several hours after catching him masturbating. Tom felt that he could trace his own sexual hang-ups to that particular sexual trauma endured by his father. Every time a situation with a woman started to get sexual, Tom would get anxious and awkward, especially when he very much desired the woman. That's how powerfully these multigenerational patterns are locked into our bodies. Tom's father was punished and shamed as a child for sex and he, in turn, punished and shamed his son, making him sexually insecure.

Among the many concerns that people typically have about their sexuality—whether it's about a lack of sexual interest, performance fears, inability to have orgasms, or sexual addiction—almost all of it can be traced to pleasure-anxiety. It can be found in their inability to just be at any level, not just in sex. It shows up in their patterns of thought, which keep them stuck in their head or defended in their heart. But most specifically, pleasure-anxiety translates into a fundamental, largely unconscious, fear of being overwhelmed by sexual excitement.

Unfortunately, we all have some sexual inhibition by virtue of having been raised in a society where sex is considered "dirty." However, most of the time we may not be in touch with our pleasure barriers because, generally, we don't go anywhere near the intensity of pleasure that would test our limits. Instead, whenever there is any possibility of intense sexual arousal, we may automatically hold sexual feelings down with a physical reflex that grips the muscles of the torso and pelvis, holding in the ribs and shortening the breath. In effect, we allow ourselves only the degree of excitement we know we can tolerate.

When a situation does become very sexually exciting, however, pleasure-anxiety too can become more intense. As Tom started to observe in himself, it was when he was most turned on to a woman that he was also most mentally obsessed, physically stressed, and unable to act on his desire. He didn't trust himself to relax and give up control.

If you meet up with pleasure-anxiety at your own upper limits of excitement, it can feel like a panic attack—your heart beats wildly, you feel faint, and you think you're dying. When your entire body hits that level of excitement, letting go of control and being swept away is, short of real death, the ultimate surrender. In fact, in French, orgasm is sometimes referred to as *le petit mort*, the little death. For many of us raised to hold sexual feelings back, the more you feel yourself melt into someone's arms, the more it can bring up feelings of mortality and the fear of death.

We all have personal stories of how we learned to inhibit ourselves sexually. We may have been shamed as young children for any display of sexual interest or were punished when caught experimenting. Women and men molested as children are likely to feel some fear during sex and often have learned to cut themselves off from the sensations in their bodies and put their minds elsewhere. But early traumas or not, even for those of us who do enjoy sex, there are still plenty of ways we may inhibit ourselves sexually.

One major way people hold themselves back is to be performance-driven rather than experience-drawn. Both women and men can be more focused on how they appear to their partner than how good it feels to be with him or her. For example, you may feel tense because you don't like your body and feel embarrassed rather than excited at being seen nude, even by your own husband or wife. You may have set images about how sex is supposed to be and concerned that aspects of your sexual desires or fantasies may not be considered normal. You may tell yourself you won't be able to please your partner. In each case, you're focusing on the other person's experience rather than your own. Being more concerned about your sexual performance than your sexual experience is often an unconscious way to keep a lid on uncomfortably expansive sexual feelings.

Sexually Liberated and Still Not Free

Sheila was a tall, attractive, single woman in her early thirties who had achieved quite a bit of success as a stockbroker. Everything was going well for her, and she had just started to see a man to whom she felt very attracted, physically as well as emotionally. She yearned for this relationship with Eddie to work out, but when they started to be sexually active, Sheila felt very disappointed. Though she prided herself on being "a sexual woman" and enjoyed dressing in sexy lace teddies, frilly garter belts, and stockings, Sheila regretfully admitted that she didn't get very turned on with Eddie, and as usual, she couldn't have an orgasm.

When Sheila and I talked about her family background she revealed that her father had left her mother when she was only two. Though her mother dated occasionally, she never remarried and had very little good to say about men. Sheila knew that she had bought into her mother's distrust of men, and that, even though she claimed to like them, she still thought of men as insensitive brutes. Nevertheless, as shallow as she felt most men were, she still felt she had to prove herself worthy of them.

In one session, as I watched Sheila's mannerisms while she talked, her gestures seemed overly feminine, almost as though she was striking poses. She sat with her chest thrust forward and her back slightly arched, punctuating her words with shoulder gestures that reminded me of old Betty Boop cartoons. I asked her to pay attention to her body language, and, though she protested at first, she began to catch herself playing the vamp. She realized she had picked up this ultra-feminine way of acting from the movies, hardly ever seeing real men and women interact who genuinely cared about one another.

Sheila was aware that she rarely just relaxed with Eddie, feeling like she had to be "on" with him, to entertain him to keep him interested. So just as I had asked her to observe her poses in my office, I asked her to pay attention to how she kept herself on edge when she was around Eddie. I suggested that she pay particular attention to her breathing and to look for how she may be tensing her body while she and Eddie made love.

The next time I saw her, Sheila told me that she did, in fact, notice that she often posed during sex, held her breath, and kept her buttocks and thighs tight. She admitted that she also tended to hold in her stomach because she felt a bit heavier than she'd like to be. I suggested that she might also be afraid of letting go, and that holding her belly tight was part of a whole pattern of muscle control she had been unaware of that was keeping her from getting fully aroused sexually.

The more Sheila paid attention to her mannerisms, especially during sex, the more she saw how her self-conscious body language projected a tacit message that proclaimed, "I don't trust you enough to relax and enjoy myself with you. Looking good is more important to me than feeling good." As Sheila examined her programmed feelings toward men, she decided to risk being her "own true self with Eddie—whatever that is." When she did, she discovered that without all that body stiffness she was indeed the authentically sexy woman she always knew she could be.

Sexual Potential: When the Focus is on Experience

Like Sheila, most of us at one time or another have been concerned about our sexual performance, not just in terms of how our partner will judge us, but also for how we rate ourselves as a sexually adequate male or female. Men want to be able to have strong erections and to postpone their ejaculation so that they won't disappoint their partner. Women want to be sexually responsive and to enjoy orgasm, not just for their own pleasure, but often because it would please their partners.

Sex therapy, too, has emphasized performance in offering to help people achieve "sexual adequacy" and only recently have sexologists begun to move away from the narrow emphasis on defining and treating performance difficulties and moved into the vast world of human sexual potential. To Dr. David Schnarch, a leading figure in this new development in sexology, great sex is not, as it's usually defined, about having intense orgasms. Rather, it's about increasing the capacity for intimacy and eroticism within the context of a committed relationship.

Schnarch suggests that when people put up with sex that is not great but "good enough," they do so because they are unwilling to go through the personal development and growth within a relationship that can enable them to tolerate more intense sexual feeling. Just as children grow by mastering appropriate developmental tasks such as learning to walk or being able to play with others at certain stages of their young lives, the ability to enjoy deeply fulfilling sex with someone you love, to Schnarch, is one of the most important developmental tasks of adult life.

Wilhelm Reich, probably the original pioneer in the field of sexual potential, was concerned mostly with what he called "orgastic potency"—the capacity to surrender to the flow of biological energy without any inhibition. Reich observed that when sex partners allow their excitement to build gradually, energy flows from the genitals into all areas of the body and results in a melting kind of sensation, which he called "streamings." When these "oceanic" or wavelike streamings are allowed to flow through the entire body, not just in the pelvis, the capacity to surrender is complete and results in what he called "total orgasm," involuntary pleasurable spasms of the musculature that envelop the entire body. Reich emphasized the importance of strong orgasms to mental and physical well-being. But he also believed this kind of orgasm could happen only between people who loved each other and who could express genuine feelings to one another.

In fact, there's now evidence to suggest that the lack of loving sensations during sex can affect the health of the heart as well as prevent fulfilling sexual experience. In his investigations, Dr. Alexander Lowen has collected research showing that the inability to experience emotional satisfaction during sex can have a negative impact on the heart. In several studies on coronary patients, about 66 percent of men and women hospitalized for heart attacks admitted to being sexually dissatisfied in the weeks or months just prior to their attack compared to 24 percent in the control group.

While it is possible to reach a physical climax without feeling any emotional satisfaction, Lowen suggests that the inability to surrender emotionally during sex prevents the fullness of discharge in the coronary muscle that would release tensions in the heart. On the other hand, when the chest muscles and heart are relaxed, and love is felt as a genuine sensation, orgasm releases energy from both the heart and genitals at the same time. The result is an extraordinarily loving experience of fulfillment through sex.

Sex therapist and researcher, Dr. Jack Morin, takes a somewhat different approach to investigating sexual potential. Morin is one of the key figures today working at expanding the scope of modern sex therapy by investigating, not problem sex, but peak sexual experiences. Morin developed a survey questionnaire that enabled him to ask anonymous respondents to disclose intimate details of their most memorable sexual encounters and to say what they thought made these events so exciting.

When Morin analyzed the data, he found that the answers most often included several basic ingredients. Their peak sexual experiences were likely to be intensely physically arousing—they talked about how hot they got and how much desire they felt for their partners. Their experience often involved strong emotion—the lovemaking had some

special significance for them; often it was particularly loving or intimate, but sometimes there was an element of anger or fear present that
charged the air and turned up the intensity several notches.
It was very erotic—with some kind of sexy drama or adventure about
it or even a degree of risk that intensified their sexual longing. Frequently, they had explosive orgasms. And sometimes they said the
experience transcended ordinary reality—describing it as something
magical, mystical, spiritual, or as an altered state of consciousness.

Obviously, reaching your pleasure-potential in sex involves
becoming more expansive on many different levels. When you and
your partner are ready to be more experimental with one another,
however, you need to start by looking at a very key issue: how you
define sex.

The Penetration Imperative

Most of the time when we make love, it's not to bring a new life into
the world but to bring new life into ourselves. We're not looking to
make babies but to enjoy the physical replenishment and emotional
connectedness that good lovemaking nurtures. But the way we typically make love more closely supports the objectives of a procreative
rather than a re-creative sexuality.

When a couple starts to play sexually, there's a consistently held
belief that the activity should proceed toward penetration. Yet, nothing interferes more with enjoying the emotional and physical pleasures of re-creative sex than compulsive intercourse, what I think of as
the "penetration imperative."

For couples, the sex-equals-intercourse equation means that unless they're willing to go the whole nine yards they won't go an inch.
They won't be sexually playful unless they're available for intercourse
because they don't want to lead their partner on. But then, this attitude places a greater burden on them when they are available. At that
point, they have to build up their arousal from zero to whatever
heights they can reach in an encounter that may last, from initial kiss
to afterglow, all of ten to twenty minutes long.

All-or-none sex can't help but lead to sexual stagnation because doing the same old routine can be as exciting as watching grass grow. It reminds me of a story a young comedian told. He asked his father if he had been following the recent news on same-sex marriages. His father grimly responded, "I know all about it. Your mother and I have been having the same sex for years."

Many sexually vital singles also inhibit their sexual pleasure with all-or-none thinking. If they're not willing to go all the way, they may deny themselves the thrill of the turn-on, of kissing and holding someone they like but may not love. Or just the opposite, they may end up in premature intercourse when what they really wanted was affectionate human connection.

How much more spontaneous it can be when a couple is playful in sexually arousing ways without immediately moving into intercourse and orgasm. When energy is allowed to build over several days or even longer, they can reach a level of genuine intensity that makes intercourse infinitely more exciting. However, this does mean that they need to be willing to end a sexual encounter while still turned on, and for a lot of people, this won't be easy.

Why are we so afraid to stay turned on? Is it the Victorian in us that demands we get rid of the excitement once it's there? Or else what? . . . that we won't be able to think or work? . . . that we'll turn into a sex fiend? . . . that we'll grab a stranger off the street to have sex with?

On the contrary, sexual energy is the life force made manifest. It is the ultimate creative drive that inspires and animates us. Arousal is not something we have to shake. What we have to shake is old-concept sex.

Eroticism: The Pleasures of Highly Arousing Sex

It takes time to kindle a spark into a heat that sizzles through your entire body. It takes time to experience your love, to get into your anxious excitement, or to take advantage of the sensuous and erotic opportunities of the moment. Only when you carefully and thoroughly build your arousal to new heights can your orgasms become explosive, or are you likely to reach the quality of emotional and spiritual connection where you and your lover can experience an altered state of consciousness together.

To explore highly arousing sex and tap your full sexual potential, your focus has to be on getting hot and staying hot. The typical way of thinking about sex is that when you're hot you're hot, and when you're not you're not. What nonsense! Sexual excitement is not on a toggle switch, like a lamp that can either be turned on or off. There are gradations of excitement and you want to allow yourself the opportunity to experience that arousal grow every single step of the way.

Eroticism is any activity you engage in for the purpose of raising sexual excitement. Some situations are spontaneously erotic and you find yourself caught up in some scenario that very naturally electrifies your passions. It's different when you're in a committed relationship. Your willingness to engage in erotic activity often has to be very deliberate and done with the playful intention of stepping up your sexual wattage with your committed partner.

I call it "sex without sex" when the appeal of your sexual contact is eroticism and not intercourse. When you postpone intercourse and focus your attention on bringing your arousal up to the point where you and your partner passionately yearn for one another, you will find that your entire experience of your sexuality changes. It's a positive new way to think about the postponement of gratification: learning to savor the state of need.

This is a valuable attribute to have not just in sex but in all aspects of life. Abraham Maslow, in his studies of self-actualization, found that among the most fulfilled people there was a consistent ability to enjoy the state of need. They tackled issues with a curious mind and a determined spirit and didn't get frustrated when they didn't achieve immediate goals. As with the urge to create or to solve a mystery, having a challenge sets up pleasurable tensions, and a speedy resolution is not only unnecessary, it's not even desirable.

"Pleasurable wanting," when it comes to sex, involves the same kind of ability: purposely letting a need grow and relishing the craving. The higher the arousal, ultimately, the more intense the release—emotionally, physically, and spiritually.

The Sexual Excitement Continuum

Think of your sexual turn-on not so much as light versus darkness, but more as a vivid rainbow that grows increasingly more brilliant over time. A rainbow is a continuum of color, ranging from red, the longest wavelength in the visual spectrum of light, to violet, the shortest.

When we look at sexual excitement as a continuum of sexual experiences, we can identify five distinct phases of turn-on—interest, desire, lust, passion, and ecstasy. Each phase is as critical as the next, a whole realm to explore with a unique terrain of its own to be relished before entering into the next.

Concentrate on building interest, desire, and lust before you consider aiming for release. If you're single and you practice "sex without sex," it will allow you to have all of the excitement of hot sex in today's risky sexual climate without taking any chances with your health. If you're in a committed relationship, it enables you to build your excitement over time, engaging in a variety of sexual contacts daily, without being afraid to start something you can't finish.

Sexual energy goes through natural peaks and valleys. When enjoying sex play with a partner, the most intensely pleasurable experiences occur if you allow your excitement to ebb, let yourself relax, then find new avenues for erotic contact. On the other hand, if things become too intense, you may want to move back, take a few slow breaths, and recoup your energy before going on.

This procedure of moving away, breathing and relaxing into the excitement, and then coming back again for more is critical to expanding your potential for pleasure in sex. Giving yourself permission to stop and take a few breaths enables you to push past your pleasure limits by helping you to sustain your excitement while building to the next level.

Each phase of sexual excitement has its own potential for drama, humor, emotional meaningfulness, expressions of love, challenge, conquest and submission, and physical release. To maximize your sexual pleasure, you need to linger and fully savor the topography of each region along the full range of the continuum.

Interest: The Realm Of Seduction

You're in a situation where you're not particularly thinking about sex when something stirs you to take notice. Perhaps it's a lingering look or a passing touch from someone that perks you up and turns a non-sexual situation into one with a sudden sexual pizzazz. It could be your mate, an acquaintance, or a stranger who sets you off and makes you want to draw closer and continue a playful contact.

What you will do under the circumstances actually bears a remarkable consistency with how potential lovers all over the world send messages of availability and sexual interest. According to anthropologist Helen E. Fisher, we typically proceed along a series of stages that involve first, looking: getting the attention of the other through exaggerated body movements; then, talking: idle, essentially meaningless banter in soft, dulcet tones; then, "accidental" touching that becomes more deliberate and lingering. By the time we unwittingly begin to synchronize our body movements—moving toward and away from each other in perfect rhythm, our eyes locked, our faces close—some kind of erotic physical contact is almost inevitable.

If you're in a new relationship, this usually happens automatically. But don't leave this step out if you are in a long-term relationship. Committed couples are often not sexually playful unless they're available for intercourse—and then they may be overly acquiescent. Rather than flirt, act seductive, or woo their partners into bed, they'll agree to sex beforehand and then meet in the bedroom to play out a tacitly accepted formula. But without flirting, teasing, and seduction, a couple is missing out on something very basic to our human sexuality.

Some couples have told me they hardly ever allow their excitement to build beyond this phase of interest before they have sex. When that's the case, though, a couple ends up having intercourse at minimal levels of arousal, resulting in lovemaking that is uninspired and climaxes that are anticlimactic.

Desire: The Realm of the Senses

The sensuous pleasures play a key role in inflaming desire. You touch his arm, and his warm, silky skin makes your flesh tingle. She steps closer and her smell quickens your pulse. You like looking at his round buttocks or at her shapely hips. You savor the taste of his kisses or the softness of her tongue. Your heart beats stronger in your chest. You hold each other tightly, and the sound of his breath in your ear or of her tender moans makes your body flush with heat. You pulse with excitement. You have a hunger and thirst for this person—to be enveloped by his arms or to bury your face in her breasts.

If you decide to consciously fan your desire, focus even more on the erotic stimulation being offered to each of your five senses.

Erotic Viewing

Too often, couples make love keeping their eyes closed and act as though they're in a trance, missing out on all the stimulation possible through the eyes alone. But when couples do take the time to admire each other and make frequent eye contact, the eyes become vital sexual organs.

Our visual sense whets our sexual appetite through exhibitionistic and voyeuristic type of activities. In the 1994 University of Chicago sex survey, the largest and most scientifically rigorous study of its kind, "watching my partner undress" unexpectedly turned out to be America's second favorite sex act, second only to intercourse and even more favored by both men and women than giving or receiving oral sex.

Nudity is generally not as big a turn-on as being in various stages of partial undress. Rather than undress for sex, I often suggest that people dress for sex. Lovers can then tease each other by exposing parts of their body or undergarments slowly and deliberately, by dancing erotically, and by assuming sexually explicit postures for one another. Fetishistic garments, such as the traditional stiletto heels or rubber clothing or any object that a person has idiosyncratically invested with sexual value, may also be incorporated into sex play for visual effects.

Some couples enjoy the voyeuristic pleasures of watching sexually explicit videos together. Both men and women who enjoy pornography say that, not only is it a turn-on to watch sexually adventurous scenes of lovemaking, but when the material is respectful toward women and addresses female satisfaction, it can also be valuable sex education for adults, providing a kind of road map for uncharted territories of sexual pleasure.

Sexy Sounds

Hearing certain sounds during a sexual encounter—whether it's soft music, driving rhythms, or the raspy sighs and moans of your lover—can all add intensity to any sexual encounter. But no sound quite compares to hearing your lovers desire for you in their panting breath. It's the same for sexually explicit videos—the hottest soundtrack accompanying scenes of lovemaking is always heavy breathing.

Heavy breathing is a big turn-on in another major way. Just as taking deep sighs encourages letting go of tension and resistance, the heavy breath so natural to feelings of desire also encourages the kind of letting go that leads to total emotional and sexual surrender. Consciously practicing a few charging breaths can intensify excitement enormously and help spread the energy throughout the body. Breathing heavily clearly does double duty by arousing the breather as well as the listener.

Some people have also discovered that when they or their partner deliberately talk sexy it really stirs their juices. It makes sense that this would be the case. Most of us were punished as children for using naughty language. Now, as adults, talking "dirty" may be linked for us with asserting our sexual potency. Some women report that a man whispering in her ear all of the deliciously nefarious things he is going to do to her can spur her into a frenzy. Women can likewise incite a powerful desire in their lovers by softly and imaginatively describing some sexual activity or fantasy directly into his ear.

Erotic Tasting

The mouth, of course, is one of our most erotic organs, not only in the taste of the lover's kisses, but in all the sucking, licking, and gentle biting that is usually a part of skilled lovemaking. The tongue—soft, moist, and warm—is a natural sexual stimulant. It has the power to arouse desire by making contact with almost every part of the body and is especially arousing on those parts of the body that are hairless. In one study, a high frequency of kissing was found to be a good barometer of sexual satisfaction and happiness in marriage.

Oral sex, sometimes called the genital kiss, is one of the most favored sexual activities. In the University of Chicago study, 68 percent of women in the age eighteen to forty-four group found it anywhere from somewhat to very appealing to receive oral sex, while 57 percent enjoyed giving it. Among males in the same age group, 83 percent enjoyed receiving, and 76 percent said they enjoyed giving, oral sex. The numbers who say they enjoy either act drops among older men and women, but almost one-third of older women and more than half of older men still say they enjoy giving oral sex to their partners—and, as you might imagine, substantially more say they enjoy being the recipient.

Erotic Smell

Couples may find that lighting incense or fragrant candles may stimulate their arousal. Pleasant aromas make us breathe more deeply, and anything that increases the likelihood of deep breathing during sexual contact will enhance arousal. For the same reason, dabbing a little subtle fragrance on one's neck or wrists can also encourage a partner to take deep breaths.

Some men and women report that they can actually smell their partner growing more and more aroused and that the sexual scent exuded by their partner excites them. They won't be aware of it, but their physical closeness also allows them to deeply inhale their partner's pheromones, turning them on even more.

Erotic Touching

For the imaginative lover, there are many different ways to touch, but if you don't vary the pressure and rhythms of your touch, your partner will adapt to your efforts and grow numb. There's the light feathery stroke known as *effleurage* where you just barely let your fingers skim the surface of your lover's skin. A firmer touch may involve gently squeezing or kneading a partner's flesh, especially on their arms, chest, or back.

For many people, sexual resistance results in tight buttocks, and tremendous sexual excitement can be evoked just by getting their buttocks squeezed. Gentle spanking can be a big turn-on for the same reason, and a couple may find that experimenting with light spanking can be a particularly effective way to encourage letting go of tension in the pelvic area.

Frotting—or rubbing against each other with your clothes on—can be one of the most exciting, though often neglected, erotic activities. Some of the hottest sex many of us can remember are those long make-out sessions when, as teenage virgins, we "dry-humped" to orgasm. We can still get a great deal of pleasure rubbing through various layers of clothing, particularly when the garments are silky and slide easily, and no buttons or zippers are present to interfere with the smoothness of the movements. Some of the best frotting occurs while slow dancing in each other's arms, when one partner is leaning against a wall, or to recapture earlier times, in the backseat of an automobile.

The Erotic Imagination:
The Phantom Sense Adds to Sex

Sexual fantasy entails using mental images to arouse yourself, and the ability to conjure up your own personal porn in your mind's eye is certainly a valuable skill to have. Research has consistently shown that it's not sexually frustrated people who fantasize the most but rather those who have the most satisfying sex lives and enjoy keeping themselves sexually stimulated. In fact, studies on women who have orgasms easily suggest that it may even be the tendency to fantasize about sex that enable these women to be so highly orgasmic.

Most people have their favorite fantasies, which can typically be relied upon to turn up the amps in any sexual activity. What we can do, however, is add a sensuous new component to the old tapes and see if we can get them to work for us even better. During masturbation, for example, you can picture your favorite fantasies and dress them up a little more in sexually provocative clothes and partial states of undress. You can turn up the mental soundtrack and hear more moans and sighs in your mind's ear, or vividly imagine the taste of someone's kisses and the flavor of different areas of their body, or sharpen your sense memory of their smell and their feel. If your fantasy image is a complete figment of your imagination, you can make up the sense memories and bestow on him or her a taste, smell, and feel in the same inventive way you've constructed how he or she looks.

During lovemaking with a partner, some lovers have learned to use their phantom taste sense to inspire their oral skills. They may imagine, for example, that their lover's neck is slathered in honey, or that his or her fingers have been dipped in chocolate, or the toes in peanut butter. Then they can relish their partner's body with an even greater sense of gusto and oral enthusiasm.

The mind is always activated by sexual arousal and can be a big part of the turn-on. Invoking the phantom sense is a much better use of the imagination than talking negatively to yourself and finding yourself lacking, or picturing yourself looking unattractive, or watching yourself from some imagined perch up above and rating your performance in bed. If you tend toward obsessive imagery during sex that takes you away from your partner, you might see if you can enjoy greater closeness with your partner by creatively making up and describing positive imagery to him or her.

Lust: The Realm of Longing

Lust has a bad reputation. While a lust for life is usually deemed an attribute, not so with sexual lust. According to the dictionary, sexual lust is typically defined as a craving that is excessive, unrestrained, or obsessive.

But what's excessive for one person may be just right for another. In fact, when a married couple complains of low sexual interest or lack of desire, when they spell it out, lust is usually what they're looking for. They want to crave sex with their partner.

Lust is a very special form of excitement that insecure or impatient lovers rarely get to savor. To build lust you must be ruthlessly honest with yourself to courageously explore your own idiosyncratic sexuality—the fantasies, scenarios, curious predilections, fetishes, and forbidden fruit that intensify your longing for the object of your desire.

Your willingness to do so is a big step toward honoring your true sexual nature. It involves having the courage to push the edges of your sexuality and to experiment with delving deeper into your own very personal arousal-imprints. What images, settings, circumstances, or mind-sets provide the most powerful erotic stimulants? What commands your most intense longings, your almost overwhelming yearnings for sexual contact? What sexually electrifies you so totally that the full force of it makes you abandon any guise of control?

Lust, by definition, is immoderate. When lust is nurtured to the utmost, to the point where the thrills of sexual urgency conquer all inhibition, the result is unbridled and unbounded sexual pleasure.

When Inhibition Can Sweeten Temptation

The verb *to tempt* comes from a Latin word meaning "to test the strength of" or "to stretch." When there are no obstacles to overcome on the path toward consummation of sexual desire, the strength of the sexual urge never gets tested and, as a result, is never stretched to its limit. The great paradox of lust is that when you maintain your erotic yearnings, while at the same time you struggle to resist them, the anticipation and longing for sex makes for arousal that is the most intense of all.

As a result, having to overcome social or psychological obstacles to achieve sexual goals can add enormously to lust. Based on his research into peak sex, Morin has shown that sexual arousal is, in fact, at its most intense when there is a tension between the attraction pulling us toward a partner and one or more barriers standing in the way. These barriers may involve having to overcome the lack of interest on the part of someone you desire greatly, violating a childhood prohibition or moral precept, or feeling torn or ambivalent about getting involved with a person who for one reason or another is sexually off-limits. Especially if you have to work at it for a while to overcome the barriers between you, when you do have sex, Morin says, it will have a knock-your-socks-off intensity that's hard to beat.

All varieties of lustful eroticism contain at one and the same time strongly opposing forces of intense attraction pulling the lovers together and the necessity for restraint, caution, and even defiance keeping them apart. Three of the scenarios that are most likely to drive us wild with lust usually involve some aspect of forbiddenness, sweet pain, and overcoming some challenge. Couples who enjoy incorporating erotic role play into their lovemaking often include one or more of these scenarios.

Forbidden Sex

In this case, the major element arousing intense excitement is the knowledge that any contact would violate some moral precept or personal pledge. What makes this kind of sex so hot is that it is, at the very least, a little naughty and, at its best, downright "bad." If you struggle with yourself to resist the temptation, the inner turmoil can take on the properties of an aphrodisiac. Nothing creates a more ferocious sexual need than fighting your desire until sheer lust eventually overwhelms your will to resist.

Violating a taboo is an important part of the appeal when a married person engages in infidelity, especially when sex in the marriage has grown stale and predictable. Sex with someone else may enable you to avoid confrontation, but, if all the eroticism gets played out with someone else, sex with that person, of course, can end up short-changing the sexual potential with your committed partner.

Some people, however, suggest that having an occasional fling on the side has actually contributed to their happy marriage. A seventy-six-year-old man with a gravelly Midwest accent once called me on a radio talk show to tell me that he and his wife had been happily married for more than fifty years and were more in love today than the day they were wed. But he didn't think that would be true if he hadn't periodically had sex with other women when he met someone he "fancied." Did his wife know? I asked him over the airwaves. "Hell, no!" he shouted in his high-pitched twang, "What would be the point of that?"

Several successful career women have also confided in me that a secret romance with a professional colleague, whether or not it resulted in intercourse, intensified their desire and lust with their own husband. One married woman related an experience where the sexual attraction between her and a coworker built up to the point where eventually, they began to kiss passionately and would break away from one another trembling. But she didn't want to betray her husband and decided not to have a full-blown affair. When her husband suddenly became the recipient of her lust, he felt very, very happy. At one point, he told his wife rather sternly, "I don't know what you're doing that's getting you so hot, and frankly, I don't care to know." Then with a grin he added, "Just keep it up."

The association of breaking a taboo with intensification of desire and lust is unavoidable in our society as long as childhood sexuality is prohibited. When hiding and defying authority or humiliation and discipline are paired with intense sexual arousal as it often is in children's sexual exploration in our culture, these qualities become part of the building blocks of our sexual development. Forbidden fruit tastes the sweetest because that's what we cut our teeth on. As long as our society continues to punish childhood sexuality and drive it underground, breaking taboos will continue to inspire some of the most intensely exciting sex.

Sweet Pain: When Anguish is an Aphrodisiac

Sometimes a complex linkage exists between shame and sexual arousal, and two people can become intensely excited playing out sexual scenarios that involve power games of dominance and submission. Naturally, there can be real danger in this kind of behavior if you make yourself a target for abusive behavior.

On the other hand, it is possible for people to gratify their taste for painful scenarios in playful, nonabusive ways with consenting partners. Prominent sexologist Dr. John Money, professor of medical psychology at Johns Hopkins University School of Medicine, has suggested that people who are disposed toward pain rituals can remain permanently anchored to the playful side of the fantasy. When they hook up with partners who enjoy playing out the complimentary role, they can stage their fantasies as erotic theater. Ritualized pain as mutually agreed upon theater can be a genuine source of heightened sexual arousal.

Some men and women have found that while they don't want to engage in some of the more ritualized sadomasochistic activities, still, they do sometimes enjoy a more vigorous manner—a hand's firm grasp, being squeezed and crushed in someone's strong arms, or feeling the weight of their lover pressing them into the floor, the wall, or the bed. Some people like hard kisses. Others enjoy when their behinds are slapped just hard enough to quicken the heart and make their tight butts relax, without causing more sting than they can handle.

Novelty and Challenge

There can be no doubt that sexual activity that becomes too familiar and repetitious loses its ability to arouse. Some situations can always be counted on to produce novelty, adventure, and challenge. Sex educator Carol Cassell has pointed out that sex with a complete stranger that won't lead to any long-term commitment—"no-strings sex"—may be highly erotic for some people because it is only when there is no emotional entanglement that they can allow themselves to focus on and revel in their own pleasure.

When people need unfamiliar partners to stay interested in sex, however, eventually the compulsive search for novelty can itself become stale. On the other hand, it's possible to create sexual adventure in a committed relationship by taking more personal risks with your own partner. How experimental do you allow yourself to be with regard to being sexually playful? How open are you about your most secret desires and titillations? How willing are you to explore your own idiosyncratic erotic tastes?

If you are willing to explore your erotic nature and can entice your partner to explore with you, then a long-time intimacy can offer some of the most sexually adventurous opportunities of all. It takes imagination and courage to break through what may be the inhibitions of a lifetime in order to playfully build interest into desire into real lust in a long-term relationship. But the sexual rewards when a couple does break through their inhibitions may be far greater than either partner could have ever dreamed. Highly arousing sex with one's committed partner forges a deep emotional bond of love—not just because the two of them share something together that's wonderful, but also because they're usually so very grateful to one another for making it happen.

Passion: The Realm of Total Abandon

As lust moves the lovers into passion, sexual activity becomes even more energized. Whereas lust can frequently be mental and even verbal, in passion it seems as though all thought ceases and the body is shot full of electricity. There is no holding back, no boundaries to hold on to. The only thing possible to do is to completely and utterly surrender to the flood of excitement overpowering the mind and the senses. Intercourse is the natural next step.

Yet when intercourse becomes a frenzy of thrusting activity geared toward achieving orgasm, naturally it won't last very long. Even in the heat of passion, you can keep sexual arousal building by slowing down and exercising discipline and skill.

Penetration also doesn't have to be thought of in traditional terms of a penis inside of a vagina. Like gay and lesbian couples, heterosexual lovers can enjoy penetration in a variety of ways, including using fingers and dildoes.

When a man and woman make love, and it's the man who usually controls and choreographs the sex, it's logical he's going to be the one to enjoy it more. Unless she offers useful feedback, his movements can be informed only by what feels good to him.

On the other hand, if he's the type of man who is unwilling to stop the car and ask for directions when he's lost, he may also have a hard time taking direction during sex. And if she isn't that familiar with her own body, sexually, she may not know how to lead him, even if he is open to her requests. She may also voice her needs critically, sabotaging her potential for sexual satisfaction with him.

Because of any or all of these reasons, women often end up following the path of least resistance, which is to play the "responsive female" role during sex, signaling their involvement by being vocally appreciative and making complementary pelvic movements. But sometimes in their supportive role, women don't necessarily make the movements that are most exciting for them.

What works best, and makes for hotter sex, is for lovers to alternate "running the sex." That way each can take turns leading as well as surrendering, finding rhythms that please them, and seeing if these movements will also feel good to the partner. While men who are insecure about their masculinity may be uncomfortable giving up the lead and assuming the more submissive role, a man may also become highly impassioned by witnessing a woman so thoroughly enjoying his body.

Some women, too, don't like leading because their narrow sex drive is relegated to laying back and being done to. However, being on your back with your legs up—in what I call "the dead cockroach position"—usually affords a woman very little direct stimulation in the places likely to do her the most good.

Orgasms and Intercourse for Women

In some ways, it's a strange turn of events that many women don't have orgasms as easily as men. After all, only the female of our species has a clitoris, the sole organ in the human body whose only known function is to give pleasure.

Women's lesser likelihood of consistently enjoying strong orgasms can be related to several important factors. For one, simply on a biological level, women have a more complex system of blood vessels in the pelvic area than men do, which need to become fully engorged to trigger the orgasmic reflex. For another, women also often require more emotional connection during sex than do men—sexy conversation or romance that embeds the sexual activity in a relational context—and standard sex more often resembles a trance where people move around with their eyes closed, relating very little to one another in a spontaneous interaction.

Another often overlooked factor is that, typically, women who don't have orgasms also don't masturbate. One of the most success-ful treatments in sex therapy, developed by therapist and researcher Dr. Lonnie Barbach, has been to teach women who have never had an orgasm to become orgasmic through learning how to masturbate.

I think a large part of women's greater difficulty to orgasm is the real lack of awareness about what gives a woman sexual pleasure, even among women themselves. Most women, after all, learn how to be sexual from men. Men are supposed to be the sex experts in our culture. But we have inherited a sexuality that, for hundreds of years, favors the man's pleasure, his orgasm, and not coincidentally, baby-making sex.

Until recently, there was very little sexual information about what pleases women that came directly from women who enjoy them-selves sexually. This is now changing, and several valuable studies on contemporary female sexuality have been very illuminating.

In one study on easily orgasmic women (women who were able to achieve orgasm in at least 75 percent of their sexual contacts with many of them multiply orgasmic in an average encounter), husband and wife investigators, Marc and Judith Meshorer, found that most of these women prepared themselves in advance when they anticipated an afternoon or evening of lovemaking. They had a kind of "toilette" or personal ritual that enabled them to relax and focus in on their bodies.

They might take a bath and think pleasant thoughts about their partner's body and have arousing fantasies about them. Often they touched themselves sensuously while smoothing oil or lotion on themselves. Not uncommonly, they masturbated, sometimes to orgasm. They deliberately dressed in sensuous fabrics and sexually alluring lingerie or outfits, not only for their partner's appreciation but to sensually arouse themselves. In other words, by the time the woman got together with her lover, she was already "starting on warm."

Sex researcher Shere Hite, in a survey of more than 3,000 women, has also shown that there appear to be some definite differences between what brings a woman to orgasm as opposed to what works best for men. Only 30 percent of women in her sample could regularly orgasm through intercourse alone. Most orgasmed through oral or manual stimulation of the clitoris either before or after intercourse. But of the few who did have orgasms during intercourse, most were able to do so primarily by being the more active one while the man became passive to her movements. Being on top of the man, instead of pinned down by his weight, the women said, gave her greater freedom to move in ways that were more likely to result in her own satisfaction.

Many of the orgasmic women also reported that the rapid thrusting movements that result in a man's orgasm often didn't work for them. The kind of thrusting many of these women preferred was smooth, continuous, and unhurried. What was particularly effective in bringing a number of women to orgasm was deep penetration with slow grinding movements.

In her studies of sexually satisfied women, sex researcher and therapist Dr. Gina Ogden has found that for these women, emotional intimacy was a crucial factor in enjoying their greatest lust and passion. Under such circumstances, many of these women were able to experience orgasm from being touched in places other than their genitals—like fingers, toes, or earlobes—and an astonishing 64 percent said they could have a spontaneous orgasm through fantasy, without any touch at all.

Evolving the Orgasm for Both Sexes

Experimental studies have shown that there are actually many different routes to orgasm. For women there are clitoral orgasms and vaginal orgasms—what are sometimes referred to "G spot" orgasms. For men there can be orgasms with or without ejaculation and orgasms that result from stimulating the penis or from stimulating the prostate. For each sex, there can be blended orgasms where both areas are stimulated at once; sequential orgasms where another, often weaker, orgasm occurs soon after the first; or multiple orgasms where each subsequent orgasm is more intense than the last.

While multiple orgasms have been seen to be largely a female skill, researchers Drs. William Hartman and Marilyn Fithian have discovered that some men can learn to be multiorgasmic by developing the ability to withhold their ejaculation during orgasm. This husband and wife team has trained men to masturbate in such a way that they can learn to anticipate and to stop sexual activity just prior to "the point of inevitability," when ejaculation is imminent and uncontrollable. Building and containing excitement in this way has been shown to enhance the possibility of multiple orgasms for men.

For women, the possibility for multiple orgasms is even greater. Dr. Mary Jane Sherfy, a psychiatrist who did one of the earliest scientific research projects on female sexuality, provided a host of material from physiological, anthropological, and primate studies to support her contention that with continuous stimulation most women are capable of having one orgasm after another literally until she and her partner drop. Sherfy asserts that when a woman is aroused to her maximum, an orgasm can actually increase, rather than decrease, the flow of blood into the pelvis and trigger another orgasm. Under optimal circumstances, a woman may not feel completely satiated until she is physically exhausted.

Solitary Sex

Artist and writer Betty Dodson is one of the pioneers in the field teaching women and men to celebrate their sexuality through masturbation, used as a meditation on self-love. With skillful masturbation, men can learn to slow down and enjoy their excitement, while practicing to withhold ejaculation. Women can practice different ways of touching themselves, stimulating both the clitoris and vagina at the same time. They can each pass their discoveries on to their partner, helping them to develop greater skills for giving added enjoyment.

Contrary to popular opinion, all research studies show that people who say they masturbate because they have no sex partner actually masturbate the least. People who masturbate the most are often those who are also most likely to be satisfied with their sex partners and their love lives.

Ecstasy: The Realm of Transcendence

Typically, when the man ejaculates, the sex is over for both partners. When both partners are multiorgasmic, having a single orgasm does not necessarily end the sex but can take them into a new realm of pleasure—into ecstasy. But it isn't only the intensity of the orgasm that can take a couple into an experience of sex that is like an altered state of consciousness. One of the most critical issues is knowing the difference between tension-reduction and ecstatic sex.

Tension-reduction sex is where having an orgasm is an important way to relieve not just sexual need, but more often than not, generalized stress accumulated during a tense day. For some people, tension-reduction sex is a way to get a good night's sleep without taking a sleeping pill.

Ecstatic sex is more like a death-rebirth-into-a-higher-plane experience than a one-bright-moment-then-total-wipeout kind of thing. This is the kind of sexual experience most likely when a couple practices sex without sex. In ecstatic sex, pleasure is not just the release of pressure but also something powerfully expansive—physiologically, emotionally, and spiritually.

Margo Anand, a writer and Tantric practitioner, has pointed out that the key to ecstatic sex is the ability to stay relaxed and aware in high states of sexual arousal. In ordinary sex, she says, relaxation often occurs only after orgasm. But in ecstatic sex, you relax into the excitement, letting it spread throughout the body and sustaining the experience for a longer than usual period of time. Clearly the formula for greater overall vitality—learning to relax as you become more stimulated—also works for sexual vitality.

When the sex is especially good and there's a genuine emotional communication between lovers, they are likely to reach a level of intensity where their heart and their genitals reach orgasm together. If you've ever had this experience, you know that the sensation is extraordinary. You feel like you're melting into your lover. Feelings of love and gratitude are palpable as emanations from the heart, and exquisite spasms of pleasure surge through your body in waves.

This is the best kind of simultaneous orgasm. Not where two people have genital orgasms together but where, for each of them, their own heart and genitals fire together. Usually, however, both people do have the experience together because they are so joined energetically, one bioelectric current shoots through them both. I think of this as the heart-gasm. It happens only when sex is an expression of love.

Spiritual Sex

Ecstatic sex can generate such intense arousal that the lovers lose any sense of a separate self; joining in a profound spiritual and mystical union with one another. The abandonment may be so complete that it feels like a merging not only with one's partner but with "all things"—a direct experience of the eternal.

Sometimes, lovers can feel as though they've soared to the center of the universe and back. They may describe it as seeing all the colors of the rainbow or hearing the music of the spheres, and of having such a deep sense of love for their partner that they felt like their bodies were interchangeable. Afterward, some say they were awestruck and cried tears of joy.

The experience can bear a remarkable similarity to mystical experiences resulting from other kinds of spiritual practices. In Zen, it's called *satori*; in Buddhism it's called enlightenment; in Tantra it's called ecstasy or cosmic union. It's also been called bliss, liberation, *samahdi*, the awakening, transcendence of space and time, and oneness with all things. Georg Feuerstein, a yoga scholar, who has researched the connection between profound spiritual experience and sexuality, has found this phenomenon in ordinary people's accounts of blissful, mystical experiences through sex, some of which resulted in an altered state of consciousness that lasted for several weeks. Many of the people who report such an experience during sex are often those who have spent some time in meditation, who have practiced quieting their mind in order to gain that very quality of emptiness, nonself, nonduality, and oneness.

But even among people who have had the experience, it's not something that happens very often. Some who have had it, see it as a once-in-a-lifetime event, a youthful time of highly charged sexual energy, and a fluke of history. For others, it may be something to aspire to and a hope that someday it can happen again.

Getting Better As We Get Older

There is no reason to assume that our ability to enjoy sexual pleasure necessarily diminishes with age. Research suggests that people who stay sexually active can continue to enjoy their sexuality for the rest of their lives. In one 1992 survey, 37 percent of married people older than sixty said they made love once a week, while 16 percent made love more frequently. In another study, two-thirds of unmarried people older than seventy said they were sexually active, defined by either partnered or solitary sex.

The overwhelming evidence shows that the majority of men and women older than fifty are sexually active, and many of them say that their sex lives are more loving and rewarding than ever. For many sexually motivated unmarried seniors, their biggest sex problem— other than finding suitable partners, which can be a challenge at any age—was that they felt they had to be secretive about it with their friends and particularly with their grown children who were most likely to disapprove.

Based on his studies, sexologist Schnarch suggests that few people even approach the heights of enjoyment of their sexual relationship until they reach their fifties or sixties. It makes a lot of sense when you consider that, for most people, the most profound sexual experience is also their most emotionally authentic one. Schnarch has found that couples in long-term marriages have the greatest probability of reaching their sexual potential because they have the highest capacity for the quality of intimacy that makes for great sex.

Not only do healthy older people have more and better sex than previously imagined, but good sex also has a very beneficial effect on overall health. A satisfying sex life can boost the immune system, decrease tension, strengthen the heart, diminish arthritis, and relieve migraines, insomnia, and aches and pains of all kinds. Moreover, according to a survey of more than 38,000 people conducted by San Francisco's Institute for the Advanced Study of Human Sexuality, being sexually active is good for mental health as well. People with fulfilling sex lives are found to be less anxious and hostile, and they are less likely to blame their difficulties on others.

Apparently, good sex is good medicine at any age, and passionate love can exist between lovers who keep their youthful vitality all through their years.

Personal Experiments in the Sexual Excitement Continuum

. . . .

These experiments are geared toward being in touch with the experience of sexual arousal moment-by-moment. They are meant to be present-centered—focusing your attention on the sensations in your body, your enhancing or intrusive thoughts, the variety and quality of connections you make with your partner, and the pleasure you derive from it all.

It's essential that you remember to use your breath to support you. Take cleansing breaths to relax and focus. Take deep sighs to feel your feelings more keenly. Take several quick charging breaths to intensify your sensation and to encourage surrender.

The experiments are appropriate for singles, new couples, long-term couples, gay and straight couples, for men and for women. They can help you see more clearly what evokes your sexual self and how you may be able to entice the sexual self of your partner.

Most importantly, don't be relentless. Remember, to build your excitement slowly and steadily—approach, back off, and let the other draw you back. That's when sex is a genuine energy exchange and not just one person imposing his or her sexuality on another. Practice sex without sex by exploring the exercises in interest, desire, and lust before moving on to passion and the potential for ecstasy.

Interest: The Art of Flirting, Teasing, Seducing, and Wooing

A couple of caveats: If you're single, be sure you're being appropriate and won't be charged with harassment if you demonstrate your sexual attraction to someone. Give respectful signals and wait for distinct signals back that invite you to proceed. For committed lovers, make sure you have a clear understanding that starting a flirtation doesn't mean that the countdown has begun to full frontal nudity; it's just an opportunity to play "no-strings sex" for lively lovers. Remember: A kiss is just a kiss—not a contract.

1. Practice projecting your interest nonverbally. Nothing is a bigger turn-on than being able to see that someone finds you attractive. If you find someone attractive, make eye contact. Let him or her see your appreciation in your eyes, in your smile, and in your body language.

2. Articulate your attraction, softly with feeling. Take some deep breaths and feel your excitement. Focus on what attracts you to this person. Is it in the way she smiles, the way he stands, or in his or her animation and easy laugh? Move closer and in a quiet voice describe what draws you to him or her and how that makes you feel.

3. Move away and see if you're invited back. The key is to make contact, then withdraw, and reconnect only if you're welcome.

4. For long-term lovers, practice love bytes. Every so often, when you are together, make a point of appreciating your lover's attractive qualities. Make eye contact. Let your eyes linger and see if you can contact genuine sensations of love and appreciation in your chest and heart. Let your face relax and be a reflection of your warmth.

Desire: Explorations in Erotic Sensuality

When you and your partner are ready to move into the next phase, get closer. Hold your partner, feel your arousal spreading through your body, and let your senses become erotically attuned.

1. Breathe and relax. As your sensual exploration of one another grows more intimate, you'll want to be able to stay open to the increasingly intense sensations of arousal. Feel where in your body you can sense the warm, tingly glow of desire. Keep letting go of tension so that excitement can build. See if you can shuttle back and forth in your concentration between the sensations in your body and your sense awareness and appreciation of your partner. If your partner is holding his breath, you can encourage him to breathe more deeply by gently massaging his chest, shoulders, and arms. Make sure your own deep breaths are audible.

2. Stimulate your erotic eye. Dress for sex, dance for each other, touch yourself sensually while your partner watches, and wear sexy garments. Admire each other slowly. Make frequent eye contact.

3. Be ear now! Talk sexy; listen for sounds of arousal; make sounds of appreciation. Talk "dirty" if your partner likes it. Describe softly and directly into her ear what about her turns you on. Play evocative music.

4. Taste your lover's kisses and the sweetness of his or her body. Nibble, suck, lick, and gently bite him or her all over, especially on those areas of the body that rarely get any attention like the back of the forearm or the knees. Be imaginative in how you practice oral sex, slowly tracing the contours of his body with your tongue. Use your phantom senses to inspire your orality, imagining her body is dripping in a delectable jam. A deft tongue can feather, flick, lick, lap, and artfully paint sensuous masterpieces with long, sweeping brush strokes.

5. Nuzzle and sniff each other. Run your nose along his skin at different parts of his body and drink in his sexual aromas and potent pheromones. Wear only light fragrances; burn scented candles.

6. Touch consciously and imaginatively. Caress, fondle, stroke, and embrace while breathing into your touch. See if you can feel your partner's responsiveness energetically, through your hand, and communicate your conscious presence through your fingers and palms. Knead tense muscles. Vary the pressure and rhythms of your contact. Move from a firm grip to a feathery effleurage. Use your fingertips, the back of your hand, your wrists, forearms, cheek or chest, or your hair and move along all different parts of your lover's body. Silky clothing, scarves, flowers, feathers, and fur remnants can also be swept ever so lightly across the skin so that only the hairy fuzz on the surface of the skin stirs. Explore the pleasures of frottage—rubbing against one another to arouse excitement.

Lust: Experiments in Eroticism

Here are some opportunities to be lustfully immoderate with your partner and to create "improvisational erotic theater" together.

1. Set the scene. Just like any good improvisational theater, you need some good themes, stimulating characters with real chemistry to interact on those themes, the proper staging and lighting, and an appreciative audience who, in this case, is usually just the actors themselves. If you can agree to do this together, be sure you trust each other and that you are respectful of each other's limits. You want to agree to stop the game whenever one person gives a clear message of wanting to end it—perhaps even a code word that signals, "This is for real. I really do want to stop now."

2. Share a sexual fantasy. Collaborate with your partner on an erotic fantasy you can act out together—for example, the two of you are teenagers fooling around at one of your homes while your parents are out. Describe it in a sexually arousing way. How can each of you add to the fantasy? Can you remember what it was like to be a nervous, excruciatingly desirous teenager? Can you find the body memory of that trembling and longing along with the fear of getting caught? Breathe into that feeling.

3. Role play your part. Once you agree to a theme, you can start to play it out like children playing house. You need to adopt an erotic persona—like, "a sex-starved teenager"—which is the specific sexual self you would be tapping. You may want to wear something that fits this erotic persona, to create or find the right setting, and to let the scene play out like an "improv" neither one of you can fully control.

4. Notice what makes you most lustful. See what quickens your breath, makes your heart pound, clutches your gut, gnaws at your belly, and tweaks your genitals. Those are the places to embellish. Let your breath be your guide and your support.

Passion: Studies in Total Abandon

To get the most out of your experience of intercourse and orgasm, practice a range of activities to intensify your excitement.

1. Experiment with solitary sex. Practice making sex an opportunity to give yourself self-love. Make it special. Create a pleasing environment for yourself as though you were preparing to enjoy an imaginative lover. You are. Conjure up vivid fantasies and take the time to stimulate yourself with your hands, a vibrator, and/or a dildo.

Take deep sighing breaths, let your belly grow round and full with each inhale, and see if you can feel your breath moving into your lower abdomen, genitals, and buttocks. Use massage oil and discover new ways of touching yourself. Practice changing positions to become less habitual about your pleasure.

Women can practice using both hands, stimulating the clitoris and the inside of the vagina at the same time. Men can practice bringing themselves to the point just before inevitability, then stopping and regaining control by breathing into the excitement, exercising a more relaxed and better choice over when to ejaculate.

2. Practice the Kegel exercises. Both men and women can strengthen the pubococcygeous muscles—the muscles in the genitals you clench to stop the flow of urine midstream. On elevators, waiting in line at the supermarket, or whenever you can remind yourself, practice tensing and quickly releasing those muscles. Do it ten times, then relax a few seconds and do it again. Or tense and hold for a full ten seconds, release ,and do that again. (No one will ever know.) Doing the Kegel exercises regularly can strengthen genital muscle tone and result in more satisfying orgasms and better choice over when to orgasm.

3. Practice erotic breath control. When you're by yourself, practice taking deep sighs, inhaling through the nose, and as you fill with air, imagine that you are drawing the sensations in your pelvis up through the center of the body into your belly, chest, and throat. Exhale all at once in a warm huff through the throat.

When you are with your lover, breathe and relax. Remember that you're not responsible for anyone's turn-on but your own. Be aware of sniffing the air as you inhale to encourage opening of the nostrils and to bring in sexy, sensuous smells. Vigorously drawing in air can also bring in more of those sex-happy pheromones that are floating around your most intimate spaces. When you breathe and relax into your body, your boundaries become more permeable, and thrilling feelings can pass more easily between your two bodies.

Listen to your partner's breath as well as to your own. If the two of you have distinctly different rhythms, you're not tuned into each other. See if you can "find" your lover by listening for his breath and matching your breath to his, inhaling when he inhales and exhaling when he exhales. Be genuinely in touch with the pleasurable sensations in your body and be grateful that you have someone to share this with. As your excitement intensifies, you may find that your breathing rhythms seem to naturally synchronize.

If your partner is holding her breath, encourage her to breathe by gently massaging her chest, diaphragm, and shoulders. Make sure your own deep breaths are audible while you do.

As your excitement builds, your breath will naturally quicken. Consciously practice the charging breath, inhaling and exhaling more rapidly through the mouth. Shuttle back and forth in your concentration between the sensations in your body and your sense awareness and appreciation of your partner. See if you can use your breath to continually keep your muscles open and flexible, expanding as the excitement grows. Every so often slow down the breath for a few moments and practice relaxing while holding on to the excitement.

4. Practice skilled intercourse. Some of the most thrilling and passionate moments during intercourse involve slow, deliberate movements where you breathe deeply and focus in on the "oceanic streaming"—waves of pleasurable sensation flowing in currents through your body.

Experiment with slow entry, becoming more experimental and conscious of the moment of penetration. Or you may enjoy teasing each other by almost pulling out very slowly and then pushing back in. You can explore different angles, depths, speeds, and rhythms of penetration.

When the man runs the sex, the combinations of his movements can be infinite—he can point up or down, he can be inside of her partially or deeply, using short and quick, long and slow, wavelike or circular movements, hitting the front wall of the vagina where her G spot is located. Each motion stimulates differently and can bring new sensations to both partners.

When the woman is on top of the man, she is in a good position to explore the deep grinding movements that bring enormous pleasure to so many women. She can also explore finding her own best angles, tempos, and depths. It takes concentration on her part to discover her own genuine, unique-as-a-fingerprint sexuality and a responsive lover who will follow her lead and complement her movements just as she does for him.

Make frequent eye contact and communicate your feelings for your lover through your eyes. See if you and your lover can maintain eye contact when you have an orgasm.

Ecstasy: Explorations in Spiritual Sex

1. Practice emotional surrender. Continually remind yourself of what you are particularly grateful for in your lover. Enjoy giving up control. Take direction.

2. Experiment with sex as a meditation. Give yourself the opportunity to enjoy penetration without movement. Relax into your excitement, breathe, and communicate energetically with your partner directly through your heart and genitals. Maintain eye contact. Feel your love and gratitude. Appreciate him or her as the essence of man and of woman.

Chapter 12

Spiritual Pleasures: Back to the Beginning

The joys of a buoyant spirit

. . . .

Truth is always new;
it is to see the same smile and see that smile newly,
to see the same person and see that person anew,
to see the waving palms anew, to meet life anew . . .
When the mind is free from all its projections, there is a
state of quietness in which problems cease, and then
only the timeless, the eternal comes into being.

—*J. Krishnamurti*

Years ago, while I was teaching a summer course at Naropa, a Buddhist institute in Boulder, Colorado, I found myself walking home one afternoon behind two young women who had apparently just discovered spirituality. They were having an animated conversation, relaying their insights to one another with the enormous enthusiasm that comes with being very young and believing you have found the truth. Just as I stepped around to pass them, I overheard one share a serious problem she had and the recent revelation that enabled her to let go of it. She said quite earnestly, "I thought to myself, what's the worst thing that could happen? Well, I could die. But now I know, that's not so bad after all!"

Unfortunately, my barely stifled giggle gave me away as an eavesdropper. But I thought about my reaction later. Couldn't she, even at that age, have brief glimpses of what it would be like to transcend that great separatist, the ego? The ego that is the target of all spiritual practice. The ego that supposedly dissolves with the grand insight of "the unity of all things" and which, when this enlightenment comes, results in the loss of the fear of death. Or was she only too happy to deny her own deepest fears and blindly accept as gospel the words of the guru of the year?

The more I thought about it, the more I realized that it didn't really matter either way. Glimpses of an alternative reality change the way we see things, even for just a little while. And for however long the awareness lasts, we get an intuitive feel for how it's possible to be goal-oriented without struggling, aiming for a particular result but doing it without trying to resist the way things currently are.

We may all enjoy moments like these in the presence of a spiritual teacher, or a friend talking from the heart, or by witnessing a birth or a sunset. Even if it's only temporary, such moments put us in touch with our spiritual nature. Why not assume that these satisfying joys of the spirit are not just isolated experiences but can eventually become the directing force that integrates all our different parts into a greater sense of internal unity?

Spiritual pleasures are the most opening, most liberating pleasures of all. They start with the simple contentment of peace of mind, a sense of belonging, and faith in the future, and take us to the most sublime joys of reverence, rapture, and bliss. But from one extreme to the other, all spiritual pleasure comes from a genuine, undeniable sensation of knowing—in your heart and gut—that you are a part of something good that is larger than yourself.

Why is this such a powerful pleasure? On the simple end of the continuum, the total sense of safety that spiritual pleasure provides is very reassuring. If you believe in a loving God or a universal principle uniting all of creation, you don't feel so all alone in the world or in so much potential danger. Maybe your faith in a God who watches over and protects you spurs you forward during difficult times and gives you strength to muster your resources and to prevail. Or maybe you have a deep sense of kinship with good people who have the same core values as you do, who stand by their friends, and who provide you, as you do them, with the solid emotional support to move through challenging times. Having faith in a higher power, feeling a part of a spiritual community, and sensing yourself as a part of a larger unseen whole are all tremendously pleasurable experiences.

On the other end of the continuum, the pleasures of the spirit can also provide some of life's most extravagant, most exciting joys—altered states of consciousness that can be profound, thrilling, and electrifying. For some people, this first glimpse of an alternative reality is drug-induced. However, based on the teachings of the mystics of all the great religions as well as on the personal stories of ordinary people who have had spiritual experiences, often the most intense pleasures are not drug-induced but depth-induced.

Yet they do take some practice. Times of profound well-being—when everything crystallizes into a sense of rightness with the world—appear to be primarily a function of looking inward from a particular vantage point. Rather than be locked in mortal combat within oneself, the man or woman who values spiritual pleasure devotes some time everyday to giving up mental chatter and judgments about the past or the future. And, for the moment, also absolves him or herself of all obligations, guilt, anger, and fear—anything and everything divisive—and simply bears witness to it all, as it unfolds internally, moment-by-moment. With practice silencing the multitude of inner voices, a moment of stillness comes, and in that moment may be the realization of the interconnectedness of all things.

That moment can happen on different levels, from a calm knowing to an insight of great magnitude that changes forever how you understand your life. The most vivid of these experiences has been called *satori, samadhi,* or enlightenment. Such intense states of spiritual pleasure are described by those who have had them as often accompanied by rapturous emotion, sensations so expansive that the individual feels transported out of ordinary experience into supreme states of joy.

These states, however, are rare experiences. Yet there are many pleasures of a spiritual nature that can be enjoyed on a daily basis—and doing so contributes greatly to our overall level of happiness. We can think of it as the spiritual aspect of an expansive lifestyle; it has to do with living daily with an ongoing sense of connection, purpose, and meaning. Two basic spiritual pleasures we can cultivate on a daily basis involve seeing oneself as a part of a larger whole and living a lifestyle that invites inspiration.

Cultivating a Larger Sense of Sense

If "spiritual" means that you know in your heart and gut that you are a part of something good that is larger than yourself, then to be attuned to your spiritual nature means identifying with others. Who are these others? Your immediate family? Your friends? Your neighborhood or community? How wide a scope can you see yourself a part of?

Somewhere in most of us is a tendency to separate ourselves along narrow definitions of self-interest that can create an unfriendly environment. As children, it's certainly critical for our well-being to build up a sense of ego and of individual worth. As adults, however, if we stay overly focused on our individual selves, we can end up spending a lot of our vital energy just watching our backsides, or continually doing battle with other islands of self-interest. There may be some dark pleasures that come from becoming skilled at making war, but ultimately, constant conflict is isolating and bleak. The wider the range of humanity, or even life in general, that we can identify with, the more our efforts can count for something enduring and of lasting value.

If we define for ourselves a set of higher values that constitutes the core of what we believe in, then we can have something to live for that is bigger than our own individual fight for survival. We can enjoy a personally grounded sense of inner guidance that gives a tremendous fullness of well-being. All it takes is to align ourselves with what is life affirming—what we believe in as doing the greatest good, not just for ourselves and loved ones, but for the community at large, and perhaps even for our whole, splendid, planet Earth.

The challenge for all of us is to ask ourselves: Am I willing to invest some energy in developing that larger sense of self? Or even more: Despite the great variety in the human race, how much of our experience is universal, and what of their life story can I personally identify with? Can my spiritual identity even extend beyond humans to include all of life on Earth, from the baboon to the worm to the redwood? How about all life forms not only on Earth but also on Mars and on any of the other planets revolving around the sun? Or how about even beyond that: as a glowing participant in an entire universe illumined with a consciousness of itself?

It's hard to explain, but something very peaceful and reassuring happens to us when we broaden our definition of self. Paradoxically, the smaller our individual ego becomes, the more expansive we feel in the recognition that we are part of the whole and not separate from it. No doubt, this can be one of life's most sublime joys. Anything that can help us let go of our tunnel vision and comprehend that bigger picture can contribute to a clearer sense of spiritual identity and open up the possibilities for experiencing some of these highest of all pleasures.

Inviting Inspiration and Revelation

You can be inspired in many different ways. At the top end of the scale, there's that glorious moment when you feel like you've been struck by a thunderbolt, and you have a brilliant insight that has a momentous consequence on how you see and do things from that instant on. Where there was doubt before, now there is none. You feel like you've been given a sign pointing you in a direction and showing you the path to get there. I had that kind of insight in Woodstock when I realized I needed to concentrate on what I found good about me and then building on that, rather than continually doing battle with my demons.

But it doesn't have to be a life-altering event. We can also be enriched by daily opportunities for inspiration. For example, when a decision needs to be made, inspiration can come from spending time alone to reflect in a relaxed and intuitive mode. Creative people—writers, painters, poets, musicians—look for another kind of inspiration, an illuminating vision that throws light on a blank page or canvas and offers an original way of expressing a private thought or feeling. Especially during troubled times, people can find inspiration from prayer or meditation.

The word *inspiration* is derived from the Latin word *inspirare* meaning "to breathe in or to blow into." To the ancient Greeks, the Muses—Zeus' nine daughters—were said to be the impelling influence behind any creative work in literature, the arts, and the sciences. In classic paintings, they are often depicted as beautiful pagan nymphs, seductively half-dressed, whispering or singing into the ear of the artist. We also hear of inspiration as a religious or spiritual revelation that may come through fervent worship, vision quests, or shamanic rituals that can have a sudden and profound impact on a person's faith in a divine plan.

Today, the social scientist has caught up with the poet and mystic. We now have a base of research evidence that shows that inspiration isn't just reserved for geniuses and zealots. Inspiration may actually play a critical, though often overlooked, role in our emotional health.

Dr. Tobin Hart, a psychology professor at the State University of

West Georgia, conducted in-depth interviews with seventy participants from a broad rage of professions, socioeconomic levels, ages,
and interests, all of whom had had an experience of inspiration.
Subjects were asked to describe the experience in detail, the context in
which it took place, and the significance it held for them. Several distinct characteristics of inspiration emerged in analyzing the data that
were present to varying degrees in every description.

People who had enjoyed moments of inspiration invariably mentioned a sense of connection—it might be a feeling of unity with ideas
or with nature, a merging with another person, or in the most expansive experiences a connection with everything. They said they felt
open—as though they had let go of all struggle and become a channel
through which their insights and creativity flowed. They reported a
tremendous sense of clarity—not only was their thinking clear but
also they felt very highly attuned to their senses—and many said that
their inspiration was strangely like a reminder of something they
already knew. All subjects said their experience of inspiration gave
them enormous energy; and while they felt elated, at the same time
they said they were very much at peace—the calm excitement that we
know to be a key aspect of vitality.

One of the most valuable insights to come out of Dr. Hart's
research is the relevance of such experiences to daily life. When people were asked to describe what their life would be like without any
moments of inspiration, they said it would be flat, boring, and empty,
suggesting that inspiration may be an important source of emotional
and spiritual sustenance. Many of the study's participants suggested
that not having times of inspiration would make them feel depressed,
their minds dull, and their lives seem hopeless.

Dr. Hart proposes that while inspiration can't be controlled, it can
be cultivated. We can do that by developing the kind of mindset that
keeps our lives open to inspiration. For one thing, we need to maintain a focus on the issue where we are looking for inspiration, and we
can do that through prayer, meditation, retreat, or healing rituals. We
also need to believe in our inherent ability to find a solution. I think of
this as "trusting the process"—having faith that if you stay focused on
the issue in a relaxed frame of mind and body, you'll come up with

the right answer. And you'll know it's true because you can feel it in your body, deep in your heart and gut.

Especially, we need to listen carefully to ourselves and to honor our insights, particularly when exciting, though uncharacteristic, new ideas present themselves.

Everyday Spiritual Pleasures

These two joys—feeling a part of a larger whole and leading a life that invites inspiration—benefit from connecting with one's spiritual nature everyday. It's not enough to contact our spirituality once a week at a religious service. When we think of the spirit as a once a week deep encounter, we compartmentalize our lives and segregate and separate the one aspect of ourselves that could potentially integrate us into a complete and fulfilled whole. Instead, the route to the most expansive pleasures of the spirit involves the same kind of daily discipline to let go and to surrender the inner conflict and physical tension that enhance the other pleasures. What follows are some of the ways we can reinforce the capacity to enjoy pleasures of the spirit on a daily basis.

Breath

The word *spirit* comes from the Latin root meaning "breath." Like inspiration, breath is a core feature of being in touch with the highest principle of the life force. It's no accident that most of the Eastern spiritual practices emphasize an awareness of the breath. In meditation, for example, the most commonly used mantra to anchor your mind to and to achieve that state of focused awareness often called mindfulness is the breath.

Breath control, as we have practiced it in all the other pleasures we've explored, is particularly useful in the spiritual dimension. Taking a few cleansing breaths periodically throughout the day and checking in with your body can be very centering. If you're floundering a bit, breath control can connect you with your inner compass. If you're confused, it can link you up to what you can be absolutely certain of, what you're body is telling you. If you find yourself being negatively motivated, or acting in ways you don't feel particularly proud of, deep breathing can release you from the grip of your lesser self and connect you to your higher, more principled side.

Most spiritual disciplines practice a variety of different kinds of controlled breathing techniques, from *hatha* yoga, which practices the cleansing breath, to *pranayama,* which is a more advanced approach to a wide scope of breathing practices, to *chi gung,* which combines several different breathing rhythms with slow movements. For thousands of years, the breath has been recognized as an important route to a more spiritual awareness.

Meditation: The Pleasures of a Quiet Mind

Many years ago, when I first became interested in meditation, I went to a meditation retreat in the Berkshire Mountains in Massachusetts. It was a crisp autumn, and I recall walking around the grounds admiring the last colors of fall and watching the gray skies as flocks of geese and other migrating birds headed south for the winter. There were about twenty of us on retreat, and we were encouraged to spend our week in complete silence, devoting about six hours a day to sitting and walking meditations and refraining from conversation with each other at meals and during rest periods. As beautiful as the natural setting was, it was hard to escape from my mental chatter, though it did get easier as the days passed.

The form of meditation we were practicing is known as *Vipassana* or Insight Meditation. The discipline requires sitting in an alert posture and quieting the mind by anchoring your attention to the motion in your chest as you inhale and exhale. With the incoming breath, your chest rises and you make a mental note of it by saying to yourself "rising;" with the outgoing breath your chest falls and you say to yourself "falling." Whenever you notice that your mind has drifted and you're daydreaming—making a plan or reminding yourself about a resentment or feelings of remorse—you simply notice where your mind has taken you, by repeating to yourself "thinking, thinking" and then gently returning your attention to the movement of the breath in the chest. "Rising, falling" or "thinking, thinking" are your mantras.

The many years I spent practicing this twenty-minute meditation every morning and evening enabled me to experience a state of inner quiet unlike anything I had ever before known. A daily meditation can be particularly valuable to anyone with an overactive, obsessive mind because it provides a kind of reference point for inner peace. Once you have experienced that internal state of tranquility, you know what it's like, and that makes it easier to find it again.

Another great value of meditation is that it helps you develop that state of mind known as the "impartial witness." Marshall McLuhan, the brilliant analyst who identified the cultural revolution brought about by the electronic media, once noted, "I don't know who discovered water, but I'm sure it wasn't a fish." A fish is totally submerged in his medium, and the only way he can discover water is to jump out of it for a moment or even just stick his tail out. Most of the time we're very much like the fish—so totally immersed in our habitual ways of seeing things that we can't observe ourselves or anyone else objectively.

Meditation is an elegant method for impartially witnessing the moment-to-moment mind-body process without identifying with either the contents of the mind or the sensations in the body. An impartial witness is one who observes without judging; a witness who judges is not much of a witness, since bias makes you look for confirmatory evidence and discount the rest. Impartial witnessing is an important skill because, as we saw in Chapter 8, when you judge yourself you're completely immersed in the duality of the inner critic and that part of yourself you condemn. But when you are an impartial witness of your own inner process, the ability to simply observe, from that place of inner unity, can lead to inner peace.

Some of the most exquisite pleasures involve the serenity of having few thoughts or, on rare occasions, no thoughts at all. People who meditate for ten, twenty, thirty minutes or more relish those brief interludes when their mind actually goes silent, and they aren't talking to themselves or evaluating their lives, their present discomfort, or egotistically congratulating themselves on achieving a state of egolessness.

Though it's difficult to keep the mind quiet without falling asleep, people who maintain a daily meditation practice find that it's possible to develop some skill at emptying the mind of thoughts while remaining relaxed and alert. Ability to concentrate improves, and they feel more clear-minded and less stressed. Research has shown that there are many benefits of meditation to physical health, particularly to the health of the heart, through a dramatic reduction in blood pressure and heart rate.

I have found that while some people are willing to alter their lifestyle to accommodate a daily meditation practice, those who are not may still be willing to sit quietly for only one minute at a time—and that can be quite good enough. One minute of anchoring your mind to your breath and noticing your inhales and exhales without controlling them can give you a quick taste of the impartial witness. Clearing your head for as many of those sixty seconds as you can goes a surprisingly long way toward achieving the pleasures of a quiet mind—especially if you do it several times a day.

Prayer

You don't need to be religious to derive the benefits of prayer. In fact, in one national poll, while 70 percent of people who believe in God pray daily—so do 10 percent of people who say they're not believers. Anyone who prays accesses a heartfelt faith that someone compassionate is listening, even if that "someone" is just you. In the British movie, *The Ruling Class*, the lead character played by Peter O'Toole is a charming madman, the sudden heir to fortune and peerage, who thinks he's God and relaxes by hanging draped on a man-sized wooden cross affixed to the wall of his manor. When someone asks him, "How do you know you're God?" he exuberantly replies, "Because when I pray, I find I'm talking to myself."

That's true for all of us. Maybe there's a God listening and maybe not. But certainly someone deep inside is listening, and in prayer it is a more compassionate and accepting side of oneself. When you are struggling with some inner dilemma or turmoil, it can feel very pleasurable and inspiring to articulate to yourself, slowly and even poetically, your fears, hopes, and desires, to be humble yet courageous and to put your faith in a spiritual force listening in to help you through.

Norman Vincent Peale, the pastor and inspirational writer, considered prayer to be a significant aspect of the power of positive thinking. But to Peale, it was the manner in which people prayed that was most critical. He suggested that when you pray, ask God for nothing; rather thank him for everything you want, in advance. That way you get to believe that it has already happened, and you act accordingly. To Peale, prayer allows you to empty your mind of defeatist attitudes and negative emotions that make problems seem overwhelming and to tap into the enormous problem-solving potential that is built into each one of us.

In fact, there's a good deal of evidence to show that there are definite health benefits to prayer. Harvard cardiologist Herbert Benson, who has run many studies over the years on both meditation and prayer, has shown that both methods slow down breathing and heart rate and lower both blood pressure and metabolic rate—resulting physiologically in what he called the relaxation response. This is the direct opposite to the stress reaction of the fight or flight response. Benson even found that when people meditated as they ran their bodies were more efficient. He suggested that runners might also benefit from trying "aerobic prayer"—keeping cadence with their running by saying words of devotion.

Solitude

No mother would react happily to her child's kindergarten teacher saying that her little one tends to play alone. In our society, people who keep to themselves are thought of as loners, potential serial killers, or disgruntled employees who may shoot up the office at any moment. And while nobody thinks she's raising a mass murderer, neither does she want to rear a child who can't get along with others.

We learn our childhood lessons well. Our culture so highly values fitting in and belonging that by the time we're adults often the thought of spending time alone feels more like a banishment than an opportunity to catch our breath and relax. I know many single people who dread being home alone, who feel that they wouldn't have to be alone for an evening or a Sunday, if they had someone to love them—or if their friends really cared enough to reach out. On the other hand, I know many couples who don't understand or accept their needs for time alone and wouldn't feel right asking for some space. So instead, they end up picking fights with one another and get their needed distance by being nasty.

Loneliness, that often intensely painful mix of anxiety and sorrow that makes us long for company, comes from many sources, some natural and some self-induced. Humans are social animals—we're meant to live together in families and tribes, to give each other comfort and companionship. We have a strong drive for love and closeness, which draws us to others. But we also have an opposing drive to be alone and independent; we need time to withdraw into ourselves or to be creative.

When people don't get enough love in their lives, or don't make authentic contact with friends and family, they often have a hard time being alone because they feel, and truly are, emotionally deprived. To compound the difficulty, lonely people often take their aloneness as a sign that they're inadequate, often spending their alone time berating themselves, wallowing in self-pity and self-doubt. No wonder they don't want to be alone with themselves—they're terrible company. Better to be distracted by the most insufferable bore than to be alone with their critical inner dialogues and endless self-torture!

Marilyn Monroe, who got plenty of adoration in her short lifetime but not enough love, apparently knew that sometimes no matter how lonely you may be, solitude can be more desirable than being with just anybody. She once declined an invitation with the remark, "If I'm going to be alone, I'd rather be by myself."

I think of solitude as time that you set aside to be with yourself. It's not that you're alone because nobody else wants you. Rather, solitude is about choosing aloneness. There are many good reasons to take time alone: to decompress after a hectic day; to move at your own pace; to relax; to reflect on how you handled something and how you feel about it now; to come to terms with a sad event; to allow time for your creative imagination to inspire you; to express yourself artistically.

Solitude is an opportunity to enjoy the present moment—to blessedly have nowhere to go and nothing to do. In fact, when people tell me they're lonely, I see it as a sign that while they may indeed need to develop more authentic relationships with others, perhaps more importantly they need to cultivate a more authentic relationship with themselves. The best way to do that is to spend quality time alone. And that doesn't even have to mean spending a lot of time all by yourself. It could also be just a half hour sitting quietly by yourself on a park bench feeding the pigeons.

Solitude is one of the most effective ways to enjoy a sense of the spiritual. Being alone enables you to remove yourself, temporarily, from all requirements to perform in a particular way. When you give yourself the opportunity for it, you can use your aloneness to quiet your mind or to talk to God, the Goddess, or your own godly self and be at peace.

Nature

Nature is hiking a trail in Colorado, surrounded on all sides by vistas of the snow-capped Rocky Mountains, the smell of pine filling your nostrils, the only sounds being the wind in the trees and the occasional flap of wings of a passing bird. Nature is sitting by a lake on a small island off the coast of Washington State watching the ripples of water gently lap the grassy shore, and, only a few feet away, a family of deer crackle slowly through the brush, sniffing the ground, remarkably unconcerned by your presence. Being in a setting of quiet natural beauty is one of life's most glorious pleasures and an opportunity to be in touch with something in the physical, perceptible world that is undeniably good and very much larger than ourselves.

The indigenous people of all nations understand themselves, in their very identity as human beings, to be spiritually connected to the land. Frank Waters, the great American author who wrote of the West and the native people he lived among and admired, described a disparity between "two views of nature"—what he saw as the defining difference between the white man and the Native American. In Western culture, humanity is created apart from nature, whereas to the native, humanity is a part of nature. Those of us who try to subdue nature also do battle with the instinctual and unconscious aspects of nature within ourselves. To Waters, for the people of the land, nature is the expression of "the one great unity of all Creation, imbued with one consciousness and infused with one power, of which everything in the universe is an embodied part." The beauty of nature is in our bodies!

For anyone who has spent any time in unspoiled country, there can be no doubt about the spiritual serenity that is possible just from spending quiet time in nature. In the same way that solitude of any kind can be replenishing, solitude in a natural setting can be particularly replenishing spiritually.

Public parks and gardens do a great service for the spirit of a community by providing a place of beauty and serenity where tense citizens can decompress. That way we don't have to deprive ourselves of nature until we can get away to a mountain trail or a lazy lakeside. We can build nature into our everyday lives very simply. Instead of having lunch at a restaurant, for example, we can take a brown-bag retreat in a public park or garden. We can make a point of finding out where there may be a little patch of tranquility in a natural setting near where we work; then, we can develop a routine of occasionally building in a midday break to spend a few moments alone there, just admiring the season in the trees and the songs and movements of the birds.

Kinship, Community, and Giving to Others

While enjoying solitude and being at peace with the natural environment are key features of living a life in tune with the nonmaterial world, so too is the importance of feeling a part of a community of kindred spirits. When we live our lives exclusively in the materialistic world of competition and striving for success, we may gain financial wealth but end up spiritually bankrupt. Spending regular time with people who believe in something more than material gain and whose core values and aspirations are more aligned with the common good than merely with what's-in-it-for-me can be very nurturing and fulfilling.

That's why Alcoholics Anonymous and similar kinds of groups have been so successful at helping people stay sober. There's something deeply supportive about being part of a group that reminds you of the strength you can draw from being humble and in believing in a higher power that you can connect with in yourself. For some people, these kinds of spiritual groups have taken the place of organized religion in their lives because, while the groups also promote standards of morality, they may be less judgmental and more inclusive in their belief systems.

A great gift is the special kind of kinship that comes with what we call "a soulmate," a life partner whose welfare is at least as important to us as our own. As soulmates, you know each other's deepest fears and loftiest aspirations; you know the emotional wounds that have healed and served as lessons, and those that, regrettably, may never heal or yield wisdom. As you witness each other's defeats and triumphs, however, you mourn and celebrate them together. And in the deepest parts of you both, you have a clear sense of the tremendous richness of spirit that comes with this kind of very special friendship. To be soulmates is to have it all: a meeting of hearts and minds and bodies and a connection that includes a sense of devotion to something beyond your own two selves.

We're blessed when we have a mate we can live out our lives with, until death do us part. But that kind of relationship may be rarer than we'd like to think, and whether or not we find such a life partner, we can still enjoy the blessings of closeness with one or two best friends.

Best friends aren't just for children. I think it's critical for all of us to have someone to talk to, with whom we can speak from the heart in complete safety, knowing that we will be loved and understood. One of my best friends now lives thousands of miles away from me; yet I know that anytime I want, I can pick up the phone and at least reach her message machine. And when we talk, I know our conversation will always be warm and genuine. We give each other unsolicited advice—which may or may not be taken. We empathize, sympathize, encourage, and sometimes admonish each other. We may disagree. Yet, we value one another's honest feedback. The trust between us runs deep, and our times of intimate fellowship are always gratifying.

Like the other core pleasures, spiritual pleasures also have pragmatic rewards—particularly when it comes to the health benefits of being connected with other people. I've already mentioned some of the research showing that volunteers who worked directly with those who benefited from their help enjoyed a greater immunity boost than volunteers who worked in administration. In another study, researchers in Michigan followed 2,700 people for close to ten years and found that men who did regular volunteer work had death rates two-and-a-half times lower than men who didn't.

Psychologist Robert Ornstein and physician David Sobel who collected these studies and others on the healthy effects of selflessness and altruism suggest a variety of ways in which giving to others may ultimately benefit the helper. Perhaps focusing on other people's problems takes our mind off our own troubles. Or maybe the heartfelt gratitude and appreciation we get from lending a hand infuses healing energy into our own systems.

Apparently, however, we don't even need to be the recipients of direct appreciation—we can get a booster shot merely from watching someone else do good. In a Harvard University study, students watching a film on Mother Theresa as she tended to the sick and dying of Calcutta got a boost in their own immune function, even among those who were not particularly fans of Mother Theresa.

A little known benefit of giving to others, according to Ornstein and Sobel, is what they call the "helper's high." When hospital volunteers described their feelings about helping others, they often spoke of a kind of euphoria they felt when they were giving. They talked about feeling a warm glow in the chest and about that deeply gratifying pleasure of vitality—being both calm and energized at the same time.

Like a runner's high, genuinely giving from the heart no doubt triggers endorphins—which would account for the fact that nine out of ten volunteers consider themselves as healthy or healthier that other people their age.

You don't have to deprive yourself to be a truly giving person. In fact, it may be impossible for altruism to be a completely selfless act since, because of all the health benefits, the one who ends up getting the most from a good deed may, ultimately, be the good Samaritan.

Fashioning an Afterlife We Can Live With

Fear of death is the terror of the end of the self and of eternal darkness. If there is something more—some kind of eternal light—we are likely to see it as a place of joy and love, enjoying the camaraderie of kindred souls. However, many people find they can't accept a belief in the kind of afterlife offered by most organized religions. Mark Twain once poked fun at our concepts of life after death, in the character of archangel Satan who visits Earth and writes letters about it to Saint Michael and Saint Gabriel in heaven. How strange, writes the visitor, that the best heaven humans can conceive of contains not a single feature humans actually value—like making love—and consists of nothing more than diversions they care nothing about, like walking around all day playing harps and singing hymns. Yet somehow they're convinced they would like it in heaven!

Maybe loose robes and sandals and an endless diet of light amusement was the best vision our toiling and embattled ancestors could come up with. In any event, the real challenge is to achieve a spirit of lightness here on earth. Meditating or praying; enjoying solitude, kinship, and time in nature; giving ourselves opportunities to be inspired creatively and spiritually can all go a long way to keeping our spirits light.

For most of us, however, to feel truly in touch with our spiritual nature, we need to come to terms with our mortality. Some people say they don't mind thinking that when the end comes, it's all over. They don't believe in heaven or hell, in reincarnation, or in anything at all after death—you did what you did, you had what you had, and you're done. Other people say they can't live that way; they find comfort believing in an eternal soul—that they will be reincarnated, as Buddhism and Hinduism teach, and come back for another life. Still others do gain comfort from organized religion because they find solace in believing in a heaven where they will reconnect with loved ones and they look forward to the opportunity to stand before their Maker.

When it comes to dealing with your mortality, what's most important is to have something that you can believe in that works for you, something that gives you "existential courage"—the emotional fortitude to live in a way that is true to yourself. You may be fine thinking that your innermost soul is as finite as your flesh, and you can still live a brave and decent life. But if that's not enough for you, you may need to believe in something more enduring.

Since we really don't know anything about death and probably can never really know about it, as an absolute fact, why not consciously fashion an afterlife you could believe in and could invest yourself in? There are good reasons for seriously examining the kind of afterlife you'd prefer to believe in—in terms of what would positively motivate you the most and bring out the best in you. For one, whether you're right or wrong, you're likely to meet with the same fate after death anyway. If your belief system doesn't change your after-death experience, why not choose one that can impact your before-death experience—one that inspires you, gives you courage, hope, solace, and a reason for reverence? Doesn't it make sense to construct an afterlife you can live happily with now?

Besides, maybe visualization is an even more powerful aptitude than we've ever imagined—not just in terms of our ability to determine the course of our lives, but also in determining the course of our afterlives. The Buddhists believe that your thought at the point of death propels you to a particular Bardo, a kind of way station for souls at a particular stage of consciousness. According to this practice, you prepare all your life to enter a higher Bardo—from which your soul will be drawn—so that in your next life you will come back to Earth at a higher stage. It's an interesting notion. Maybe in death, as in life, what you see is what you get! Wouldn't it make sense, then, to fully see what you most fervently wish for death to be, and to invest yourself in that spiritual vision?

For me, I take comfort in the belief that there really is an eternal soul. That death is not the Big Sleep, but rather the Big Awakening. I enjoy the words of the Bhagavad Gita, the sacred Hindu text, that proclaim, "We are born into the world of nature; our second birth is into the world of spirit." Since the death that is most discomforting for me is one that is filled with darkness, cold, and isolation, my most personally empowering vision for an afterlife—other than coming back to Earth knowing everything I know now and getting a chance to do a few things differently—is sunshine, warmth, and the company of kindred spirits.

Many years ago, I saw a documentary about the life of Carl Jung, the eminent Swiss psychiatrist who included religious and mystical motifs in his understanding of the human mind. Jung, who was by then an old man with sparse gray hair and a bit of a tremor in his gestures, had been interviewed at various points throughout the film, but I was most struck by his comments during the closing frames. He sat in a broad wooden chair in his study, surrounded by the books and relics he had collected over his long life. His back was slightly rounded but he held his head up; his right arm rested on the arm of the chair, and his left hand rested on the cane he gripped just to the side of his knee. He had a pleasant smile on his face, and his eyes squinted to see the interviewer off-camera who was bringing the session to an end. "Dr. Jung," he said, "one last question: Do you believe in God?" Jung's face lit up, his eyes widened, his back straightened, and he started to gently laugh. "Believe in God?" he asked almost incredulously, as though the question was some kind of joke. "Believe in God?" he repeated, his eyes darting back and forth as he savored the moment. "No," he said finally, solemnly staring at the carpet and shaking his head slowly from side to side, "I don't believe in God." Then, looking up with his eyes glistening and a big warm smile, he said softly, "I know!"

Now that kind of faith is inspiring.

There is, however, an afterlife that doesn't rest on faith and is completely indisputable—and that's the afterlife of what we leave behind us when we go. The one afterlife we can surely anticipate is that we will live on in the people who love us and who have been enriched by our being here. Our mate, children, family, friends, neighbors, and all those we interacted with day to day, will miss us and probably, on occasion, will tell warm or funny stories about us. We'll also live on in anything that we have created—anything fashioned by our own hands and visions, and anything we've amassed over the course of our years and valued.

In truth, the only afterlife we can be sure of is that we will live-after in the hearts, minds, and treasured mementos of those whose lives we've touched. Hopefully, we'll be remembered with love, and the legacy of our having been here will continue to do good even after we're gone. That's the one afterlife we can prepare for, and, despite the ultimate mystery of it all, it's the one afterlife we can anticipate with absolute certainty.

Personal Experiments

· ·

1. Practice breath control periodically throughout the day. Use conscious breathing to support connecting with your larger sense of self, your ability to be inspired, and your highest principles. Take a few cleansing breaths to blow out tension, take inventory of the sensations of your body and stretch out any kinks, and focus your mind. Use the deep sighing breath to feel your feelings more keenly. Take five deep charging breaths when you need some quick energy.

2. Practice one-minute meditations a few times a day, particularly when you're tense. Sit in an alert but relaxed position, your chin parallel to the floor and follow your breath without controlling it as it rises and falls in your chest. See if you can let go of your narrative thoughts and simply be an impartial witness for a minute. Notice your body sensations, whatever thoughts rise up, and the sounds around you—without having to do anything but to merely witness it all.

3. When in doubt, pray for guidance. You don't have to believe in God to pray. Believe, at least, in a higher power in yourself, a source of wisdom and integrity, that can direct you to your intuitive truth.

4. Spend some time alone in nature to mellow out and just be. Let your senses be keenly alive and in the moment. See yourself as a part of it all.

5. Write a letter of affection and gratitude to someone you love. Write about what you most love and appreciate in him or her. Then read it to the person.

6. Assist someone in need by your actions rather than money. Be a Big Brother or a Big Sister and mentor a disadvantaged child; prepare some meals for AIDS patients or the elderly; serve the homeless at a mission on Thanksgiving Day; teach an adult to read; make it an instant priority to give solace to anyone who turns to you for comfort.

7. With a mate or friend, volunteer together to assist in a community project. Get involved in a community effort you believe in.

8. With a mate or friend, discuss your spiritual beliefs. Describe for each other what your purpose is in life; what gives your present life the most meaning; what is your notion of a higher power; how you feel about death.

9. Give it some thought and construct for yourself an afterlife you can believe in. See if these new convictions give you added strength.

10. Be sure to take a little time everyday to enjoy and be enriched by life's simplest joys—a warm heart, a peaceful mind, and a calm energetic body.

A Last Word

. . . .

I hope I have inspired you to expand your notions of pleasure and to make some truly wonderful discoveries for yourself. To let go and be happy, you have to believe in your heart of hearts that, if you don't resist it, happiness is the natural state of our human organism. I believe that's true, and that if we didn't struggle so hard to fight ourselves, we'd be more peace loving with others.

As our globe shrinks and we come into greater contact with one another, I'm counting on this new respect for pleasure as the *embodiment* of happiness to continue to gain momentum. Increasing numbers of people are recognizing that the more fulfilled each of us is—in our bodies, as well as in our minds, hearts, and souls—the healthier we'll be, and the more civil, patient, and loving we'll be with the people we encounter. Ideally, more and more of us will forge the courage to be authentic, to choose enthusiasm and good feelings, and to be motivated positively, toward what genuinely inspires us.

My most ardent wish for you, as for myself, is that we keep learning and practicing it all—that we will keep reminding ourselves to *carpe' diem,* dammit! And to:

Breathe and relax. Stretch. Witness it all. Surrender to what is truly sweet and good in yourself. Be playful and expressive. Laugh. Think good thoughts and make good pictures. Have faith in yourself. Trust the process of growth. Be loving and appreciative of the love that's given you. Be more sensuously alive. Be more sexually turned-on and more passionately fulfilled. And most especially, lighten up! Let your spirit soar!

References and Bibliography

Ackerman, Diane. *A Natural History of the Senses*. New York: Random House, Inc., 1990.

Anand, Margo. *The Art of Sexual Ecstacy*. Los Angeles: Jeremy P. Tarcher, Inc., 1989.

Anderson, Walter Truett. *Reality Isn't What It Used to Be*. New York: HarperSanFrancisco (a division of HarperCollins Publishers), 1990.

Andreas, Steve. *Is There Life Before Death?* Moab: Real People Press, 1995.

Aron, Elaine and Aron, Arthur. "The Influence of Inner State on Self-Reported Long-Term Happiness" in *Journal of Humanistic Psychology*, vol. 27 (2), 1987.

Barbach, Lonnie. *For Each Other*. New York: Anchor Press/Doubleday, 1982.

Beck, Deva and Beck, James.. *The Pleasure Connection*. San Marcos, CA: Synthesis Press, 1987.

Becker, Ernest. *The Denial of Death*. New York: The Free Press, 1973.

Benson, Herbert. *The Relaxation Response*. New York: Avon Books, 1975.

Branden, Nathaniel. *The Psychology of Romantic Love*. Los Angeles: Jeremy P. Tarcher, Inc., 1980.

Cassell, Carol. *Swept Away*. New York: Simon & Schuster, Inc., 1984.

Csikszentmihalyi, Mihaly. *Flow*. New York: Harper & Row Publishers, Inc., 1990.

DeAngelis, Tori. "Should Wellness Model Replace Disease Focus?" in American Psychological Association *Monitor,* December 1990.

Dodson, Betty. *Sex for One*. New York: Harmony Books, 1987.

Eisler, Riane. *Sacred Pleasure*. San Francisco: HarperSanFrancisco, 1995.

Feuerstein, Georg. *Sacred Sexuality*. Los Angeles: Jeremy P. Tarcher, Inc., 1992.

Fisher, Helen E. *Anatomy of Love*. New York: W. W. Norton & Company, 1992.

Flew, Anthony. *A Dictionary of Philosophy*. New York: St. Martin's Press, 1979.

Foucault, Michel. *The Use of Pleasure, The History of Sexuality*, vol. 2. New York: Random House, Inc., 1990.

Frankl, Viktor E. *Man's Search for Meaning*. New York: Washington Square Press, 1965.

Freud, Sigmund. *Civilization and Its Discontents*. London: Hogarth Press, 1930.

Friday, Nancy. *Women on Top*. New York: Simon & Schuster, Inc., 1991.

Fromm, Erich. *The Art of Loving*. New York: Harper & Row Publishers, Inc., 1956.

Goldstein, Joseph and Kornfield, Jack. *The Path of Insight Meditation*. Boston: Shambhala Publishing, 1995.

Goleman, Daniel. *Emotional Intelligence.* New York: Bantam Books, 1995.

Hart, Tobin. "Inspiration: Exploring the Experience and its Meaning" in *Journal of Humanistic Psychology,* (in press).

Hartman, William and Fithian, Marilyn. *Any Man Can.* New York: St. Martin's Press, 1984.

Hayden, Tom. *The Lost Gospel of the Earth.* San Francisco: Sierra Club Books, 1996.

Hite, Shere. *The Hite Report.* New York: Dell Publishing Company, Inc., 1976.

Hutchinson, Michael. *The Book of Floating.* New York: Quill, 1984.

Jacobson, Edmund. *Progressive Relaxation.* Chicago: University of Chicago Press, 1942.

Johnson, Robert A. *Ecstasy.* New York: Harper & Row Publishers, Inc., 1921, 1987.

Karlen, Arno. "Appreciating the Sexual You" in *Modern Maturity,* April-May, 1992.

Kepner, James I. *Body Process.* New York: Gardner Press, 1987.

Krishnamurti, J. *Total Freedom.* San Francisco: HarperCollins Publishers, Inc., 1996.

LaBerge, Stephen. *Lucid Dreaming.* Los Angeles: Jeremy P. Tarcher, Inc., 1985.

Ladas, Alice Kahn; Beverly Whipple; and John D. Perry. *The G Spot and Other Recent Discoveries About Human Sexuality.* New York: Holt, Rinehart, and Winston, 1982.

Lawrence, Raymond J. Jr. *The Poisoning of Eros.* New York: Augustine Moore Press, 1989.

Liebowitz, Michael R. *The Chemistry of Love.* Boston: Little, Brown and Company, 1983.

Liedloff, Jean. *The Continuum Concept.* Reading, MA: Addison-Wesley Publishing Company, Inc., 1977.

Locke, Steven and Douglas Colligan. *The Healer Within.* New York: E. P. Dutton, 1986.

Lowen, Alexander. *Love, Sex, and Your Heart.* New York: Macmillan Publishing Company, 1988.

Lowen, Alexander. *Pleasure.* New York: Penguin Books, Inc., 1970.

Marcuse, Herbert. *Eros and Civilization.* New York: Random House, Inc., 1955.

Markowitz, Laura. "Minding the Body, Embodying the Mind" in *The Family Therapy Networker,* September-October 1996.

Marks, Linda. *Living with Vision: Reclaiming the Power of the Heart.* Indianapolis: Knowledge Systems Inc., 1989.

Maslow, Abraham H. *Toward a Psychology of Being.* Princeton, NJ: D. Van Nostrand Company, Inc., 1962.

Mazur, Thomas. "Children and Sex" in *Human Sexuality.* (eds., Bullough and Bullough) New York and London: Garland Publishing, Inc., 1994.

McCraty, Rollin; Mike Atkinson; William A.Tiller; Glen Rein and Alan D. Watkins. "The Effects of Emotions on Short-Term Heart Rate Variability Using Power Spectrum Analysis" in *American Journal of Cardiology,* 1995:76(14): 1089-1093.

McLuhan, Marshall and Quentin Fiore. *The Medium Is the Massage.* New York: Bantam Books, 1967.

Meshorer, Marc and Judith. *Ultimate Pleasure.* New York: St. Martin's Press, 1986.

Michael, Robert T.; John H.Gagnon; Edward O. Laumann; and Gina Kolata. *Sex in America.* Boston: Little, Brown and Company, 1994.

Miller, Alice. *For Your Own Good.* New York: Farrar, Straus & Giroux, 1983.

Money, John. *Lovemaps.* Irvington Publishers, Inc., 1986.

Morin, Jack. *The Erotic Mind.* New York: HarperCollins Publishers, Inc., 1995.

Murphy, Michael. *The Future of the Body.* Los Angeles: Jeremy P. Tarcher, Inc., 1992.

Nadel, Laurie. *Sixth Sense.* New York: Prentice Hall Press, 1990.

Needleman, Jacob. *A Little Book on Love.* New York: Doubleday/Currency, 1996.

Ogden, Gina. *Women Who Love Sex.* New York: Pocket Books, 1994.

O'Hara, Maureen. "Divided We Stand" in *The Family Therapy Networker,* September/October 1996.

Ornstein, Robert and David Sobel. *Healthy Pleasures.* Reading, MA: Addison-Wesley Publishing Company, Inc. 1989.

Peale, Norman Vincent. *Positive Imaging.* New York: Fawcett Crest, 1982.

Perls, Fritz. *Ego, Hunger, and Aggression.* New York: Random House, Inc.,1969.

_____. *The Gestalt Approach & Eye Witness to Therapy.* Palo Alto, CA: Science and Behavior Books, Inc., 1973.

Prescott, James W. "Physical Affection and the Origins of Violence." in *The Futurist.* April, 1975.

Randles, Jenny. *Sixth Sense.* Topsfield, NJ: Salem House Publishers, 1987.

Reich, Wilhelm. *The Function of the Orgasm.* New York: Farrar, Straus & Giroux, 1961.

Rein, Glen; Mike Atkinson and Rollin McCraty. "The Physiological and Psychological Effects of Compassion and Anger" in *Journal of Advancement in Medicine.* volume 8, number 2, Summer 1995.

Rosenberg, Jack Lee; Rand, Marjorie L. and Asay, Diane. *Body, Self & Soul.* Atlanta, GA: Humanics Limited, 1985.

Ruch, Theodore C.; Harry D. Patton; J. Walter Woodbury and Arnold L. Towe. *Neurophysiology.* Philadelphia & London: W. B. Saunders Company, 1965.

Saint Exupéry, Antoine de. *The Little Prince*. New York: Harcourt, Brace & World, Inc., 1943.

Samuels, Mike and Nancy Samuels. *Seeing with the Mind's Eye*. New York: A Random House/Bookworks Book, 1975.

Scheff, Thomas (principal investigator, The Laughter Project). *Laughter and Stress*. Santa Barbara, CA: University of California, 1984.

Schnarch, David M. *Constructing the Sexual Crucible*. New York: W. W. Norton & Company, 1991.

Seligman, Martin E. P. *Learned Optimism*. New York: Simon & Schuster, Inc., 1990.

Selye, Hans. *The Stress of Life*. New York: McGraw-Hill Book Co., 1956.

Sherfey, Mary Jane. *The Nature & Evolution of Female Sexuality*. New York: Random House, 1966.

Siegel, Ronald K. *Intoxication*. New York: E. P. Dutton, 1989.

Stern, Daniel N. *Diary of a Baby*. New York: HarperCollins, 1990.

Thoreau, Henry David. *Walden*. New York: A Signet Classic, The New American Library, 1942.

Thomas, Lewis. *The Lives of the Cell*. New York: Viking Penguin, 1978.

Trungpa, Chögyam. *Meditation in Action*. Berkeley, CA: Shambala, 1970.

Twain, Mark. *Letters from the Earth*. New York: Harper & Row Publishers, Inc., 1962.

Villee, Claude A. *Biology*. Philadelphia and London: W. B. Saunders Company, 1985.

Waters, Frank. *Pumpkin Seed Point*. Athens, OH: Ohio University Press/Swallow Press, 1981.

White, Michael and David Epston. *Narrative Means to Therapeutic Ends*. New York and London: W. W. Norton & Company, 1990.

Index

A Note from the Author

. . . .

I'd like to hear from people whose lives have been meaningfully affected by what you've read in this book. Write to me and tell me your story.

Dr. Stella Resnick
P. O. Box 1543
North Hollywood, CA 91614

A variety of workshops on pleasure are available, including professional seminars and couples' groups co-led with my husband Alan Kishbaugh. Write for a brochure or to arrange a workshop in your area.

Beginning in the fall of 1998, with Dr. Marjorie L. Rand as co-director, The Los Angeles Living Arts Center will begin to offer classes and gatherings focused on healthful body-mind awareness and identifying and building our community. Write for information and a copy of the newsletter.

Conari Press, established in 1987, publishes books on topics ranging from spirituality and women's history to sexuality and personal growth. Our main goal is to publish quality books that will make a difference in people's lives—both how we feel about ourselves and how we relate to one another.

Our readers are our most important resource, and we value your input, suggestions, and ideas. To receive a complete catalog of our books and be placed on our mailing list, contact us at:

Conari Press
2550 Ninth Street, Suite 101
Berkeley, CA 94710-2551

800-685-9595   Fax: 510-649-7190
E-mail: Conaripub@aol.com